# GREAT LIVES OBSERVED

Gerald Emanuel Stearn, *General Editor*

EACH VOLUME IN THE SERIES VIEWS THE CHARACTER AND ACHIEVEMENT OF A GREAT WORLD FIGURE IN THREE PERSPECTIVES—THROUGH HIS OWN WORDS, THROUGH THE OPINIONS OF HIS CONTEMPORARIES, AND THROUGH RETROSPECTIVE JUDGMENTS—THUS COMBINING THE INTIMACY OF AUTOBIOGRAPHY, THE IMMEDIACY OF EYEWITNESS OBSERVATION, AND THE OBJECTIVITY OF MODERN SCHOLARSHIP.

ALLEN J. MATUSOW, *the editor of this volume in the Great Lives Observed series, is Associate Professor of History at Rice University, Houston, Texas. He has written several books and articles on United States' administrations, most notably that of Harry Truman.*

GREAT LIVES OBSERVED

# JOSEPH R.
# McCarthy

### Edited by
### ALLEN J. MATUSOW

*No bolder seditionist ever moved among us—*
*nor any politician with a surer, swifter*
*access to the dark places of the American mind.*

—RICHARD ROVERE

A SPECTRUM BOOK

PRENTICE-HALL, INC., ENGLEWOOD CLIFFS, N.J.

The quotation on the title page is from
Richard Rovere, *Senator Joe McCarthy*
(New York, 1959).

Copyright © 1970 by PRENTICE-HALL, INC.
*Englewood Cliffs, New Jersey.*

A SPECTRUM BOOK

Current printing (last number):

10  9  8  7  6  5  4  3  2  1

C 13–566729–1

P 13–566711–9

*Library of Congress Catalog Card Number: 73–104846*

Printed in the United States of America

PRENTICE-HALL INTERNATIONAL, INC. (*London*)
PRENTICE-HALL OF AUSTRALIA, PTY. LTD. (*Sydney*)
PRENTICE-HALL OF CANADA, LTD. (*Toronto*)
PRENTICE-HALL OF INDIA PRIVATE LIMITED (*New Delhi*)
PRENTICE-HALL OF JAPAN, INC. (*Tokyo*)

973.921
M434j

# Contents

v

24975

## 4

## PART TWO
## McCARTHY APPRAISED

## PART THREE
## WHO WERE THE McCARTHYITES?

GREAT LIVES OBSERVED

# JOSEPH R. McCARTHY

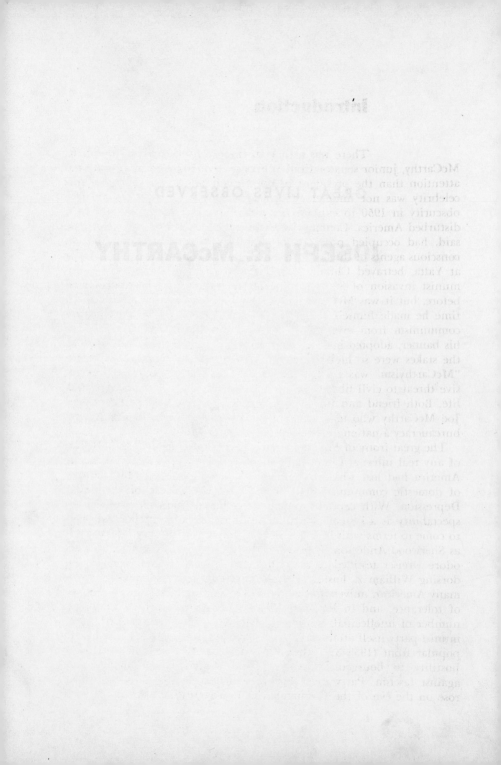

# Introduction

There was a time in the early 1950s when Joseph R. McCarthy, junior senator from Wisconsin, commanded more national attention than the president of the United States. In one sense this celebrity was not undeserved, for McCarthy emerged from relative obscurity in 1950 to explain the catastrophes of recent history to a disturbed America. Communists, subversives, and fellow travelers, he said, had occupied positions of power in the government and, as conscious agents of the Soviet conspiracy, had sold out Eastern Europe at Yalta, betrayed Chiang Kai-shek, and in 1950 invited the Communist invasion of South Korea. Similar views had been expressed before, but it was McCarthy who won for them a mass audience. In time he made himself the leader of a reckless crusade to eliminate communism from every facet of American life. Millions rallied to his banner, adopted his view of the current world crisis, and because the stakes were so high, forgave his every excess. To other millions, "McCarthyism" was a slanderous assault on innocent citizens, a massive threat to civil liberty, and a debasement of the nation's political life. Both friend and foe would agree on at least one point: it was Joe McCarthy who made the subject of security risks in the federal bureaucracy a national obsession from 1950 to 1954.

The great irony of McCarthyism is that it developed in the absence of any real internal Communist menace; for by 1950 communism in America had lost whatever influence it once possessed. The heyday of domestic communism had occurred in the decade of the Great Depression. With capitalism then in collapse, Marxism attained respectability as a system of explanation, and serious intellectuals had to come to terms with it. Thus in 1932 important literary figures such as Sherwood Anderson, Erskine Caldwell, Edmund Wilson, and Theodore Dreiser testified to the temporary appeal of Marxism by endorsing William Z. Foster of the Communist party for president. In many American universities in the 1930s Communists found a climate of tolerance, and in left-wing liberal circles they turned up a fair number of intellectuals willing to defend Stalinist crimes. The Communist party itself attained its greatest popularity in the period of the popular front (1935–39), when on orders from Moscow it muted its hostility to bourgeois democracy and sought class collaboration against fascism. Party membership, which was only 7,500 in 1932, rose on the eve of the German-Soviet non-aggression pact in 1939 to perhaps 80,000. To generate an atmosphere favorable to the popular front, the Reds manipulated front groups such as the American League Against War and Fascism and the National Negro Congress—organizations that attracted liberals but served in part the ends of Communists. But Communist inroads among middle-class intellectuals were never more than marginal and did not threaten the hold of Franklin Roosevelt on most socially concerned progressives.

More important in the thirties were Communist gains in the labor movement. John L. Lewis, leader of the Congress of Industrial Organizations, needed skilled organizers to help unionize the mass production industries. By 1937 Lewis was saying, "I'll work with anyone who'll work with me," and he struck up a quiet alliance with his old enemies, the Communists, whose past adventures in the union movement left them with a cadre of experienced labor organizers. After helping to form new industrial unions, the Communists planted colonizers in them to foster friendly factions. In his book, *The Communist Party vs. the C.I.O.*, Max Kampleman estimated that Communists for a time had complete or partial control "in at least 40 per cent of the C.I.O. unions," including the United Auto Workers, the United Electrical Workers, the Newspaper Guild, and several others. Communists also obtained important positions in the C.I.O.'s national office. Lee Pressman, the C.I.O. general counsel, and Leon De Caux, editor of the *C.I.O. News*, both owed allegiance to the party.

In the 1930s the Communists scored one other significant gain: they successfully penetrated the federal bureaucracy. Under the supervision of J. Peters, head of the Communist underground in the United States, Communist employees of the government met secretly in study groups and sometimes performed acts of espionage. Though the number of Communists in the government during the New Deal remains unknown, Whittaker Chambers, the confessed underground agent, later estimated that the so-called Ware group with which he was connected had 75 members. During World War II Communist espionage attained its greatest successes. Assisted by the spirit of Soviet-American military collaboration, the Red apparatus in the government penetrated, among other agencies, the War Production Board, the Office of Strategic Services, the Treasury, the State Department, and counter-intelligence of the War Department. Through its espionage activities the underground supplied great quantities of secret information to Soviet Russia.

At the end of World War II American communism seemed to have a hopeful future. But between 1945 and 1949 steadily mounting resistance would eradicate all the former achievements of the party and leave the movement in a shambles. The Communists themselves took the first step toward their own isolation when they abandoned the wartime campaign for national unity and in 1945 again declared war on American capitalist imperialism. Liberals, meanwhile, forgot the popular front, became caught up in the emerging Cold War and were soon criticizing Russian transgressions in Eastern Europe. On January 4, 1947, the growing anti-Communist impulse among liberals received organizational form with the founding of the Americans for Democratic Action. The A.D.A. was dedicated to the proposition that liberalism and communism were irreconcilable enemies, and it fought against former Vice-President Henry A. Wallace and his followers on the left who still believed that some accommodation with Russia was possible. In 1948 Wallace, preaching liberal capitalism, ran for president as the candidate of the new Progressive party, an organization in which Communists exercised considerable influence. One meaning of Wallace's disastrous defeat at the polls was that, by 1948, America's liberals and intellectuals had joined up with the rest of the country for the duration of the Cold War.

In these same years Communists in the C.I.O. suffered a series of devastating reverses. In 1946 Walter Reuther, a militant anti-Communist, defeated the Communist faction in the United Auto Workers and became the union's new president. The long-time head of the National Maritime Union, Joseph Curran, ended an alliance with the Communists in his union and was soon leading a purge against them. And at the C.I.O.'s 1946 annual convention, delegates passed a resolution against efforts of the Communist party "to interfere in the affairs of the C.I.O." When Communist-controlled unions in the C.I.O. went for Wallace in 1948, they met fierce resistance from the bulk of the federation, which remained loyal to the Democrats. At the beginning of 1949 only 15 per cent of C.I.O. workers belonged to unions still under Communist influence. In November of that year, at the C.I.O. annual convention, the open break between the Communists and non-Communists at last occurred. The convention expelled the United Electrical Workers, the largest of the Red unions, and in 1950 severed connections with four smaller Red unions. In a few more years hardly a vestige of the once powerful Communist presence in the C.I.O. remained.

The early postwar period also saw the government take drastic steps to tighten its security procedures. Until 1939 the loyalty of every government employee was simply assumed. But in that year Congress provided in the Hatch Act that federal employment be denied anyone belonging to an organization which advocated overthrow of the government. In World War II Congress and the president experimented with piecemeal loyalty and security measures, but these were sometimes unfair to employees and usually ineffective in protecting the government. Then, in February, 1945, government agents turned

up more than a thousand classified documents in the offices of
*Amerasia,* an allegedly pro-Communist magazine. The State Department in the meantime discovered employees who were clandestine
members of the Communist party. Most shocking of all was an
announcement from the Canadian government in February, 1946,
that it had uncovered an extensive Soviet spy ring. In a report published a few months later, a Canadian royal commission said that
at least fourteen Canadian "public officials and other persons in
positions of trust" gave valuable secret data to the Russians. Among
the contributions that Canadian spies made to Soviet science were
samples of enriched Uranium 235 and information vital to the development of radar. Prodded in part by nervous Congressmen, President Truman decided that the time had come to tighten government
security.

In 1946 Truman appointed a Temporary Commission on Employee Loyalty and, on the basis of its report, issued a famous
executive order in March, 1947, establishing a new loyalty program
for the federal government. Truman's order enumerated the grounds
on which an employee could be removed as a loyalty risk. These
included espionage, advocacy of revolution, and membership in or
"sympathetic association with" organizations deemed subversive by the
Attorney General. Truman called on the FBI to check the names
of all government workers against FBI files and, upon turning up
derogatory information about an employee, to inform the appropriate
agency. If the agency chief determined that an FBI report warranted
further action, he appointed a loyalty board composed of employees
within the agency. The accused had the right to a hearing before a
loyalty board and was entitled to counsel. Should a loyalty board
decide against an employee, he could appeal first to the agency chief
and then to a newly created Loyalty Review Board of the Civil Service
Commission. As for security risks, sensitive agencies, including the
State Department, already possessed Congressional authorization to
dismiss them summarily. (A security risk was not necessarily disloyal,
but because of his associations, his personal life, or psychological
peculiarities, he was not regarded as trustworthy.) In practice, after
1947, federal agencies with loyalty as well as security programs handled both kinds of cases in the same way, except that security risks
could not appeal to the Loyalty Review Board.

From the beginning the president's program met considerable criticism, especially from liberals. Defenders of civil liberties argued that
the program's loyalty standards were vague. Moreover, by denying the
accused the right to confront and cross-examine his anonymous
accusers, the program violated the principles of Anglo-American
justice. The government, the critics said, would ever after conduct

secret investigations into the beliefs and personal affairs of its employees. And, wrote Alan Barth in *The Loyalty of Free Men,* "The mandate which the executive order gives the Attorney General to designate voluntary associations as subversive is perhaps the most arbitrary and far-reaching power ever exercised by a single public official in the history of the United States." Heedless of these criticisms, the administration put the program's machinery into operation. From 1947 until May, 1953, when President Eisenhower created his own program, the FBI ran 4,772,278 name checks on both government employees and job applicants and conducted 27,326 full field investigations of suspect persons. The government denied employment to 575 on loyalty grounds, 3,634 employees quit before their cases were adjudicated, and 2,748 others resigned while still under investigation. It is impossible to evaluate these figures. On the one hand the program did not uncover a single spy and rested primarily on the doubtful practice of examining the political ideas and associations of government employees. On the other hand there can be little doubt that, for whatever reason, after Truman's order took effect the violations of national security so widespread in the war years soon became rare indeed.

The government was not content with mere defensive measures and decided to strike a blow directly against the American Communist party. In July, 1948, the Department of Justice obtained indictments charging the eleven members of the party's national board with violating the Smith Act of 1940 by teaching and advocating the overthrow of the government. The defendants were not accused of participating in an illegal plot or committing revolutionary acts; they were tried for advocacy of proscribed ideas. The Communist party tried to convert the trial, which consumed nine months of 1949, into a vehicle for its own propaganda, and while pickets paraded in front of the courthouse, defense lawyers turned the courtroom into a circus. In the end the jury found the Communists guilty as charged. In 1951 the Supreme Court upheld the convictions and the Smith Act in the case of *Dennis et al.* v. *United States.* To justify its decision, the Court had to reckon with Justice Holmes's declaration in the Schenck case (1919) that speech could be outlawed only in circumstances "as to create a clear and present danger." Referring to Holmes's dictum, the Court majority said, "Obviously, the words cannot mean that before the Government may act, it must wait until the *putsch* is about to be executed, the plans have been laid and the signal is awaited. If Government is aware that a group aiming at its overthrow is attempting to indoctrinate its members and to commit them to a course whereby they will strike when the leaders feel the circumstances permit, action by the Government is required." In his dissenting opinion Justice William O. Douglas denied existence of a clear and present danger. "To believe," he said, "that petitioners and their following are placed in such critical positions as to endanger the Nation is to believe the incredible." (In 1957 in *Yates* v. *United States,* the Court retreated from the Dennis decision and held that mere speech divorced from action enjoyed the protection of the First Amendment.)

But in 1949, even as the party was staggering from this succession of blows, public anxieties about domestic communism began to assume irrational proportions. In large measure public concern with subversives was the work of two former Communists, Elizabeth Bentley and Whittaker Chambers, who appeared in August, 1948, before the House Un-American Activities Committee (HUAC) to tell about their days in the underground. Miss Bentley, naive and somewhat confused, told how she was lured into espionage by her lover, a Russian-born agent named Jacob Golos, and how she collected secret documents for the Red underground from two government cells from 1941 to 1944. Chambers, a senior editor of *Time* in 1948, was a more compelling and sophisticated witness. The product of a scandalous youth and a repentant middle age, Chambers presented himself as an agent of destiny in the struggle against communism. The essence of his dramatic testimony before HUAC was that from 1933 to 1937 he collected dues from Communists who were on the way up in the federal bureaucracy. In all, Chambers and Bentley named some fifty persons who had allegedly participated in covert Communist activities in the 1930s and 1940s. Among those named were Laughlin Currie, once a White House assistant to FDR; Harry Dexter White, a former assistant secretary of the treasury; and Alger Hiss, former high-ranking career official in the State Department and, since 1946, president of the Carnegie Endowment for International Peace. Thus began the famous Hiss Case, an important milestone on the road to McCarthyism.

Two days after Whittaker Chambers made his accusations against him before HUAC, Hiss voluntarily appeared as a witness to reply. Hiss was a man of enviable reputation and impeccable social credentials. He swore now, "I am not and never have been a member of the Communist party," and he went on to deny Chambers' statement that "we were close friends." After Chambers repeated his accusations on the radio, Hiss instituted libel proceedings against him and thereby began a chain of events that culminated in his own ruin. On November 17, 1948, when Hiss's lawyers privately asked Chambers whether he had evidence to substantiate his story, Chambers is supposed to have replied, "Only these." Chambers thereupon produced copies of secret State Department documents, which, he said, Hiss had transmitted to him in the 1930s. These documents, of course, linked Hiss with espionage, but they also raised doubts about Chambers' own veracity. For Chambers had previously told HUAC that he had not collected espionage material in his work for the underground. Moreover, he had testified that he had broken with the party in 1937; since the documents that he now produced were dated early 1938, he had to change that part of his story. Chambers had still other surprises to spring. On December 3, 1948, he led two HUAC investigators to the garden in the rear of his Maryland home, thrust his hand into a scooped-out pumpkin, and brought forth rolls of microfilm, containing pictures of still more documents allegedly supplied by Hiss from the State Department's files. On December 15, 1948, a federal grand jury indicted Alger Hiss for perjury for denying that he ever transmitted secret papers to Whittaker Chambers.

The trials of Alger Hiss (the first ended in a hung jury) were the sensation of 1949. It was not merely that one of these fascinating and complex men was engaged in a monstrous lie. It was, as James Reston wrote in *The New York Times* (June 9, 1949), "that Mr. Hiss has become elevated by partisan minds into a symbol of the controversial group of young New Dealers who came to Washington in the 1930's and remained to administer a revolution in the nation's domestic and foreign policy." (To right-wingers it was almost too good to be true that Hiss had been a member of the U.S. delegation at Yalta.) As for Hiss's trials, they were a jungle of tangled issues, but on one point there could be little doubt. Hiss's defense failed to explain satisfactorily how some of the copies of the stolen State Department documents came to be typed on a typewriter once owned by the Hisses and kept in their home. When at last, in January, 1950, a jury found Alger Hiss guilty, the verdict was more than a personal tragedy for Hiss. No other episode in the postwar period did more to convince the public that, after all, treason had once reached into high places and perhaps was still there.

The year 1949 was not a happy one for the American nation. In the midst of Hiss's first trial, the public learned about Judith Coplon of the Foreign Agents Registration Division of the Department of Justice. A trusted employee with access to certain secret FBI reports, she had been making copies of some of these since 1946 and passing them to a Soviet intelligence contact named Valentin Gubitchev. In 1948 the FBI discovered the leak and eventually traced it to Miss Coplon's desk. On March 4, 1949, the FBI arrested her in the act of giving documents to Gubitchev. Though convicted of espionage by a federal jury, higher courts freed her on technicalities. But as the public understood only too well, Judith Coplon was undoubtedly guilty.

The event that most frightened the American people in 1949 and opened the way for a witch hunt was the victorious advance of Mao's guerrillas across mainland China. The Republican right wing, which had been confined to the political wilderness for two decades, its counsel ignored or scorned, now mounted a furious attack against the administration's China policy. On April 15, 1949, Senator Styles Bridges of New Hampshire called for a congressional investigation of the State Department and accused Secretary of State Dean Acheson of "what might be called sabotage of the valiant attempt of the Chinese Nationalists to keep at least part of China free." On April 21, Senator William Knowland of California likewise demanded an investigation and said, "If ever a government has had the rug pulled out from under it, if ever a non-Communist government in the world has reason to feel betrayed, that government is the Republic of China." The public, which was not well informed about events in China, suddenly became aware on August 5, 1949, of the tremendous change about to occur in world politics. The State Department released its white paper on China, a huge volume that was both a history and a justification of U.S. policy. Unfortunately for the administration, the white paper only alarmed the public and enraged Chiang Kai-shek's American friends. Four pro-Chiang senators denounced the white paper as a "whitewash of wishful, do-nothing policy which has succeeded only in placing Asia in danger of Soviet conquest." The most ominous criticism came from former U.S. ambassador to China, General Patrick Hurley. In November, 1945, Hurley had blamed the failure of his mission in China on State Department career officials who, he said, "sided with the Chinese Communist armed policy." Few then paid much attention. Now Hurley called the white paper "a smooth alibi for the pro-Communists in the State Department, who had engineered the overthrow of our ally, the Nationalist Government of the Republic of China and aided in the Communist conquest of China." This time his words found a receptive audience.

As 1949 came to a close and the Nationalists transferred their capital to the island of Formosa, revulsion against U.S. policy increased. On January 2, 1950, former President Herbert Hoover and Senator Robert A. Taft of Ohio demanded American naval protection for Chiang's regime on Formosa. Three days later Truman barred further military aid to the Nationalists. Senator Taft, "Mr. Republican" to millions in his party and a man famous for his integrity, rose in the Senate to say, "the State Department has been guided by a left-wing group who obviously have wanted to get rid of Chiang, and were willing at least to turn China over to the Communists for that purpose." The ingredients for the witch hunt had begun to brew.

In the midst of the furor over China, and one day after a federal judge ordered Judith Coplon to stand trial for espionage, the jury in the Hiss case returned its verdict. Four days later, on January 25, 1950, Secretary Acheson answered a question at his press conference about Hiss and left Democratic politicians, according to *The New York Times*, "aghast." Acheson, who had known Hiss for years, said, "I should like to make it clear to you that, whatever the outcome of any appeal which Mr. Hiss and his lawyers may take in this case, I do not intend to turn my back on Alger Hiss." Republicans, who were trying to link Hiss with the Democrats, seized gleefully on Acheson's statement and made the most of it. "I don't know," said Congressman Robert F. Rich of Pennsylvania, "if we have anybody working with Joe Stalin more than the Secretary of State."

Worse was yet to come. On the last day of January, 1950, President Truman announced that the U.S. had decided to build hydrogen bombs, which were potentially a thousand times more powerful than the A-bomb. Scientists forecast that the Russians too would soon have H-bombs, and Albert Einstein went on television to warn, "General annihilation beckons." Then on February 3, the British Government released the news that it had arrested Dr. Klaus Fuchs, one of Britain's top atomic scientists, for giving atomic secrets to the Russians. The British had sent Fuchs to the United States from 1943 to 1946 to work on the A-bomb, and while in this country he had transmitted secret atomic data to an underground courier named Harry Gold. (Eventually the confessions of Fuchs and Gold implicated others, including Julius and Ethel Rosenberg, who were later executed in the U.S. for their treason.) The right wing immediately exploited the Fuchs case for its partisan purposes. Senator Homer Capehart of Indiana announced, "There are other spies, too, and there will continue to be as long as we have a President who refers to such matters as 'red herrings' and a Secretary of State who refuses to turn his back on the Alger Hisses." The Republican party issued a "Statement of Principles and Objectives" on February 6, 1950, that, among other points, made clear a developing interest in the issue of subversion:

> We deplore the dangerous degree to which Communists and their fellow travellers have been employed in important Government posts and the fact that information vital to our security has been made available to alien agents and persons of questionable loyalty. We denounce the soft attitude of this Administration toward Government employees and officials who hold or support Communist attitudes.

Three days later, Senator McCarthy traveled to West Virginia and made his bid to become the spokesman for the right wing.

Fifth of nine children, Joseph R. McCarthy was born November 14, 1909, near Grand Chute, a township one hundred miles north of Milwaukee. His father, Timothy McCarthy, was a stern and hard-working farmer, half-Irish and half-German in ancestry. His mother, Bridget, was an Irish immigrant who, according to the McCarthy legend, made Joe her favorite child. The family, devout Catholics, worked together on 142 acres and managed to rise a bit above poverty. McCarthy was apparently shy and awkward as a boy, but he was also diligent at his chores, a good student, and anxious for independence. At age fourteen he quit school, rented an acre of land from his father, and went into the business of raising chickens. For five years he devoted himself to his flocks and gradually achieved some prosperity. But when he became ill and had to rely on outside help, his chickens began dying of disease and neglect, and at the age of nineteen McCarthy was ruined. He decided then to abandon the farm.

McCarthy moved to Manawa, a small town twenty miles from his home. He had by now developed a gregarious, flamboyant personality and, as manager of the Cashway market in Manawa, he immediately became a local notable. With encouragement from the town's high school principal, he decided to continue his education, and in one year completed a four-year high school course. Now twenty-one, he entered Marquette University, a Jesuit institution in Milwaukee, where he began as a student of engineering and after two years switched to the law school. He was too busy to be anything but a mediocre student. Working at a variety of odd jobs, he found time to become class president and a varsity boxer known for his slashing, wide-open style. In 1935 McCarthy received his law degree and opened a law office in the town of Waupaca, Wisconsin. According to Jack Anderson and Ronald W. May in their book *McCarthy: The Man, the Senator, and the "Ism"*, McCarthy's first months of practice were so unprofitable that he survived financially only through his skills at the poker table. In February, 1936, he moved from Manawa to Shawano to take a job with Mike G. Eberlein, a successful lawyer and a minor power in the state Republican party.

McCarthy's real passion was politics. Six months after he moved to Shawano he was elected president of the Young Democratic Clubs of Wisconsin's seventh district. Now twenty-seven years old and in possession of a political organization, he decided to run for district attorney of Shawano County. Democrats had no chance to win anything in Shawano, but McCarthy nevertheless made a strong showing.

In the next three years he apparently extended his friendships and did well enough at the bar to become Eberlein's partner. He also switched political loyalties. In 1939 McCarthy announced that he was going to run in the Republican primary for judge of Wisconsin's tenth circuit. McCarthy's declaration was especially surprising to Mike Eberlein, who had already informed McCarthy privately of his own desire to run for the office. The partnership of McCarthy and Eberlein dissolved a short time later. After winning the primary, McCarthy ran a strenuous campaign that stressed the age of the incumbent, Judge Edgar V. Werner, "my 73-year-old opponent." Werner was actually 66. McCarthy won handily.

McCarthy never intended to make a career of the bench and began immediately to turn his new eminence into publicity. To dispose of a large backlog of cases, McCarthy specialized in "quickie" divorces and sometimes kept his court in session till midnight. In a few months his calendar was cleared and, better still, he had won the attention of the state's newspapers. Not everyone admired his judicial performance, however. In one notorious case, McCarthy inexplicably refused to enjoin a Wisconsin dairy company from breaking a state law. When the case reached the Supreme Court, it was discovered that McCarthy had actually destroyed part of the case record. The Supreme Court rebuked McCarthy for his decision and deemed his destruction of the records "highly improper."

Six months after World War II began, McCarthy asked the other judges of Wisconsin's circuit courts to take over his work load and took a commission as an officer in the U.S. Marines. (Before he left for basic training, he had himself photographed hearing a case in a cash-and-carry uniform.) For most of his tour of duty, McCarthy served in the South Pacific as an intelligence officer whose responsibility was to interview pilots returning from combat. But sometimes he received permission to go along on combat missions and, sitting as a passenger in the tail gunner's seat, he got to shoot the guns. He later boasted that he was known throughout the Pacific as "Tail Gunner Joe." In 1951, claiming that he had flown thirty combat missions, he asked for and eventually received the Distinguished Flying Cross. Though McCarthy also said later that he had suffered a leg wound in combat, his only wartime injury resulted from a freak accident incurred on a navy ship during an equator-crossing party. However exaggerated McCarthy's later recollections of his military exploits, he did impress his superior and friend, Marine Major E. E. Munn. It was Munn who obtained for McCarthy a citation from Admiral Chester Nimitz, praising McCarthy for his contributions on combat missions and for continuing to perform his duties while "suffering from a severe leg injury." Throughout his stay in the Pacific, McCarthy made sure that the home folks back in Wisconsin were treated to news stories about their soldier-judge.

McCarthy's real goal was the U.S. Senate. In 1944, while still in the Pacific, he opened a campaign to win the Republican primary against incumbent Alexander Wiley. McCarthy ignored both a state law forbidding state judges to run for other offices and a military regulation barring servicemen from speaking on political issues. McCarthy got a thirty-day pass to go home to campaign, and though Wiley defeated him, McCarthy made a respectable showing. When the Marines subsequently refused to give McCarthy a three-month pass to run for re-election as circuit judge, he resigned his commission and in February, 1945, returned to civilian life. McCarthy won re-election easily and laid plans to capture the Senate seat of "Young Bob" LaFollette.

Robert M. LaFollette, Jr., was the son of "Fighting Bob" LaFollette, the great progressive leader of the early twentieth century. Since 1925 Young Bob had occupied his father's seat with quiet distinction and had several times been selected the outstanding senator by the Washington press corps. In March, 1946, LaFollette recognized that Wisconsin's Progressive party, which had for years returned La-Follettes to office over Republicans and Democrats alike, was now moribund. Against the opposition of organized labor, LaFollette persuaded the Progressive party convention of 1946 to endorse a movement into the Republican party. LaFollette himself entered the Republican primary to seek the party's senatorial nomination. His opponent was thirty-seven-year-old Joseph McCarthy, whose slogan was "Congress needs a Tailgunner."

While LaFollette stayed in Washington to work on his monumental congressional reorganization bill, McCarthy stumped the state. Successfully straddling the main issues of the day, he spent most of his effort in attacking his version of LaFollette's record. McCarthy accused LaFollette of making "war profits" from his part ownership of a Wisconsin radio station, of drawing fat rations "while 15,000,000 Americans were fighting the war," and of staying on his "Virginian plantation" instead of explaining his sorry record to the people of Wisconsin. Regarded as an easy winner, LaFollette returned home only two weeks before the primary, spoke in generalities, and ignored McCarthy's charges. Seasoned observers predicted that McCarthy might carry rural Wisconsin but that he would lose the election in the industrial counties of Racine, Kenosha, and Milwaukee, where LaFollette had swamped his opponent in 1940 by 60,000 votes. It did not happen that way. LaFollette actually defeated McCarthy by a small majority in the rural counties, but the expected avalanche of labor votes for LaFollette never materialized. McCarthy won the state by 5,400 votes out of 410,000 cast.

McCarthy's stunning upset has frequently been ascribed to a Communist plot. It is true that Communists were outraged by LaFollette's recent criticism of Soviet foreign policy, that they exercised great influence in the Wisconsin C.I.O., and that on the eve of the primary the *Wisconsin C.I.O. News* attacked the Senator and recommended that its readers "take proper action at the next election." But the defection of the labor vote from LaFollette had more complex causes than communism, for A.F. of L. unions and railroad brotherhoods in Wisconsin also joined the C.I.O. in refusing to endorse LaFollette. Regardless of ideological differences, all elements of Wisconsin labor turned against LaFollette because he had failed to repudiate an endorsement from the conservative Senator Robert A. Taft and, most of all, because he defied labor's wishes and took the remnants of his Progressive following into the Republican instead of the Democratic party. In the primary election of 1946, organized labor worked neither for LaFollette nor McCarthy. It spent its money and its energy to swell the vote for liberals running in the Democratic primary. Thus in the three big industrial counties, Howard J. McMurray, unopposed for the Democratic senatorial nomination, polled 40,000 votes, many of which in other years would probably have gone to LaFollette.

In his race against McMurray, McCarthy charged that his opponent's campaign was part of a Communist conspiracy and that if Wisconsin sent a tail gunner to Washington, he would "make every effort toward removing the vast number of Communists from the public payrolls." On the eve of the election McCarthy exhorted the voters not to vote Democratic, for while "all Democrats are not Communists," enough Democrats were voting "the Communist way to make their presence in Congress a serious threat to the very foundation of our nation." The Republican tide was running strong nationwide in 1946, and in any case Wisconsin was not then in the habit of voting for Democrats. McCarthy won in a landslide.

Without much background or experience, McCarthy amassed a record in his early senatorial years that was at best undistinguished. After a few days in Washington he made *The New York Times* by demanding that Truman draft John L. Lewis of the United Mine Workers and court-martial the union chief if he refused to call off the coal strike. Throughout the next three years he continued to make enough news to avoid obscurity and in fact earned a certain notoriety in Washington through the causes which he championed, the company which he sometimes kept, and the crudeness of his political style. Particularly notable was his penchant for entwining his legislative interests with his personal finances.

In 1947, for instance, McCarthy became a specialist of sorts on the problem of sugar rationing. As a member of the Senate Banking and Currency Committee's subcommittee on sugar, McCarthy sought increased sugar allocations for industrial users and an early end of government rationing. In one wild debate on the sugar question, two of McCarthy's fellow Republicans, Charles Tobey of New Hampshire and Ralph Flanders of Vermont, accused McCarthy of juggling figures and of falsely reporting a phone conversation he claimed to have had with the secretary of agriculture. McCarthy's zeal on the subject of rationing apparently owed as much to his private avarice as to his conception of the public good. Known in certain circles as the Pepsi Cola Kid, McCarthy was a friend of Russell M. Arundel, a Pepsi Cola lobbyist who once endorsed a $20,000 bank note for the senator at a time when McCarthy was financially embarrassed. Pepsi Cola, of course, stood to gain from an early end of sugar rationing.

McCarthy's special legislative interest was the housing problem. In 1947, as a freshman senator, he executed a clever parliamentary maneuver at the expense of Senator Tobey and won the vice-chairmanship of a special congressional committee on housing. In a short time he became a real authority on the subject. Opposed to public housing, McCarthy advocated government aid to private manufacturers of prefabricated homes as the best way to end the nationwide housing shortage. Again, however, his conduct made him vulnerable to charges of profiting from statesmanship. As a member of the Senate Banking and Currency Committee, he helped oversee operations of the Reconstruction Finance Corporation, which made large loans to the Lustron Corporation, builder of prefabricated homes. At a time when he desperately needed money, McCarthy asked Lustron to pay him $10,000 for a 36-page booklet that he had written on the subject of housing. Without consulting the company's other officers, the president of Lustron paid McCarthy the money.

McCarthy had other interests in these years, including Wisconsin furs, veterans, the Marine Corps, and the case of the Malmédy Massacre. In 1949 the Malmédy case became practically an obsession with McCarthy. Malmédy was a crossroads town in Belgium where, late in the war, German S.S. troops gunned down eighty American prisoners of war. After the war forty-three German soldiers were sentenced to die for this crime. In time the condemned men charged that the U.S. Army had obtained their confessions through intimidation, deception, and even torture. McCarthy, apparently to please pro-German constituents in Wisconsin, made himself the Senate champion of the Malmédy Germans. He discussed their case on the Senate floor, took over an Armed Services subcommittee investigation of the affair, and browbeat Raymond Baldwin of Connecticut, chairman of the subcommittee. (McCarthy quite properly objected to Baldwin's participation on the grounds that one of the original prosecutors of the Malmédy Germans was a partner in Baldwin's law firm.) McCarthy's treatment of witnesses, his abuse of the army, and his exaggerated rhetoric were without doubt outrageous, but the case that McCarthy argued was not without merit. The army itself had by early 1949 commuted most of the death sentences and would in time commute more.

Only once in these early years did McCarthy concern himself in the Senate with communism. On March 27, 1947, he proposed an amendment to a pending labor bill that would soon become the Taft-Hartley Act. McCarthy proposed permitting unions the right to persuade employers to dismiss any worker who was a "member of the Communist Party or [is] actively and consistently promoting or supporting the policies, teachings, and doctrine of the Communist Party . . . ." Senator Taft thought that McCarthy's amendment contributed nothing to his bill, and after a short debate it was voted down.

In retrospect the most interesting aspect of McCarthy's early senatorial performance was his style. From the beginning he displayed only contempt for the traditions of the Senate, defied powerful colleagues, and indulged in debating tactics that other senators sometimes found irresponsible. McCarthy was, therefore, kept on the fringe of the Senate, far away from the centers of real influence and power. And on the fringe he might have remained, except that in 1950 more circumspect right-wing senators found his peculiar gifts useful to their cause. Some of these same senators would soon learn, however, that McCarthy would be the servant of no one's purposes but his own. The documents that follow will trace McCarthy's career as an anti-Communist crusader, examine some of the reactions he provoked, and explore the fascinating problem of who it was who rallied to his cause.

# Chronology of McCarthyism

| | |
|---|---|
| **1909** | (November) McCarthy born in Grand Chute, Wisconsin. |
| **1935** | Begins law practice in Wawpaca. |
| **1939** | Elected circuit judge. |
| **1942** | Enters Marine Corps. |
| **1944** | Loses Wisconsin Republican senatorial primary. |
| **1945** | (February) Classified documents discovered in *Amerasia* offices. |
| **1946** | (February) Canadian government reveals Soviet spy ring. (November) McCarthy elected to U.S. Senate. |
| **1947** | (March) Truman initiates tough loyalty program. |
| **1948** | (July) Top communists indicted for violating Smith Act. (August) Whittaker Chambers accuses Alger Hiss. |
| **1949** | (August) State Department issues white paper on China. McCarthy defends Malmédy Germans. |
| **1950** | (January) Hiss found guilty. Truman decides to build H-bomb. (February) Klaus Fuchs arrested for atomic espionage. McCarthy makes his first charges of Communists in the government. (June) North Korea invades South Korea. (July) Tydings committee denounces McCarthy's charges. (November) Tydings defeated for re-election to Senate. Red China enters Korean conflict. (December) McCarthy blames Korean disaster on State Department. |
| **1951** | (April) Truman recalls MacArthur. (June) McCarthy links General Marshall to Red plot. (August) Senator Benton moves McCarthy's expulsion. |
| **1952** | (July) McCarthy receives ovation at Republican convention. (October) McCarthy on TV accuses Stevenson of aiding Reds. (November) McCarthy re-elected Senator. |
| **1953** | (January) McCarthy becomes chairman of Government Operations Committee. (April) Cohn and Schine go on famous junket. (July) Army drafts Schine. (October) McCarthy seeks Reds in Army Signal Corps. |
| **1954** | (February) Eisenhower breaks with McCarthy. (March) Army-McCarthy hearings begin. (July) Senator Flanders moves McCarthy's censure. (December) Senate censures McCarthy. |
| **1957** | (May) McCarthy dies. |

# McCARTHY'S ANTI-COMMUNIST CRUSADE, 1950–1954

# 1

## McCarthy and the State Department

### FIRST CHARGES

*McCarthy began his career as the nation's leading Red hunter on February 9, 1950, in a speech in Wheeling, West Virginia. Controversy about what McCarthy actually said in this speech would rage for years. According to a report the next day in the* Wheeling Intelligencer, *McCarthy stated, "I have here in my hand a list of 205 that were known to the secretary of state as being members of the Communist Party and who, nevertheless are still working and shaping the policy of the State Department." McCarthy subsequently denied making that charge. In his book* McCarthyism: The Fight for America, *McCarthy recalled that he had used the number 205 at Wheeling because in 1946 Secretary of State James F. Byrnes admitted dismissing only 79 of the 284 Departmental employees known to be security risks. That left 205. "I said that while I did not have the names of the 205 referred to in the Byrnes letter, I did have the names of 57 who were either members of or loyal to the Communist Party." And no one disputes that the day after his Wheeling speech, McCarthy said in Salt Lake City that he had "the names of 57 card-carrying members of the Communist Party."*

*In the days that followed, McCarthy's charges against the State Department became national news and provoked denials from the president and the State Department. On February 13, 1950, to reassure the public, the State Department issued a statement summarizing the results of its loyalty-security program. Since 1947 the FBI had checked 16,075 departmental employees.*

*Of these only two had been "separated" from service as security
risks, and none had been found disloyal. In addition 202 employees on "whom security questions had been raised have left
the Department . . . either through resignation or reduction
of force." The department assured the country that it "knows
of no Communists who are presently employed."*

*With interest in McCarthy and his charges rapidly increasing,
he took to the Senate floor on February 20, 1950, to make a full
statement of his case. In the course of his remarks he put into
the* Congressional Record *a copy of what he claimed was his
Wheeling speech of February 9. Even L. Brent Bozell and William F. Buckley concede in their book* McCarthy and His Enemies, *a defense of the senator, that he was obviously in error.
Making no reference at all to 205 loyalty or security risks, the
speech in the* Record *was not the one McCarthy delivered
at Wheeling. Buckley and Bozell suggest that it was actually
the transcript of a speech that McCarthy made a few days
later at Reno. Regardless of where it was delivered, this address,
reprinted below, is a good sample of McCarthy's case against
the State Department.*[1]

Ladies and gentlemen, tonight as we celebrate the one hundred
and forty-first birthday of one of the greatest men in American history, I would like to be able to talk about what a glorious day today
is in the history of the world. As we celebrate the birth of this man
who with his whole heart and soul hated war, I would like to be able
to speak of peace in our time, of war being outlawed, and of world-
wide disarmament. These would be truly appropriate things to be
able to mention as we celebrate the birthday of Abraham Lincoln.

Five years after a world war has been won, men's hearts should
anticipate a long peace, and men's minds should be free from the
heavy weight that comes with war. But this is not such a period—
for this is not a period of peace. This is a time of the "cold war."
This is a time when all the world is split into two vast, increasingly
hostile armed camps—a time of a great armaments race.

Today we can almost physically hear the mutterings and rumblings
of an invigorated god of war. You can see it, feel it, and hear it all
the way from the hills of Indochina, from the shores of Formosa,
right over into the very heart of Europe itself.

The one encouraging thing is that the "mad moment" has not yet

[1] U.S., Congress, Senate, *Congressional Record,* 81st Cong., 2d sess., 1950, 96,
1954, 1946, 1957.

arrived for the firing of the gun or the exploding of the bomb which will set civilization about the final task of destroying itself. There is still a hope for peace if we finally decide that no longer can we safely blind our eyes and close our ears to those facts which are shaping up more and more clearly. And that is that we are now engaged in a show-down fight—not the usual war between nations for land areas or other material gains, but a war between two diametrically opposed ideologies.

The great difference between our western Christian world and the atheistic Communist world is not political, ladies and gentlemen, it is moral. There are other differences, of course, but those could be reconciled. For instance, the Marxian idea of confiscating the land and factories and running the entire economy as a single enterprise is momentous. Likewise, Lenin's invention of the one-party police state as a way to make Marx's idea work is hardly less momentous.

Stalin's resolute putting across of these two ideas, of course, did much to divide the world. With only those differences, however, the East and the West could most certainly still live in peace.

The real, basic difference, however, lies in the religion of immoralism—invented by Marx, preached feverishly by Lenin, and carried to unimaginable extremes by Stalin. This religion of immoralism, if the Red half of the world wins—and well it may—this religion of immoralism will more deeply wound and damage mankind than any conceivable economic or political system.

Karl Marx dismissed God as a hoax, and Lenin and Stalin have added in clear-cut, unmistakable language their resolve that no nation, no people who believe in a God, can exist side by side with their communistic state.

Karl Marx, for example, expelled people from his Communist Party for mentioning such things as justice, humanity, or morality. He called this soulful ravings and sloppy sentimentality.

While Lincoln was a relatively young man in his late thirties, Karl Marx boasted that the Communist specter was haunting Europe. Since that time, hundreds of millions of people and vast areas of the world have fallen under Communist domination. Today, less than 100 years after Lincoln's death, Stalin brags that this Communist specter is not only haunting the world, but is about to completely subjugate it.

Today we are engaged in a final, all-out battle between communistic atheism and Christianity. The modern champions of communism have selected this as the time. And, ladies and gentlemen, the chips are down—they are truly down.

Lest there be any doubt that the time has been chosen, let us go directly to the leader of communism today—Joseph Stalin. Here is what he said—not back in 1928, not before the war, not during the war—but 2 years after the last war was ended: "To think that the Communist revolution can be carried out peacefully, within the framework of a Christian democracy, means one has either gone out of one's mind and lost all normal understanding, or has grossly and openly repudiated the Communist revolution."

And this is what was said by Lenin in 1919, which was also quoted with approval by Stalin in 1947:

"We are living," said Lenin, "not merely in a state, but in a system of states, and the existence of the Soviet Republic side by side with Christian states for a long time is unthinkable. One or the other must triumph in the end. And before that end supervenes, a series of frightful collisions between the Soviet Republic and the Bourgeois states will be inevitable."

Ladies and gentlemen, can there be anyone here tonight who is so blind as to say that the war is not on? Can there be anyone who fails to realize that the Communist world has said, "The time is now"— that this is the time for the show-down between the democratic Christian world and the Communist atheistic world?

Unless we face this fact, we shall pay the price that must be paid by those who wait too long.

Six years ago, at the time of the first conference to map out the peace—Dumbarton Oaks—there was within the Soviet orbit 180,000,-000 people. Lined up on the antitotalitarian side there were in the world at that time roughly 1,625,000,000 people. Today, only 6 years later, there are 800,000,000 people under the absolute domination of Soviet Russia—an increase of over 400 percent. On our side, the figure has shrunk to around 500,000,000. In other words, in less than 6 years the odds have changed from 9 to 1 in our favor to 8 to 5 against us. This indicates the swiftness of the tempo of Communist victories and American defeats in the cold war. As one of our outstanding historical figures once said, "When a great democracy is destroyed, it will not be because of enemies from without, but rather because of enemies from within."

The truth of this statement is becoming terrifyingly clear as we see this country each day losing on every front.

At war's end we were physically the strongest nation on earth and, at least potentially, the most powerful intellectually and morally. Ours could have been the honor of being a beacon in the desert of destruction, a shining living proof that civilization was not yet ready to destroy itself. Unfortunately, we have failed miserably and tragically to arise to the opportunity.

The reason why we find ourselves in a position of impotency is not because our only powerful potential enemy has sent men to invade our shores, but rather because of the traitorous actions of those who have been treated so well by this Nation. It has not been the less fortunate or members of minority groups who have been selling this Nation out, but rather those who have had all the benefits that the wealthiest nation on earth has had to offer—the finest homes, the finest college education, and the finest jobs in Government we can give.

This is glaringly true in the State Department. There the bright young men who are born with silver spoons in their mouths are the ones who have been worst.

Now I know it is very easy for anyone to condemn a particular bureau or department in general terms. Therefore, I would like to cite one rather unusual case—the case of a man who has done much to shape our foreign policy.

When Chiang Kai-shek was fighting our war, the State Department had in China a young man named John S. Service. His task, obviously, was not to work for the communization of China. Strangely, however, he sent official reports back to the State Department urging that we torpedo our ally Chiang Kai-shek and stating, in effect, that communism was the best hope of China.

Later, this man—John Service—was picked up by the Federal Bureau of Investigation for turning over to the Communists secret State Department information. Strangely, however, he was never prosecuted. However, Joseph Grew, the Under Secretary of State, who insisted on his prosecution, was forced to resign. Two days after Grew's successor, Dean Acheson, took over as Under Secretary of State, this man—John Service—who had been picked up by the FBI and who had previously urged that communism was the best hope of China, was not only reinstated in the State Department but promoted. And finally, under Acheson, placed in charge of all placements and promotions.

Today, ladies and gentlemen, this man Service is on his way to represent the State Department and Acheson in Calcutta—by far and away the most important listening post in the Far East.

Now, let's see what happens when individuals with Communist connections are forced out of the State Department. Gustave Duran, who was labeled as (I quote) "a notorious international Communist," was made assistant to the Assistant Secretary of State in charge of Latin American affairs. He was taken into the State Department from his job as a lieutenant colonel in the Communist International Brigade. Finally, after intense congressional pressure and criticism, he resigned in 1946 from the State Department—and, ladies and gentlemen, where do you think he is now? He took over a high-salaried job as Chief of Cultural Activities Section in the office of the Assistant Secretary General of the United Nations.

Then there was a Mrs. Mary Jane Kenny, from the Board of Economic Warfare in the State Department, who was named in an FBI report and in a House committee report as a courier for the Communist Party while working for the Government. And where do you think Mrs. Kenny is—she is now an editor in the United Nations Document Bureau.

Another interesting case was that of Julian H. Wadleigh, economist in the Trade Agreements Section of the State Department for 11 years and [sic] was sent to Turkey and Italy and other countries as United States representative. After the statute of limitations had run so he could not be prosecuted for treason, he openly and brazenly not only admitted but proclaimed that he had been a member of the Communist Party * * * that while working for the State Department he stole a vast number of secret documents * * * and furnished these documents to the Russian spy ring of which he was a part.

You will recall last spring there was held in New York what was known as the World Peace Conference—a conference which was labeled by the State Department and Mr. Truman as the sounding board for Communist propaganda and a front for Russia. Dr. Harlow Shapley was the chairman of that conference. Interestingly enough, according to the new release put out by the Department in July, the Secretary of State appointed Shapley on a commission which acts as liaison between UNESCO and the State Department.

This, ladies and gentlemen, gives you somewhat of a picture of the type of individuals who have been helping to shape our foreign policy. In my opinion the State Department, which is one of the most important government departments, is thoroughly infested with Communists.

I have in my hand 57 cases of individuals who would appear to be either card carrying members or certainly loyal to the Communist Party, but who nevertheless are still helping to shape our foreign policy.

One thing to remember in discussing the Communists in our Government is that we are not dealing with spies who get 30 pieces of silver to steal the blueprints of a new weapon. We are dealing with a far more sinister type of activity because it permits the enemy to guide and shape our policy. . . .

This brings us down to the case of one Alger Hiss who is important not as an individual any more, but rather because he is so representative of a group in the State Department. It is unnecessary to go over the sordid events showing how he sold out the Nation which had given him so much. Those are rather fresh in all of our minds.

However, it should be remembered that the facts in regard to his connection with this international Communist spy ring were made known to the then Under Secretary of State Berle 3 days after Hitler and Stalin signed the Russo-German alliance pact. At that time one Whittaker Chambers—who was also part of the spy ring—apparently decided that with Russia on Hitler's side, he could no longer betray our Nation to Russia. He gave Under Secretary of State Berle—and this is all a matter of record—practically all, if not more, of the facts upon which Hiss' conviction was based.

Under Secretary Berle promptly contacted Dean Acheson and received word in return that Acheson (and I quote) "could vouch for Hiss absolutely"—at which time the matter was dropped. And this, you understand, was at a time when Russia was an ally of Germany. This condition existed while Russia and Germany were invading and dismembering Poland, and while the Communist groups here were screaming "warmonger" at the United States for their support of the allied nations.

Again in 1943, the FBI had occasion to investigate the facts surrounding Hiss' contacts with the Russian spy ring. But even after that FBI report was submitted, nothing was done.

Then late in 1948—on August 5—when the Un-American Activities Committee called Alger Hiss to give an accounting, President Truman at once issued a Presidential directive ordering all Government agencies to refuse to turn over any information whatsoever in regard to the Communist activities of any Government employee to a congressional committee.

Incidentally, even after Hiss was convicted—it is interesting to note that the President still labeled the exposé of Hiss as a "red herring."

If time permitted, it might be well to go into detail about the fact that Hiss was Roosevelt's chief adviser at Yalta when Roosevelt was admittedly in ill health and tired physically and mentally * * * and when, according to the Secretary of State, Hiss and Gromyko drafted the report on the conference.

According to the then Secretary of State Stettinius, here are some of the things that Hiss helped to decide at Yalta. (1) The establishment of a European High Commission; (2) the treatment of Germany —this you will recall was the conference at which it was decided that we would occupy Berlin with Russia occupying an area completely circling the city, which, as you know, resulted in the Berlin airlift which cost 31 American lives; (3) the Polish question; (4) the relationship between UNRRA and the Soviet; (5) the rights of Americans on control commissions of Rumania, Bulgaria, and Hungary; (6) Iran; (7) China—here's where we gave away Manchuria; (8) Turkish Straits question; (9) international trusteeships; (10) Korea.

Of the results of this conference, Arthur Bliss Lane of the State Department had this to say: "As I glanced over the document, I could

not believe my eyes. To me, almost every line spoke of a surrender
to Stalin."

As you hear this story of high treason, I know that you are saying
to yourself, "Well, why doesn't the Congress do something about it?"
Actually, ladies and gentlemen, one of the important reasons for the
graft, the corruption, the dishonesty, the disloyalty, the treason in high
Government positions—one of the most important reasons why this
continues is a lack of moral uprising on the part of the 140,000,000
American people. In the light of history, however, this is not hard to
explain.

It is the result of an emotional hang-over and a temporary moral
lapse which follows every war. It is the apathy to evil which people
who have been subjected to the tremendous evils of war feel. As the
people of the world see mass murder, the destruction of defenseless
and innocent people, and all of the crime and lack of morals which
go with war, they become numb and apathetic. It has always been
thus after war.

However, the morals of our people have not been destroyed. They
still exist. This cloak of numbness and apathy has only needed a
spark to rekindle them. Happily, this spark has finally been supplied.

As you know, very recently the Secretary of State proclaimed his
loyalty to a man guilty of what has always been considered as the
most abominable of all crimes—of being a traitor to the people who
gave him a position of great trust. The Secretary of State in attempting to justify his continued devotion to the man who sold out the
Christian world to the atheistic world, referred to Christ's Sermon on
the Mount as a justification and reason therefor, and the reaction of
the American people to this would have made the heart of Abraham
Lincoln happy.

When this pompous diplomat in striped pants, with a phony British
accent, proclaimed to the American people that Christ on the Mount
endorsed communism, high treason, and betrayal of a sacred trust,
the blasphemy was so great that it awakened the dormant indignation
of the American people.

He has lighted the spark which is resulting in a moral uprising and
will end only when the whole sorry mess of twisted, warped thinkers
are swept from the national scene so that we may have a new birth
of national honesty and decency in Government.

### McCARTHY "DOCUMENTS" HIS CASE

*In a hectic six-hour speech that he delivered in the Sen-
ate on February 20, 1950, McCarthy attempted to demonstrate the laxity of the State Department's security procedures.*

*He cited eighty-one cases of employees whose security files allegedly proved them a menace to the nation. McCarthy noted that some of his cases were still working in the department but that others were no longer there. Some were Communists or espionage agents; others were merely security risks. McCarthy later contended that the famous fifty-seven Communists of whom he had spoken ten days before were included in his eighty-one cases, but he neglected to so inform the assembled senators. He claimed that the source of his cases was the State Department's own security files, leaked to him by "loyal" departmental employees; in reality his cases came from the files of the House Appropriations Committee, which had investigated the security program two years before. The Senator's literate defenders, Buckley and Bozell, admit that comparison of this committee's files with McCarthy's speech reveals that he exaggerated in no fewer than thirty-eight of his cases. Buckley and Bozell also claim that of the three cases which McCarthy regarded as most important, No. 1 was later suspended, No. 2 was ultimately found to be a loyalty risk, and No. 81 had been "separated" from the government four months before. Excerpts from McCarthy's February 20 speech follow.*[2]

I finally arrived at the conclusion that the only way to clean out the State Department, or any other Department which is infested with Communists, is not by the passage of any additional law. The only way it can be done is to secure the cooperation of the President. If we could get that, and he says that the information will be made available so that trusted staff members could go over the files, and we can be sure that the sources of information shall not be disclosed, we can clean house. I frankly think that is the only way. In line with that, I decided to submit to the Senate the detailed cases. Originally I was disturbed that I might give out information which would embarrass the investigative agencies by indirectly disclosing some of their sources of information, but I was told, "With so many commies over here having top positions, you need not fear giving the information to the Senate."

I have gone over it. Let me say, before starting, that I shall submit quite a large number of names. I think they are of importance. They all worked for the State Department at one time or another. Some are not there at the present time. Many of them have gone into work which is connected closely with the Department, for example, foreign trade, and some branches of the Maritime Commission.

I shall not attempt to present a detailed case on each one, a case which would convince a jury. All I am doing is to develop sufficient evidence so that anyone who reads the *Record* will have a good idea of the number of Communists in the State Department.

While I consider them all important, there are three big Communists involved, and I cannot possibly conceive of any Secretary of State allowing those three big Communists, who are tremendously important and of great value to Russia, to remain in the State Department. I do not believe President Truman knows about them. I cannot help but feel that he is merely the prisoner of a bunch of twisted intellectuals who tell him what they want him to know. To those who say, "Why do you not tell the State Department; why do you not give the names to the State Department?" I say that everything I have here is from the State Department's own files. I felt, when the State Department asked for the names, without being willing to cooperate or to work with us, it was saying, "Tip us off; let us know on whom you have the goods."

*Case No. 1.* The names are available. The Senators may have them if they care for them. I think, however, it would be improper to make the names public until the appropriate Senate committee can meet in executive session and get them. I have approximately 81 cases. I do not claim to have any tremendous investigative agency to get the facts, but if I were to give all the names involved, it might leave a wrong impression. If we should label one man a Communist when he is not a Communist, I think it would be too bad. However, the names are here. I shall be glad to abide by the decision of the Senate after it hears the cases, but I think the sensible thing to do would be to have an executive session and have a proper committee go over the whole situation. . . .

I was very happy to hear the Senator from Massachusetts say that he would move that the Foreign Relations Committee appoint a subcommittee to go into the cases.

The man involved in case No. 1 is employed in the office of an Assistant Secretary of State. The intelligence unit shadowed him and found him contacting members of an espionage group. A memorandum of December 13, 1946, indicates that he succeeded in having a well-known general intervene with an Assistant Secretary in behalf of one man who is an active Communist with a long record of Communist Party connections. There is another individual who is very closely tied up with a Soviet espionage agency. There is nothing in the file to indicate that the general referred to knew those two individuals were Communists.

That is a part of the usual modus operandi. If there is one Communist in the Department, he will get some other individual to recommend another Communist so that the breed can be increased.

This individual was successful in obtaining important positions for other Communists. They were finally ordered removed from the Department not later than November 15 of the following year. Subsequent to that time, however, both of them still had access to secret material.

A memorandum of November 2, 1946, pointed out that this individual and the previously mentioned Communists whom he succeeded in having placed were connected with an alleged Russian espionage agency. Nevertheless, this individual still occupies an important position in the State Department. I should like to point out at this time, however, that the security group, which was then operating in the State Department, was apparently doing a good job. It presented the entire picture to the Secretary of State. This individual who, the investigative agency of the State Department says, is a Communist, got a general innocently to bring two other Communists into the State Department, and he is today in the State Department and has access to the secret material. As I say, his name is certainly available to any Senate committee that wants it. . . .

*Case No. 7.* This individual was an associate business economist to August 1944; with FEA from August 1944 to August 1945, and then transferred to the State Department as an economist. This individual is a member of the Young Communist League. He was affiliated with four other organizations which are named by the Attorney General as having been Communist fronts. This individual admits membership in the Young Communists, and in the other Communist-front organizations, but claims to have changed his view since that time, and therefore was given top secret clearance by the State Department. I may say incidentally I am using the pronoun "he" in all these cases, although some of the individuals are not of the male sex. . . .

I may say that I know that some of these individuals whose cases I am giving the Senate are no longer in the State Department. A sizable number of them are not. Some of them have transferred to other Government work, work allied with the State Department. Others have been transferred to the United Nations. But I think the cases are important whenever we find that an individual, despite his Communist connections, has been given top-secret clearance. That gives an idea what is going on.

Here is one which I think the Senate will enjoy:

*Case No. 9.* This individual, after investigation, was not given security clearance by the State Department. After failing to obtain clearance by the State Department he secured a job in the Office of the

Secretary of Defense. And where do Senators think that man is today? He is now a speech writer in the White House. That is case No. 9. I will secure a little more information on that case if I may.

So that there may be no question about this, we will refer directly to the investigative file. I think I am doing Mr. Truman a favor by telling him this. I do not think he knows it. I do not think he would have this individual there writing speeches for him if he knew it.

Both the individual referred to and his wife—this is in the file of the investigative agency—are members of Communist-front organizations. He has a relative who has a financial interest in the Daily Worker. But in any event the State Department used good judgment not to clear this individual. . . .

*Mr. McMahon:* In the cases the Senator has recited, has the Senator simply read the derogatory information that was in the files or has the Senator attempted to give the full contents of the file in each case? . . .

*Mr. McCarthy:* The Senator asks whether I have complete State Department files. The answer is "No."

*Mr. McMahon:* Has the Senator the complete files in any one of the 34 cases?

*Mr. McCarthy:* Eighty-one cases.

*Mr. McMahon:* The Senator said he had presented 34 cases so far.

*Mr. McCarthy:* Yes.

*Mr. McMahon:* I take it the Senator is going through all 81. I merely say that when the Senator reaches case No. 81 I hope to be home in bed. That is beside the point. I want to find out from the Senator if in the cases he has read or in the cases that are to be presented, the Senator is able to give the Senate both the derogatory information that is in the file and any contradictory information that indicates that the derogatory information may be in question.

*Mr. McCarthy:* Let me answer the Senator.

*Mr. McMahon:* That is a yes-or-no question. Would the Senator give this information if he had it in his possession?

*Mr. McCarthy:* Does the Senator want the answer?

*Mr. McMahon:* Yes.

*Mr. McCarthy:* The answer is that I obviously do not have photostats of all the files.

*Mr. McMahon:* Has the Senator got——

*Mr. McCarthy:* Let me finish. I do not have a counterespionage group of my own. All I can do is pick up the information, check, and make sure it is confirmed by something in the State Department file. The Senator understands I do not have complete State Department files in these matters. I very greatly wish I did. That is one of the things I hope one of our committees will succeed in getting. . . .

*Mr. McMahon:* The Senator does not have in his possession any information which will indicate that that derogatory statement is true. Does not the Senator realize that if I were to send investigators into his State, perhaps I could obtain 105 or perhaps 1,005 witnesses who would make statements about the Senator that would be totally untrue and incorrect, and the same investigators might go to 2,000 other persons who would say, "Those 105 people are not telling the truth at all. They are very angry with the Senator because he voted for this bill or that bill that they did not like." . . .

[*McCarthy*]: Here is a rather important case. In fact, they are all important. This is case No. 53, involving an individual who has been named by a confessed Communist spy as part of his spy ring. Prior to that time, on August 19, 1946, another governmental agency received information to the effect that he was a recognized leader of the Communist underground. This individual is, in my opinion, Mr. President, one of the most dangerous Communists in the State Department. . . .

Next, Mr. President, I come to case No. 81. I think this individual has been doing this Nation untold damage because of the high position she holds in the Voice of America. This individual was in the Voice of America project, in the New York office, until some time ago. She was transferred to Europe, technically under control of the Commanding General, in the same type of work as the Voice of America, and subsequently the entire project was transferred back to the State Department, and she is today in the State Department. . . .

I should like to read this material. Incidentally, this is the last case we have.

The file in this case contains a wealth of information indicating that this individual is an extremely dangerous and active Communist, completely disloyal to the United States, and loyal to Soviet Russia. Much of the information here, however, was given in strictest confidence but I shall try to give somewhat of a picture of this person.

It is perhaps sufficient to point out that the witnesses without exception have stated in essence that this individual has collected in her office a mixture of fellow travelers and pseudo liberals and outright Communists. These witnesses indicate that the group is close knit and attempts a vicious character assassination of anyone who attempts to disagree with them, and apparently rather successfully so. . . .

Mr. President, since this paper was dictated night before last I find that she is back in the State Department.

Immediate steps should be taken, in my opinion, to obtain not only the discharge but the prosecution of this individual.

Mr. President, I may also say that I feel very strongly that cases Nos. 1, 2, and 81 should not only be discharged but should be immediately prosecuted. However, unless the President will cooperate with us in that, the possibility of a successful prosecution is rather remote, because of the complete iron curtain of secrecy.

I wish to thank very much the Senators who very patiently have remained here and have listened to what may have been somewhat tedious during the last 8 hours.

I assure them that I tried to keep my remarks as brief as possible, while at the same time giving Senators all the pertinent information from the files.

### "IT MIGHT AS WELL BE ME"

*On March 8, 1950, a subcommittee of the Senate Foreign Relations Committee, chaired by Millard Tydings, Democrat from Maryland, opened hearings to investigate McCarthy's charges against the State Department. In a rare exercise of autobiography, McCarthy recalled in his book* McCarthyism: The Fight for America *the thoughts that he entertained as he got ready for his committee appearance on that fateful day.[3]*

When the inter-office buzzer across the room on my desk sounded, it seemed as though only ten minutes had passed since I had stretched out on the leather couch in my office after a night's work.

Actually, an hour had passed since I had asked my office manager to wake me at 10:15.

It was now 10:15 A.M.

This was March 8, 1950.

In fifteen minutes I was due in the Senate Caucus room to begin testifying before the Tydings Committee.

My office manager walked into the room and placed a pot of coffee on the desk. "Everything you dictated last night is typed," he said. "Still a few more pages to put in order, but by the time you're ready to go, we'll be set."

I quickly shaved and checked through my briefcase to see that the documents, photostats, and other exhibits were all there.

On my way to the corridor I detoured through the outer office. To my surprise I found even those members of the staff who had been alternately typing and taking dictation practically the entire night, still on duty—sleepy-eyed but going strong. I shall never cease to be amazed at the pace which the office set in those early days in 1950— a pace which they have maintained ever since. Without the day and

[3] Joseph R. McCarthy, *McCarthyism: The Fight for America* (New York: Devin-Adair, 1952), pp. 1–2. Editor's title. Footnotes have been omitted for reasons of space.

night work of my loyal and efficient office staff, my task would have been impossible.

As I walked down the long marble corridors to the Senate Caucus room, I wondered if I would be able to accomplish what I had set out to do.

The Senate had authorized the Tydings Committee to investigate Communist infiltration of government. The Senate had given that committee power, investigators, and money to run down every lead on Communists in government which I gave them. Today, March 8, 1950, my task was to give the committee the leads which would be a basis for their investigation.

In the back of my mind there was faintly echoing the chairman's statement, "Let me have McCarthy for three days in public hearings and he will never show his face in the Senate again."

Over two weeks had elapsed since my Senate speech which had forced the creation of the Tydings Committee. Already it had become very apparent that this was to be no ordinary investigation. It was to be a contest between a lone Senator and all the vast power of the federal bureaucracy pin-pointed in and backing up the Tydings Committee.

The picture of treason which I carried in my briefcase to that Caucus room was to shock the nation and occupy the headlines until Truman declared war in Korea. But there was nothing new about this picture. The general pattern was known to every legislator in Washington, except those who deliberately blinded their eyes and closed their ears to the unpleasant truth.

As I walked toward the hearing room, many things crossed my mind. For example, in a few seconds I relived the first trip which I had taken in the rear seat of an SBD to divebomb Japanese anti-aircraft on the then southern anchor of the chain of Japanese Pacific defenses at Kahili on the southern tip of Bougainville. Apparently I had complained too much about the lack of photo coverage for our dive and torpedo bombing strikes for I suddenly found myself the Pacific's most reluctant "volunteer" cameraman in the rear seat of a dive bomber. As we flew over the Japanese airfield on Ballale island that morning, a few minutes before our break-off for the dive through Kahili's anti-aircraft fire, there crossed my mind the thought: "McCarthy, why are you here? Why isn't it someone else? Why did you have to be the one who objected so much to the bad photo coverage?" But then I remembered the next thought which I had as my pilot—I believe it was little Johnny Morton—cracked his flaps and I saw the red undercover as the dive bombing brakes opened up. My thought was: "Hell, someone had to do the job. It might as well be me."

In a split second my thoughts shifted from the Pacific to the Arizona hills and I found myself riding a long-legged black mule rounding up cattle in the hills and canyons of the rim-rock country beyond Young, Arizona. It was on the ranch of Kelly Moeur, father of one of the less retiring and modest Marines of my acquaintance, who in his more generous moments admits that the Army and Navy also helped him win the war.

Ten saddle-sore days which I spent on that desolate but friendly cattle ranch played a most important part in my anti-Communist fight. It was a link in a chain of events leading up to that morning of March 8, 1950. Six years before, after having spent thirteen months as combat intelligence officer for Marine Dive Bombing Squadron 235, I was ordered to the Intelligence Staff of COMAIRSOLS (Commander of Army, Navy, Marine, and New Zealand aircraft in the Solomon Islands area). My major task was to study the de-coded messages from and concerning the activities of all of our search planes in the entire Pacific. That was my task under General Mitchell of the Marine Corps, General Harmon of the Army, and General Field Harris of the Marine Corps. Morning after morning I briefed some 30 of the top officers of Army, Navy, and Marine Corps on what our search planes had found throughout the entire Pacific area during the previous 24 hours.

In performing that task I came to know the Pacific and the coast of Asia almost as well as I knew Dad's farm when I was a boy. And for the first time I began to fully appreciate the great wisdom of America's long-time foreign policy on Asia—the policy of maintaining a free, independent, friendly China in order to keep the Pacific *actually* pacific in fact as well as in name.

Upon my return to the United States I discovered that our wise long-time foreign policy was being scuttled—scuttled without the approval of either of America's two great political parties. At that time, I frankly had no idea that traitors were responsible. In my campaign for the United States Senate in 1946, I referred to the State Department planners as "starry-eyed planners, drifting from crisis to crisis, like a group of blind men leading blind men through a labyrinth of their own creation." I then thought that we were losing to international Communism merely because of abysmal incompetence. At that time I had not even heard the names of many of those whom I was to later expose and force out of policy-making jobs.

Many of them I heard discussed for the first time by a man who was later to be hounded to his death by the Communists. I arrived in Washington in December, 1946, about two weeks before being sworn in as a senator. Three days later my administrative assistant and I received an invitation to have lunch with Jim Forrestal.

I have often wondered how the extremely busy Secretary of the Navy discovered that a freshman Senator had arrived in town and why he took so much time out to discuss the problems which were so deeply disturbing him. More than an equal number of times I have thanked God that he did.

Before meeting Jim Forrestal I thought we were losing to international Communism because of incompetence and stupidity on the part of our planners. I mentioned that to Forrestal. I shall forever remember his answer. He said, "McCarthy, consistency has never been a mark of stupidity. If they were merely stupid they would occasionally make a mistake in our favor." This phrase struck me so forcefully that I have often used it since.

When I took on my duties as a Senator, I discovered that certain outstanding Senators and Congressmen for years had been intelligently trying to alert the American people. They belonged to both parties. Unfortunately, when they clearly and intelligently presented a picture of incompetence or treason which should have commanded banner headlines in every newspaper, the story was found, if at all, hidden in want-ad space and type. I witnessed the frustration of those honest, intelligent, loyal Americans who were attempting to expose our suicidal foreign policy. Day after day I came into contact with convincing evidence of treason. Obviously, unless the public was aroused, the downward course upon which we were embarked would continue and at an accelerated pace. But how to arouse the public to the danger before it was too late?

The tempo of events and the pressure in Washington make difficult the careful laying of plans and drafting of blueprints for an effective fight against the inconceivably powerful Communist conspiracy.

The best place to lay the plans for this fight, I decided, was in the lonely relatively uninhabited rim-rock country of Arizona, which had been so thoroughly pictured to me by J. K. Moeur while I was in the Marine Corps. It was there in the lonely Arizona hills that I carefully laid the plans for the one great fight which, as a Senator, I had to make. There I became convinced that the American people could not be awakened by merely a discussion of traitorous policies *generally*. The men who made those policies—the specific traitors or the dupes, well-meaning as they might be—had to be exposed. Foreign policy, after all, does not just happen. It is carefully planned by men with faces and names. Those faces and names had to be exposed. As J. Edgar Hoover has said, "Victory will be assured once Communists are identified and exposed, because the public will take the first step of quarantining them so they can do no harm."

I decided that it did but little good to argue about changing our suicidal foreign policy so long as the men in charge of forming that policy were in the camp of the enemy. The change which had to be made—if this country was to live—was a change of the "experts"— the "experts" who had so expertly sold out China and Poland without the American people realizing what was happening.

The planning was made infinitely easier by my contact with real Americans without any synthetic sheen—real Americans who are part of the Arizona hills—real Americans like J. K.'s mother and his father, Kelly Moeur, like Rillabelle, old Jim Sands, and Old Jack with the hounds, whose last name I cannot recall.

All of those things crossed my mind as I headed toward the Senate Caucus room. And thoughts of those real people who are the heart and soul and soil of America; thoughts of the young people in my office, toiling night and day, some of them not even fully understanding the fight, but knowing that this fight was their fight; thoughts of the many young men, friends of mine, who went to their death in the Pacific for what they thought was a better world—those thoughts convinced me that this fight I had to win.

So it was that I walked into the huge, red-carpeted Caucus room on that Wednesday morning more than two years ago.

### "A HOAX AND A FRAUD"

*McCarthy presented 110 cases to the Tydings Committee to substantiate his charges against the State Department —the eighty-one cases he described on February 20 and more that he had uncovered since then. In the first two weeks of the hearings he did not fare well. Pressured by the committee's Democratic majority to name names, McCarthy made public charges against nine persons, none of whom was a Communist and some of whom delivered forceful rebuttals of the senator. McCarthy then retook the initiative by claiming that he would produce the name of "the top espionage agent" in the United States, a man currently connected with the State Department. "I am," he said, "willing to stand or fall on this one. If I am shown to be wrong on this, I think the subcommittee would be justified in not taking my other cases too seriously." McCarthy's man was Professor Owen Lattimore of Johns Hopkins, an occasional adviser of the State Department on Far Eastern matters. McCarthy talked about Lattimore in a four-hour Senate speech, but after J. Edgar Hoover testified that FBI files failed to substantiate McCarthy's charges, the senator had to retreat. "I may have perhaps placed too much stress on the question of whether or not he has been an espionage agent," McCarthy said. But*

*McCarthy continued to characterize Lattimore as the chief "architect of our Far Eastern policy" and blame him for Communist successes in China. Finally Louis Budenz, former editor of* the Daily Worker, *came partially to McCarthy's rescue by testifying that Lattimore was part of a Communist cell that had infiltrated the Institute of Pacific Relations in the 1930s. Budenz admitted that his testimony was based on hearsay, but to those who wanted to believe McCarthy in the first place, Budenz had invested the Senator with the credibility he so far lacked. As for Lattimore, his spirited denials of McCarthy's charges made him a hero to America's liberals, at least until a 1951–1952 Senate Internal Security subcommittee did a better job than McCarthy of raising doubts about Lattimore.*

*The Tydings Committee meanwhile decided that the best way to judge McCarthy's charges was to compare his cases against the State Department's loyalty files. Though Truman at first refused to grant the committee's request for access to the files, he was finally persuaded to change his mind. (McCarthy thereupon charged that the administration had "raped" the files by removing derogatory material from them.) The committee's Democratic majority, hostile to McCarthy from the beginning, ended its examination of the State Department's security files more convinced than ever that the senator was a charlatan. On July 20, 1950, in his report to the Senate, Tydings roundly denounced McCarthy and his performance at the hearings.*

*McCarthy's defenders then and later contended that had Tydings been less partisan, had he attempted a thorough investigation of the department's security procedures, he would have found at least some substance to McCarthy's allegations. Buckley and Bozell claimed that of the sixty-two McCarthy cases actually employed in the State Department in 1950, forty-nine were returned to security channels within the next year, and by January, 1953, eighteen of these had left the government. "We do not know," these authors wrote, "whether they all were classed or were about to be classed, as loyalty or security risks. But the presumption lies in that direction with respect to a number of them; if for no other reason than that the turnover among McCarthy cases (eighteen out of sixty-two) is a good deal higher than that of the Department as a whole." Portions of Tydings' report are reprinted below.*[4]

[4] U.S., Congress, Senate, Committee on Foreign Relations, *State Department Employee Loyalty Investigation: Report No. 2108,* 81st Cong., 2d sess., July 20, 1950, pt. 1: 9, 10, 11, 149, 150, 151, 152, 167.

Of the 81 alleged State Department employees, only 40 were found to be employed by the State Department at the time of the review. Seven of the so-called 81 were never employed by the State Department and the remaining 33 are no longer in the Department, having been separated either through resignation, termination, or reduction in force. Specifically, of the 33 former employees, 3 were separated in 1949; 16, in 1948; 12, in 1947; and 2, in 1946. . . .

. . . We have carefully and conscientiously reviewed each and every one of the loyalty files relative to the individuals charged by Senator McCarthy. In no instance was any one of them now employed in the State Department found to be a "card-carrying Communist," a member of the Communist Party, or "loyal to the Communist Party." Furthermore, in no instance have we found in our considered judgment that the decision to grant loyalty and security clearance has been erroneously or improperly made in the light of existing loyalty standards. Otherwise stated, we do not find basis in any instance for reversing the judgment of the State Department officials charged with responsibility for employee loyalty; or concluding that they have not conscientiously discharged their duties. . . .

What the State Department knows concerning an employee's loyalty is to be found in its loyalty and security files. These files contain all information bearing on loyalty, obtained from any and all sources, including, of course, the reports of full field investigations by the FBI. Interestingly, in this regard, no sooner had the President indicated that the files would be available for review by the subcommittee than Senator McCarthy charged they were being "raped," altered, or otherwise subjected to a "housecleaning." This charge was found to be utterly without foundation in fact. The files were reviewed by representatives of the Department of Justice, and the Department has certified that all information bearing on the employee's loyalty as developed by the FBI appears in the files which were reviewed by the subcommittee. . . .

### The Facts Behind the Charge of "Whitewash"

Seldom, if ever, in the history of congressional investigations has a committee been subjected to an organized campaign of vilification and abuse comparable to that with which we have been confronted throughout this inquiry. This campaign has been so acute and so obviously designed to confuse and confound the American people that an analysis of the factors responsible therefor is indicated.

The first of these factors was the necessity of creating the impression that our inquiry was not thorough and sincere in order to camouflage the fact that the charges made by Senator McCarthy were groundless and that the Senate and the American people had been deceived. No sooner were hearings started than the cry of "white-wash" was raised along with the chant "investigate the charges and not McCarthy." This chant we have heard morning, noon, and night for almost 4 months from certain quarters for readily perceptible motives. Interestingly, had we elected to investigate Senator McCarthy, there would have been ample basis therefor, since we have been reliably informed that at the time he made the charges initially he had no information whatever to support them, and, furthermore, it early appeared that in securing Senate Resolution 231 a fraud had been perpetrated upon the Senate of the United States.

From the very outset of our inquiry, Senator McCarthy has sought to leave the impression that the subcommittee has been investigating him and not "disloyalty in the State Department." The reason for the Senator's concern is now apparent. He had no facts to support his wild and baseless charges, and lived in mortal fear that this situation would be exposed.

Few people, cognizant of the truth in even an elementary way, have, in the absence of political partisanship, placed any credence in the hit-and-run tactics of Senator McCarthy. He has stooped to a new low in his cavalier disregard of the facts.

The simple truth is that in making his speech at Wheeling, Senator McCarthy was talking of a subject and circumstances about which he knew nothing. His extreme and irresponsible statements called for emergency measures. As Senator Wherry told Emmanuel S. Larsen, "Oh, Mac has gone out on a limb and kind of made a fool of himself and we have to back him up now." Starting with nothing, Senator McCarthy plunged headlong forward, desperately seeking to develop some information, which colored with distortion and fanned by a blaze of bias, would forestall a day of reckoning.

Certain elements rallied to his support, particularly those who ostensibly fight communism by adopting the vile methods of the Communists themselves and in so doing actually hinder the fight of all right-minded people who detest and abhor communism in all its manifestations. We cannot, however, destroy one evil by the adoption of another. Senator McCarthy and McCarthyism have been exposed for what they are—and the sight is not a pretty one. . . .

**General Observations**

In concluding our report, we are constrained to make observations which we regard as fundamental.

It is, of course, clearly apparent that the charges of Communist infiltration of and influence upon the State Department are false. This knowledge is reassuring to all Americans whose faith has been temporarily shaken in the security of their Government by perhaps the most nefarious campaign of untruth in the history of our Republic.

We believe, however, that this knowledge and assurance, while important, will prove ultimately of secondary significance in contemplating the salutary aspects of our investigation. For, we believe that, inherent in the charges that have been made and the sinister campaign to give them ostensible verity, are lessons from which the American people will find inspiration for a rededication to the principles and ideals that have made this Nation great.

We have seen the technique of the "Big Lie," elsewhere employed by the totalitarian dictator with devastating success, utilized here for the first time on a sustained basis in our history. We have seen how, through repetition and shifting untruths, it is possible to delude great numbers of people.

We have seen the character of private citizens and of Government employees virtually destroyed by public condemnation on the basis of gossip, distortion, hearsay, and deliberate untruths. By the mere fact of their associations with a few persons of alleged questionable proclivities an effort has been made to place the stigma of disloyalty upon individuals, some of whom are little people whose only asset is their character and devotion to duty and country. This has been done without the slightest vestige of respect for even the most elementary rules of evidence or fair play or, indeed, common decency. Indeed, we have seen an effort not merely to establish guilt by association but guilt by accusation alone. The spectacle is one we would expect in a totalitarian nation where the rights of the individual are crushed beneath the juggernaut of statism and oppression; it has no place in America where government exists to serve our people, not to destroy them.

We have seen an effort to inflame the American people with a wave of hysteria and fear on an unbelievable scale in this free Nation. Were this campaign founded in truth it would be questionable enough; where it is fraught with falsehood from beginning to end, its reprehensible and contemptible character defies adequate condemnation.

We sincerely believe that charges of the character which have been made in this case seriously impair the efforts of our agencies of Government to combat the problem of subversion. Furthermore, extravagant allegations, which cannot be proved and are not subject to proof, have the inevitable effect of dulling the awareness of all Americans to the true menace of communism. . . .

At a time when American blood is again being shed to preserve our dream of freedom, we are constrained fearlessly and frankly to call the charges, and the methods employed to give them ostensible validity, what they truly are: A fraud and a hoax perpetrated on the Senate of the United States and the American people. They represent perhaps the most nefarious campaign of half-truths and untruth in the history of this Republic. For the first time in our history, we have seen the totalitarian technique of the "big lie" employed on a sustained basis. The result has been to confuse and divide the American people, at a time when they should be strong in their unity, to a degree far beyond the hopes of the Communists themselves whose stock in trade is confusion and division. In such a disillusioning setting, we appreciate as never before our Bill of Rights, a free press, and the heritage of freedom that has made this Nation great.

## SOME UNANSWERED QUESTIONS

*The two Republicans on the Tydings Committee, Senators Bourke Hickenlooper of Iowa and Henry Cabot Lodge of Massachusetts, viewed the recent hearings from a different perspective. Senator Lodge, who was impressed neither by McCarthy nor the security procedures of the State Department, presented his views in the form of a minority report to the Senate. Portions of his report follow:[5]*

### The 81 Loyalty Files

Much stress has been laid on the question of whether the members of the subcommittee would have access to the loyalty files. It was apparently believed that if only the subcommittee could get its hands on the files the question of past and present disloyalty in the State Department would be speedily cleared up.

But after having read a representative cross section of the 81 loyalty files, the conviction was reached that the files alone did not furnish a basis for reaching firm conclusions of any kind and that to attempt to conclude with respect to an individual case on the basis of the file alone would be a most half-baked and superficial procedure, unfair alike to the Government and to the employee in question. The files which I read were in such an unfinished state as to indicate that an examination of each file would be a waste of time. So far as is known, no one in the executive branch is required to make final decisions based on the file alone (there is always a chance to question and to interview the subject of the file) and Senators cannot be expected to do what is demanded of no one else.

There were, for example, many instances in those files which I read where hostile and serious allegations were made about the employee

[5] U.S., Congress, Senate, Henry Cabot Lodge. *Individual Views: State Department Employee Loyalty Investigation: Report No. 2108,* 81st Cong., 2nd sess., July 20, 1950, p. 2: 19, 20, 21, 26, 27.

concerned but which, insofar as the files were concerned, were left unexplained. Where one would expect to find some rebuttal or explanation, there was nothing. Summaries of the files which were prepared were inadequate from the standpoint of a Senator who was trying to come to a conclusion on the basis of the file alone. In some of the most important cases the report of the FBI full field investigation was not included.

In none of the files was there any material which would establish the credibility of the persons making the statement about the employee or the relative importance to be attached to the various people who spoke either for or against the employee. These few cases taken at random must make it obvious that a definite review of the files of the 40 persons who are still in the State Department and of the other 40 who once were in the State Department would mean that all persons making allegations would have to be investigated as to whether or not they were telling the truth and that all allegations would have to be tracked down and either disproved or confirmed. Assuming an average of 10 witnesses per case—which is a modest estimate—this would mean a total of 800 persons to be examined. This is obviously a job which is beyond the time and competence of any congressional committee, even if it could work under the most favorable conditions. It would probably take even a full-time commission of trained men a good 6 months. This consideration underlines once again the need for a trained bipartisan commission whose authority stems from an action of Congress with full power to issue subpoenas and a professional staff to run these cases down, thus taking the whole business out of politics and getting the whole truth, let the chips fall where they may. . . .

The result of all these draw-backs has become plain in the last few months. The work of this subcommittee has had a number of unfortunate results, including the besmirching of the reputations of innocent persons, the hampering of the work of the Government investigative agencies, the impairment of the position of the United States before the world, and an unjust reflection on all of the happily numerous excellent men and women who work in the State Department, with the resulting discouragement to other excellent men and women from going to work for the State Department. This is a loss to the country as a whole.

Furthermore, it is apparent that there are many vital points which the subcommittee has not covered and many basic questions which it has not even asked—let alone received answers. A few of these questions are as follows:

> What State Department officials were responsible for placing Hiss and Wadleigh in the State Department?

What person or persons were primarily responsible for sponsorship for employment of the 91 sexual perverts who were in the State Department and who were reported as having been dismissed beginning with January 1, 1947?

Were those State Department officials who opposed United States recognition of Soviet Russia and who thereafter warned against any appeasement of the Soviet regime in any way discriminated against or unfairly treated by the State Department?

What are the procedures whereby Communists gained entry into the United States upon the basis of visas obtained through our consular service abroad?

What are the facts with reference to the release of the Soviet spy named Gaik Badalovich Ovakimian on July 23, 1941?

What are the facts with reference to the release of the Soviet spy named Mikhala Nickolavich Goran on March 22, 1941?

What is the significance of the statement by Adolph Berle to the House Un-American Activities Committee that Alger Hiss belonged to the pro-Russian clique in the State Department?

Who in the State Department was responsible for obtaining the services of Frederick Schuman and Owen Lattimore as speakers for the Department's indoctrination course for Foreign Service employees?

What are the facts of the charge that a State Department security officer's decision that 10 members of the Department be discharged was subsequently reversed by higher authority?

What State Department officials were responsible for advice given higher officials that the Soviet Government would allow free elections in Poland and Czechoslovakia, Hungary, Rumania, and the other satellite countries?

What are the facts surrounding the case of Arthur Adams, an alleged Soviet spy, who was permitted to leave the United States in 1946?

It is reported that the FBI had prepared a chart which purported to show the number of "agents," "Communists," "sympathizers," and "suspects" in the State Department as of May 15, 1947. The tabulation shows:

| | |
|---|---|
| Agents | 20 |
| Communists | 13 |
| Sympathizers | 14 |
| Suspects | 77 |

It is further stated that by July 12, the number had been reduced to the following:

| | |
|---|---|
| Agents | 11 |
| Communists | 10 |
| Sympathizers | 11 |
| Suspects | 74 |

Who are these Communists and agents and sympathizers and suspects?

What are their names? Why are they there?

# 2
# At Storm Center, 1950–1952

*In the months after the Tydings hearings, McCarthy
made his bid to become a leader of the resurgent right wing.
The Korean War, which politically enfeebled the Democrats,
made his task considerably easier. By the time of the congressional elections of 1950, McCarthy had done so well that "Mc-
Carthyism" was an issue in the campaign, and millions of Americans had begun to regard him as a hero.*

*The results of the election greatly enhanced McCarthy's pres-
tige. Two of his outspoken critics, Senators Scott Lucas and
Millard Tydings, went down to defeat, and many observers gave
McCarthy the credit. McCarthy had, in fact, dispatched members
of his staff to Maryland to work against Tydings. Their labors
were so extraordinary that in 1951 a Senate subcommittee on
privileges and elections investigated the Maryland campaign.
The committee's report criticized McCarthy's staff for putting together malicious campaign literature, doctoring a photograph,
and collecting unreported campaign funds. Meanwhile Senator
William Benton, Democrat from Connecticut, charged McCarthy
with various improprieties and demanded his expulsion from
the Senate. The result was still another investigation by a Senate
committee, this one raising damaging questions about McCarthy's financial transactions but refusing to take a stand on the
question of his expulsion. McCarthy easily survived these attacks
on his integrity and solidified his hold on the rightwing public.*

## "THEY ARE HIDING BEHIND THE WORD UNITY"

*In seeking to exploit anxieties about the Korean war, which
he did brilliantly from 1950 to 1952, McCarthy had to endorse
the administration's response to aggression and at the same time
turn latent resentment about the war against the Democrats.
McCarthy made his first speech on the war in the Senate on July
6, 1950.*[1]

[1] U.S., Congress, Senate, *Congressional Record,* 81st Cong., 2d sess., 1950, 96,
9715–16.

44

Mr. President, at this very moment GI's are consecrating the hills and the valleys of Korea with American blood. But all that blood is not staining the Korean hills and valleys. Some of it is deeply and permanently staining the hands of Washington politicians.

Some men of little minds and less morals are today using the Korean war as a profitable political diversion, a vehicle by which to build up battered reputations because of incompetence and worse.

The American people have long condemned war profiteers who promptly crowd the landscape the moment their Nation is at war. Today, Mr. President, war profiteers of a new and infinitely more debased type are cluttering the landscape in Washington. They are political war profiteers. Today they are going all-out in an effort to sell the American people the idea that in order to successfully fight communism abroad, we must give Communists and traitors at home complete unmolested freedom of action. They are hiding behind the word "unity," using it without meaning, but as a mere catch phrase to center the attention of the American people solely on the fighting front. They argue that if we expose Communists, fellow travelers, and traitors in our Government, that somehow this will injure our war effort. Actually, anyone who can add two and two must realize that if our war effort is to be successful, we must redouble our efforts to get rid of those who, either because of incompetence or because of loyalty to the Communist philosophy, have laid the groundwork and paved the way for disaster.

The pattern will become clearer as the casualty lists mount. Anyone who critcizes the murderous incompetence of those who are responsible for this disaster, anyone who places the finger upon dupes and traitors in Washington, because of whose acts young men are already dying, will be guilty of creating disunity.

Already this cry has reached fantastic pinnacles of moronic thinking. Take, for example the local *Daily Worker,* that is, the *Washington Post.* The other day this newspaper ran an editorial in effect accusing the University of California of injuring the war effort by discharging 137 teachers and other employees who refused to certify that they were not members of the Communist International conspiracy. This, Mr. President, would be laughable if it came merely from the Communist Party's mouthpiece, the *New York Daily Worker,* and its mockingbirds like the *Washington Post.* Unfortunately, a few of the Nation's respectable but misguided writers are being sold this same bill of goods, namely, that to have unity in our military effort the truth about Communists at home must be suppressed.

I should like to call the attention of those misguided individuals to three simple facts:

First. Highly placed Red counselors in the State Department are far more deadly than Red machine-gunners at Suwon. Those Red counselors, by blending treachery into policy, can enslave entire nations, while the Red machine-gunners at the most can kill only hundreds or thousands.

Second. If unity is to be purchased by coddling and protecting saboteurs and Communists, then the cost is far, far too high.

Third. We need not worry about having the American people unified behind any sensible anti-Communist program. The American people were unified against international communism long before the President decided to act against communism on the military front.

Unfortunately, so far his actions against communism are directed only to the military effort. In fact, it was only the unity of purpose of the American people that finally forced the President to disregard the advice of that group of Communists, fellow travelers, and dupes in our State Department—a group who make Benedict Arnold look like a piker.

The American people are unified, not behind the Achesons, Lattimores, and Jessups, who have been selling our allies into communistic slavery, but unified behind the kind of thinking represented by MacArthur.

Republican Members of the Senate . . . have long urged that this Nation take steps to stem the flow of communism which was rolling across Asia and out into the Pacific. Mr. Truman has at a dangerously late date decided to follow the advice those men have been urging upon him for years. We welcome him even at what may be a disastrously late date.

However, we do not welcome the motley crowd that he is bringing with him to put into effect this program, the type of program against which they have dedicated themselves throughout their careers in the State Department. How can the Congress or the American people trust the shaping of this new program to men who have opposed it and who have either permitted or planned disaster to America in both the east and west?

One inescapable fact is that either Acheson has been wrong up until the Korean war started, or Truman is now wrong. Both cannot have been right. When Acheson sabotaged and vetoed the attempt of the Congress to fortify South Korea and to give aid to Chiang's anti-Communist forces on Formosa, either he was wrong then, or Truman is wrong now in extending the aid which Acheson has long opposed. Both cannot be right. Gentlemen, that follows as the night follows the day.

Either Acheson was wrong when he referred to the suggestion of the Senator from Ohio [Mr. Taft] that we aid the anti-Communist forces on Formosa as a "silly venture" or, if Acheson was then right, the President is now engaged in a "silly venture." . . .

Mr. President, it is time to serve notice upon the Communists, fellow travelers, and dupes that they are not going to be able to hide and protect themselves behind a war which would not have been necessary except for their acts.

The American people realize that we cannot invoke a moratorium on fighting Communists and traitors at home, any more than we can invoke a moratorium on fighting them abroad, without completely disastrous results. . . .

Frankly, Mr. President, I think the Communists within our borders have been more responsible for the success of communism abroad than Soviet Russia has been responsible for that success. I strongly feel, and I do not think there can be any question about it, that had it not been for the planners in our State Department, who went along 100 percent with Stalin in Poland and who went along 100 percent with him in Asia, the entire face of the world would have a different complexion, as of today.

I agree with the historian who once said:

> If this Nation is ever destroyed, it will not be destroyed by enemies from without, but by enemies from within.

Over the last few years, we have seen how dangerously true those words have been. . . .

Mr. President, in that connection I should like to call attention to what the great architect of our Far Eastern policy had to say, not 2 years or 5 years ago, but on the 17th day of July 1949, as quoted in *Compass*—Owen Lattimore, who had been advising the State Department—and this is a direct quotation:

> The problem in Korea is to allow Korea to fall, but not to let it appear that we pushed her.

That is the program that Acheson and his crowd accepted lock, stock, and barrel. That is the program they put into effect, until President Truman made the sudden change of policy 4 or 5 days ago.

If the program of Owen Lattimore—the program of allowing our friends to fall, but not making it appear that we were pushing them —had not been bought and put into effect by the State Department, the blood of American boys would not be consecrating the hills and valleys of Korea today.

Mr. President, today the same columnists who have always headed the smear brigade against those who would expose Communists and traitors at home, have now wrapped themselves in the American flag and are attempting to convince the American people—by some strange, twisted reasoning—that the best way to aid our fighting men is to protect the traitors who are responsible for sending them almost bare-handed against tanks in the mud of the valleys of Korea.

As Samuel Johnson said:

Patriotism is the last refuge of a scoundrel.

Mr. President, I think it is time for this Congress and for the 152,-000,000 normal American people to serve notice that we can successfully fight a war abroad and at the same time can dispose of the traitorous filth and the Red vermin which have accumulated at home.

### ACHESON AND "THE BLUEPRINT FOR DISASTER"

*The event that finished off the Truman Administration was the entrance of Red Chinese "volunteers" into the Korean War in late November, 1950. On December 6, McCarthy was ready with his explanation of this disaster.*[2]

Now let us look briefly at the State Department's plan for Asia insofar as it affects the life and death of this Nation and the life and death of 100,000 of our young men in Korea—the plan to turn all of Asia over to international communism, or, putting it in Lattimore's words, to "allow them to fall, but do not let it appear that we pushed them." This plan was proceeding according to schedule until Truman on June 26 ordered MacArthur to defend South Korea. This, of course, was directly contrary to Acheson's previous public statements in which he publicly assured the Chinese Communists that neither Formosa nor Korea was within our defense perimeter, thereby inviting the Communists to move into Korea and Formosa. While it appeared upon the surface on June 26 that Truman was scrapping the disastrous Hiss-Acheson-Jessup-Lattimore-Vincent plan, actually the reversal and the scrapping did not go deep. It can now be seen that the Communists sustained only a temporary, minor loss, that is, temporary and minor unless—unless at this late date we scrap the entire Acheson plan, lock, stock, and barrel, and scrap the men who were responsible for the plan.

For example, as we all recall, part of Truman's order to the Seventh

[2] U.S., Congress, Senate, *Congressional Record,* 81st Cong., 2d sess., 1950, 96, 16177, 16178.

Fleet was that it prevent the Republic of China from taking any military action against the Chinese Communists on the mainland. Truman's orders to the Seventh Fleet also were to break Chiang Kai-shek's blockade of the Communist mainland. This released over a quarter of a million Communist troops which were stationed upon the mainland of China opposite Formosa.

Strangely—and rather significantly—in Acheson's speech of last week he admitted that he knew that those troops started moving north to the Manchurian border after they were assured by the Acheson-inspired Truman order that they could safely leave the China coast and there would be no danger of Chiang Kai-shek moving over.

As a result of this Acheson-inspired Truman order, at this moment a quarter of a million troops which had been immobilized on the China coast by Chiang Kai-shek's forces are now surrounding and cutting to pieces American forces in North Korea. Those Chinese Communists are using equipment which would not have gotten to them had the American fleet not been ordered to break Chiang Kai-shek's blockade of the China coast. This double barrelled action to aid the Chinese Communists was not United Nations action. It was action taken by President Truman under the advice of Dean Gooderham Acheson. . . .

Let us keep that part of the picture clearly in mind. While the President was ordering our young men to fight and die in the battle against Communists in Korea, Acheson was saying to his Chinese Communist friends—the "agrarian reformers": "Don't worry, the Acheson hand will again be quicker than the Truman brain. I will have him sign an order under which the Seventh Fleet will make it unnecessary for you to guard the China mainland from Chiang Kai-shek's 500,000 troops on Formosa. I will insert in that order a provision forbidding the continuance of the blockade of the China coast by Chiang Kai-shek. Then you can get the necessary war matériel and oil which Chiang has prevented reaching your armies."

But that was only one of the major services which our State Department has rendered the Chinese Communists. With half a million Chinese Communists in Korea—I believe it is now 1,000,000—killing American men, Acheson says, "Now let's be calm; let's not take hasty action; let's do nothing to alienate the friendship of the Chinese Communists who are killing our men. Let's keep them friendly."

With the rim of the world on fire, with the death toll of American men mounting by the hour, the great Red Dean asks us to be calm and patient. It is like advising a man whose home is being pillaged and burned, whose family is being killed, to be calm and not take hasty action for fear he might alienate the affection of the murderers.

Such has been the blueprint for disaster. It doesn't take a military or diplomatic expert to tell the American people that if we continue with the same plans and the same planners 100,000 men will be sacrified on Acheson's altar of double dealing, and western civilization will have been dealt a staggering blow.

### "DEAN . . . YOU AND YOUR CRIMINAL CROWD BETRAYED US"

*Truman's recall of MacArthur in April, 1951, brought national anxieties about the conduct of the war to their fullest expression. No one participated more vigorously in the resulting furor than Senator McCarthy. On May 24, 1951, he delivered one of the most savage attacks that an American politician had ever made on an official of his own government.*[3]

In that connection, I think the Senator from Maryland is aware of the fact that when General MacArthur was on the stand he testified that when the Chinese Communists started to pour across the Yalu River in an undeclared war, he ordered his planes to bomb our half of the bridges across the Yalu, the purpose being to keep the Communists on their own side of the river where they belonged. As he said, they greatly outnumbered our men. The purpose was to keep them where they belonged and save the lives of American boys. Let me read his testimony on that point. This has not been contradicted at all. I read from page 49 of the testimony:

As soon as we realized that the Chinese were moving across the Yalu in force as a national—as national entities, I ordered the bridges across the Yalu bombed from the Korean side, half way to the stream. That order was countermanded from Washington, and it was only when I protested violently that I was allowed to continue my original directive.

We know that during the time that order stood countermanded, Chinese Communists poured vast numbers of troops and vast amounts of military equipment across the Yalu. We know that while that order stood countermanded, and because it was countermanded, a sizable number of American boys died.

Let me, if I may, give Senators a specific example. If we multiply this case by thousands, perhaps we can better understand why General MacArthur felt that he had a duty to bring the truth to the Amer-

[3] U.S., Congress, Senate, *Congressional Record*, 81st Cong., 1st sess., 1951, 97, 5579.

ican people even if it meant the end of his glorious military career.

Let us take the case of Bob Smith, from Middleburg, Pa. When the Communists started to pour across the Yalu Bob Smith was up at Chanjin Reservoir. He was wounded. He lay in a gutter for 3 days and nights. The Communists overran his position. He played dead. They took off his shoes and some of his clothing. Then he and some other wounded GI's crawled to a dugout or hut. A unit of Marines learned about those wounded soldiers, and slugged a bloody path through the Communist ring and rescued them.

Today Bob Smith is at home in Middleburg, Pa., but his hands and his feet are still in the hills on this side of the Yalu—a tribute to the traitorous Red Communist clique in our State Department, who have been in power ever since before the days of Yalta. I suggest that when the day comes that Bob Smith can walk, when he gets his artificial limbs, he first walk over to the State Department and call upon the great Red Dean of fashion if he is still there. He should say to him, "Mr. Acheson, I was there while MacArthur's order stood countermanded by you. I saw the Communists pour across the Yalu. I saw your agrarian reformers on horseback firing rockets at us—reincarnations of the horsemen of Genghis Khan." He should say to Acheson: "You and your lace handkerchief crowd have never had to fight in the cold, so you cannot know its bitterness."

He should say to him "You never felt the shock of bullets, so you cannot know their pain."

He should say to him, "Dean, thousands of American boys have faced those twin killers because you and your crimson crowd betrayed us."

He should say, "Mr. Acheson, if you want to at long last perform one service for the American people you should not only resign from the State Department but you should remove yourself from this country and go to the nation for which you have been struggling and fighting so long."

### DREW PEARSON: "AN IMPORTANT PLACE . . . IN THE COMMUNIST SCHEME OF PROPAGANDA"

*McCarthy fought an unending war against hostile newspapers and reporters. Drew Pearson wrote columns so annoying to the senator that at a Washington party in December, 1951, McCarthy got into an argument with Pearson and ended the evening by slapping and kicking him. ("When are they going to put you in the booby hatch?" Pearson managed to ask.) The next day McCarthy took his feud onto the Senate floor and, as usual, attempted to link his adversary with the Communist conspiracy.*[4]

Mr. President, the other night I told one of my fellow Senators that today I intended to discuss the background of one of the cleverest men who has ever prostituted one of the noblest professions—a man, who, in my opinion, has been and is doing an infinite amount of damage to America and all of the institutions of our form of Government. When I told the Senator this, he said: "McCarthy, don't do it." He said it would be like having stood in the mouth of the Cloaca Maxima and having tried to stop the flow. He said: "You will be merely inundated by the slime and smear and he will still go on every day and every week polluting otherwise fine newspapers and poisoning the air waves."

I realize that the task of exposing this man, or perhaps I should say this person, will be an unpleasant, disagreeable task, which will leave me more than a bit bloodied up also, but as I told the Senator the other night—when I was a boy on the farm my mother used to raise chickens. From those chickens the groceries for a large family were supplied, as well as mother's Christmas money. The greatest enemy the chickens had were skunks. In order to protect mother's chickens my three brothers and I had to dig out and destroy those skunks. It was a dirty, foul, unpleasant, smelly job. We learned early in life that the jobs that most badly need doing and are so often left undone are often the most difficult and unpleasant jobs.

I do not agree with the Senator who advised me the other night—I do not agree that this is an impossible task. I think that while it cannot be done overnight, this man can be exposed to the American people for what he is, at which time he will no longer be dangerous.

Before discussing the important place which he holds in the Communist scheme of propaganda, I would like to describe him in the words of some expert witnesses, well known and highly respected by the Senate. . . .

It is impossible for me to understand how so many reputable newspapermen can buy the writings of this twisted, perverted mentality which so cleverly sugar-coats and disguises his fiendishly clever, long-range attempts to discredit and destroy in the minds of the American people all of the institutions which make up the very heart of this Republic.

It is difficult beyond words to understand how reputable publishers

[4] U.S., Congress, Senate, *Congressional Record*, 81st Cong., 2d sess., 1951, **96,** 16634, 16635, 16641.

and editors with such a deep obligation to their readers allow the streams of information to be polluted and poisoned by a man so thoroughly labeled and known to be a prostitute of the great profession of journalism.

So much for Pearson's disregard for truth and honesty and decency. Let us proceed briefly on to the even more dangerous part of this picture.

The heads of any of our intelligence agencies will testify that one of the principal aims of the Communist Party is to gain control of our lines of communication; that is, newspapers, radio, television, motion pictures, and so forth. It, of course, would be a miracle if they had not recognized in Pearson the ideal man for them—an unprincipled, greedy degenerate liar—but with a tremendous audience both in newspapers and on the air waves * * * a man who has been able to sugar-coat his wares so well that he has been able to fool vast numbers of people with his fake piety and his false loyalty.

Pearson has long had working for him—part of the time officially on his payroll, and part of the time in a slightly different status—one David Karr. The relationship is such that it is difficult to know who is the master and who is the servant. I may say that just what his status is is difficult to know, except that they are still working together today. I will give the Senate a complete picture of Karr's function in a minute. . . .

Incidentally, while under questioning by Dr. Matthews before the House Committee on Un-American Activities, Karr admitted under oath that he knew the American League for Peace and Democracy, whose publicity he was handling, was a Communist-controlled organization. Some of the testimony is set forth on page A876 of the *Congressional Record* for February 18, 1944.

I have discussed this man Pearson with practically every former member of the Communist Party whom I have met during my recent and present investigation of Communists in Government. Almost to a man, they were agreed on a number of things: No. 1: That Pearson's all-important job, which he did for the party without fail, under the directions of David Karr, was to lead the character assassination of any man who was a threat to international communism. No. 2: That he did that job so well that he was the most valuable of all radio commentators and writers from the standpoint of the Communist Party. No. 3: In order to maintain his value, it was necessary that he occasionally throw pebbles at communism and Communists generally, so as to have a false reputation of being anti-Communist.

It appears that Pearson never actually signed up as a member of the Communist Party and never paid dues. However, that has not in any way affected his value to the party; nor has it affected his willingness to follow the orders of David Karr, who, of course, is a most active member of the party, and who carries instructions and orders to Pearson.

I ask those who are skeptical as to whether Pearson actually has been doing a job for the Communist Party to stop and review Pearson's record over the past 10 years. You will find that he has always gone all-out to attack anyone who is attempting to expose individual and dangerous Communists, while at the same time he goes through the fakery of criticizing communism and Communists generally. The heads of the House Un-American Activities Committee have always been his targets. . . .

It is up to the American people—and above all, up to the newspapermen who are buying Pearson's column and the radio stations that are carrying his broadcasts—to see that this voice of international communism is stilled.

If the loyal American newspaper editors and publishers and radio station owners refuse to buy this disguised, sugar-coated voice of Russia, the mockingbirds who have followed the Pearson line will disappear from the scene like chaff before the wind. The American people can do much to accomplish this result. They can notify their newspapers that they do not want this Moscow-directed character assassin being brought into their homes to poison the well of information at which their children drink. They can notify the Adam Hat Co., by actions, what they think of their sponsoring of this man. It should be remembered that anyone who buys an Adam hat, any store that stocks an Adam hat, anyone who buys from a store that stocks an Adam hat, is unknowingly and innocently contributing at least something to the cause of international communism by keeping this Communist spokesman on the air.

### "A CONSPIRACY SO IMMENSE AND
### AN INFAMY SO BLACK—"

*On June 14, 1951, McCarthy offered the Senate a 60,000 word attack on General George C. Marshall.[5] Marshall had been Army Chief of Staff in World War II, Truman's special representative to China from December, 1945 to January, 1947, secretary of state in 1947–1948, and, since 1950, secretary of defense. McCarthy's speech was a rambling review of Marshall's career, unified only by its attempts to make Marshall the conscious agent of world communism. But in his remarks, McCarthy occasionally drew back from this accusation to disclaim*

[5] U.S., Congress, Senate, *Congressional Record*, 82d Cong., 1st sess., 1951, **97,** 6556, 6557, 6566, 6570, 6572, 6573, 6581, 6593, 6594, 6601, 6602, 6603.

*knowledge of Marshall's motives or merely to criticize Marshall's defective judgment. The speech was scholarly enough to prompt Richard Rovere, in his book* Senator Joe McCarthy, *to ascribe its authorship to revisionist historians at Georgetown University. Some months after McCarthy's indictment of his career, Marshall retired to private life. Whether these two events are related remains unknown. Portions of McCarthy's speech follow.*

Mr. President, in closely following the testimony before the joint committee on Foreign Relations and Armed Services, sitting jointly, which is conducting an investigation of the dismissal of Douglas MacArthur, I have become more and more impressed by two inescapable facts:

First. That it is impossible to develop the facts in the MacArthur inquiry without at the same time bringing to light some of the facts which bear on the question of why we fell from our position as the most powerful Nation on earth at the end of World War II to a position of declared weakness by our leadership.

Second. That it will be equally impossible to obtain the answers to the above without uncovering a conspiracy so immense and an infamy so black as to dwarf any previous such venture in the history of man. During the Marshall testimony, one of the Senators, obviously troubled by the odor of the conspiracy which was commencing to rise as a result of the constant probing by the members of the committee— troubled by the fringes of the conspiracy which were commencing to show—came to my office and asked me for information on a subject which was troubling and puzzling him greatly. While I cannot quote him verbatim, the questions he asked were substantially as follows:

First. Who was close to Marshall and succeeded in deceiving this great American at Yalta when his military advice was that we turn Manchuria over to Russia, thereby signing at least the first section in the death warrant of the Republic of China?

Second. Who twisted and perverted the thinking of this great American and misguided him into the folly of his disastrous mission to China?

Third. Who, of tortured disloyalty to America, succeeded in deceiving this great general during the course of World War II to the end that he always sided with Stalin and against Churchill when history's great decisions were being made—decisions which turned out so bad for the free world and so good for international communism?

Upon searching for the answers for the Senator, I found to my surprise that Marshall, who, by the alchemy of propaganda, became the "greatest living American," and the recently proclaimed "master of global strategy" for the party in power, has never had his record subjected to the searching light of any historian. In view of the fact that the committee, the Congress, and the American people are being called upon either to indorse or reject Marshall's global strategy, I felt that it was urgent that such a study be made and submitted to the Russell committee. . . .

It is needless to tell you that this was a monumental task, but one which I felt had to be done, for unless we understand the record of Marshall it will be impossible to even remotely grasp the planned steady retreat from victory which commenced long before World War II ended. Unless we carefully study the records of Marshall and Acheson, who have worked together so closely, it will be impossible to foretell the next move on the timetable of the great conspiracy.

I realize full well how unpopular it is to lay hands on the laurels of a man who has been built into a great hero. I very much dislike this unpleasant task, but I feel that it must be done if we are to intelligently make the proper decisions in the issues of life and death before us. . . .

This administration, which has given us this caricature of a war, is now bent on an even worse horror—a phony and fraudulent peace. It is planned by Secretary Marshall and the elegant and alien Acheson—Russian as to heart, British as to manner. We even hear cries for a fraudulent peace within this Chamber. In support of their campaign for a fraudulent peace, its advocates wage a campaign of fear.

The President threatens us with the destruction of our cities by Russian bombs unless we continue to pursue his empty, defeatist strategy in the Far East. The President's only answer to the splendid counsel of General MacArthur is that we must on no account offend the Soviet Union. One of the administration's two principal spokesmen on this matter seeks to frighten us with the admonition that unless we mind our P's and Q's in Korea, "This very Capitol Building, this very Senate Chamber may be blown to smithereens next week or the week after." Mr. President, that is not the great heart of America speaking.

I do not think we need fear too much about the Communists dropping atomic bombs on Washington. They would kill too many of their friends that way. . . .

We have observed what calamities might have befallen the allied cause had Roosevelt accepted Marshall's persistent demand for a "second front now." We have seen the equivocal and dangerous nature of his counsel with reference to the North African invasion. We have observed how closely he fitted his views into those of Stalin over every major issue of the war. We have seen further how in his instructions to General Deane, his refusal to exercise foresight over the corridor to Berlin, and his wish that the Russians might first enter that great and shattered city, General Marshall's decisions paralleled the interests of the Kremlin.

The Democrats at Denver may have been correct in their appraisal of General Marshall's attainments as a strategist. The question that arises, after examining the facts we have enumerated and those we shall enumerate, is, in whose interest did he exercise his genius? If he was wholeheartedly serving the cause of the United States, these decisions were great blunders. If they followed a secret pattern to which we do not as yet have the key, they may very well have been successful in the highest degree.

I do not at this time discuss the question of whether General Marshall was aware that he was implementing the will of Stalin in these matters. I do not propose to go into his motives. Unless one has all the tangled and often complicated circumstances contributing to a man's decisions, an inquiry into his motives is often fruitless. I do not pretend to understand General Marshall's nature and character, and I shall leave that subject to subtler analysts of human personality. . . .

It was Marshall who stood at Roosevelt's elbow at Yalta, urging the grim necessity of bribing Stalin to get into the war. It was Marshall who submitted intelligence reports to support his argument, suppressing more truthful estimates, as we are informed in Hanson Baldwin's book on page 81, and keeping from the stricken Roosevelt knowledge that the Japanese were even then feeling for peace in acknowledgment to defeat. . . .

It was Marshall who selected the line for the division of Korea which was chosen by the Russian Foreign Office and General Staff nearly 50 years ago. We restored their pre-1904 claims on North Korea at the Pentagon in August of 1945. . . .

I think it is now transparently clear why Marshall went to China. Having, with the Yalta crowd, framed the China policy, he was intent on executing it down to its last dreadful clause and syllable and it is, I think, significant that he tarried in China for 13 arduous months, and when he left it was obvious to all beholders that China must fall to the Russian Empire. What was his mission:

> First. To restrain the Government of China from subduing the Red forces which were sworn to bring all China within the orbit of Moscow.
> Second. To deny the Chinese Government American assistance if it attempted to master the Communist minority by force.
> Third. To insist at all times, in defiance of the lessons of Europe and the plain evidences of Russian imperial ambitions in Asia, that Chiang Kai-shek must accept the Communists into his government.

The surrender of Yalta had to be concluded and perfected. . . .

The principal advantage to the United States, as I look back over it, of the Moscow conference was that it took Marshall out of Washington while the policy of aid to Greece and Turkey was being hurriedly formed. Given his militant aversion to anything which would adversely affect Communist interest in the Mediterranean, which we have seen, and subsequent manifestations which are yet to come, we can scarcely believe that he would have been a genuine advocate of the Forrestal plan in the eastern Mediterranean. I regard the assistance we voted to Greece and Turkey the most statesmanlike approach made by the Truman administration to the whole postwar problem of the containment of Russia. The so-called Truman doctrine for Greece and Turkey, which should be rightly named the Forrestal doctrine, is perhaps the only statesmanlike enterprise which has come out of the administration. . . .

Need I point out to you that the Marshall plan made mincemeat of the Truman-Forrestal doctrine? . . . Need I elaborate the point that, whereas the Truman-Forrestal doctrine offered to give our wealth to like-minded countries, striving to combat communism, externally and internally, the Marshall plan neatly eradicates that purpose? Need I say that the one bade fair to forge the free world into a great and vital instrument with which to confront Soviet imperialism, the other reduced the whole splendid concept of Truman speaking Forrestal's mind at Cleveland into a mere charity enterprise, without political content and without use to the United States in the major crisis of these times. What Marshall did, to borrow the facetious language of some opponents of his plan, was to put Europe on the WPA.

The Forrestal plan would have strengthened us in the conflict with Russia. The result of using the Marshall plan instead of the Forrestal plan in Europe has been to make us the patsy of the modern world, to arouse the contempt and suspicion of Europe and to leave us in the summer of 1951, heavily engaged in Asia, and with no willing, reliable allies in all Europe among the beneficiaries of our bounty except Greece and Turkey and, a country that had no seat at the table at all, Spain, plus Western Germany whose resources we cannot use in the struggle against international communism because her 48,000,000 people according to the State Department are not peace-loving.

The Truman-Forrestal doctrine's means test would have included Spain. The Marshall plan excluded Spain, although it included Russia in its intent.

I do not think that this monstrous perversion of sound and understandable national policy was accidental. I think it was an evil hoax on the generosity, good will and carelessness of the American people. I think that it was the product of a will and intention hostile to this free society. . . .

Of all Marshall's significant endeavors since the early months of World War II, the derricking of the Forrestal plan ranks next, I should judge, to the Marshall policy for China in its massive helpfulness to the world ambitions of the Kremlin. That judgment is in no way impaired by the fact that Russia declined and forbade its satellites to share in the Marshall plan's bounty. . . .

The point that I want to make with all emphasis is this: Since Marshall resumed his place as mayor of the palace last September, with Acheson as captain of the palace guard and that weak, fitful, bad-tempered and usable Merovingian in their custody, the outlines of the defeat they meditate have grown plainer. The weakness of the United States in relation to the growing power of Soviet imperialism has become clearer. Our weakness has become plain to the simplest citizen, the farthest removed from the seat of Government in Washington, and would have been evident even without the shameless doubts of the President that we could win a war with Russia and the self-satisfied shocking revelations of Marshall and his place men, in their testimoney before the Russell committee.

The feeling of America's weakness is in the very air we breathe in Washington. It derives not only from the moral debility of the highest echelons of the administration, from the flabbiness and lack of resolve upon the part of the palace guard and their minions. It comes from the objective facts of the situation. . . .

How can we account for our present situation unless we believe that men high in this Government are concerting to deliver us to disaster? This must be the product of a great conspiracy, a conspiracy on a scale so immense as to dwarf any previous such venture in the history of man. A conspiracy of infamy so black that, when it is finally exposed, its principals shall be forever deserving of the maledictions of all honest men.

Who constitutes the highest circles of this conspiracy? About that we cannot be sure. We are convinced that Dean Acheson, who steadfastly serves the interests of nations other than his own, the friend of Alger Hiss, who supported him in his hour of retribution, who contributed to his defense fund, must be high on the roster. The President? He is their captive. I have wondered, as have you, why he did not dispense with so great a liability as Acheson to his own and his party's interests. It is now clear to me. In the relationship of master and man, did you ever hear of man firing master? Truman is a satisfactory front. He is only dimly aware of what is going on. . . .

What can be made of this unbroken series of decisions and acts contributing to the strategy of defeat? They cannot be attributed to incompetence. If Marshall were merely stupid, the laws of probability would dictate that part of his decisions would serve this country's interest. If Marshall is innocent of guilty intention, how could he be trusted to guide the defense of this country further? We have declined so precipitously in relation to the Soviet Union in the last 6 years. How much swifter may be our fall into disaster with Marshall at the helm? Where will all this stop? That is not a rhetorical question: Ours is not a rhetorical danger. Where next will Marshall carry us? It is useless to suppose that his nominal superior will ask him to resign. He cannot even dispense with Acheson.

What is the objective of the great conspiracy? I think it is clear from what has occurred and is now occurring: to diminish the United States in world affairs, to weaken us militarily, to confuse our spirit with talk of surrender in the Far East and to impair our will to resist evil. To what end? To the end that we shall be contained, frustrated and finally fall victim to Soviet intrigue from within and Russian military might from without. Is that farfetched? There have been many examples in history of rich and powerful states which have been corrupted from within, enfeebled and deceived until they were unable to resist aggression. . . .

It is the great crime of the Truman administration that it has refused to undertake the job of ferreting the enemy from its ranks. I once puzzled over that refusal. The President, I said, is a loyal American; why does he not lead in this enterprise? I think that I know why he does not. The President is not master in his own house. Those who are master there not only have a desire to protect the sappers and miners—they could not do otherwise. They themselves are not free. They belong to a larger conspiracy, the world-wide web of which has been spun from Moscow. It was Moscow, for example, which decreed that the United States should execute its loyal friend, the Republic of China. The executioners were that well-identified group headed by Acheson and George Catlett Marshall.

### "ALGER—I MEAN ADLAI . . ."

*McCarthy played an important role in the presidential election of 1952. At the Republican convention he received an ovation and delivered an attack on the treason of the Democrats. McCarthy was not enthusiastic about Eisenhower's nomination but was prepared to campaign for him anyway. As for Eisenhower, he found McCarthy a continual embarrassment but shied away from an open break. McCarthy's major service for the Republican campaign was a nationally televised speech attempting to raise doubts about the loyalty of the Democratic nominee. Up for re-election himself in Wisconsin in 1952, McCarthy won without difficulty but ran far behind Eisenhower. Excerpts from*

*McCarthy's famous speech on Adlai E. Stevenson are reprinted below.*[6]

Thank you, fellow Americans. I am deeply grateful, very deeply grateful to all of you who have made this night possible.

We are at war tonight—a war which started decades ago, a war which we did not start, a war which we cannot stop except by either victory or death. The Korean war is only one phase of this war between international atheistic communism and our free civilization.

And we've been losing, we've been losing that war since the shooting part of World War II ended, losing it at an incredibly fantastic rate of 100,000,000 people a year.

And for the past two and a half years I've been trying to expose and force out of high positions in Government those who are in charge of our deliberate planned retreat from victory.

Now this fight, this fight against international communism, should not be a contest between America's two great political parties. Certainly, after all the millions of Americans who've long voted the Democratic ticket are just as loyal, they love America just as much, they hate communism just as much as the average Republican.

Unfortunately, the millions of loyal Democrats no longer have a party in Washington. And tonight, tonight I shall give you the history of the Democratic candidate for the Presidency who endorsed and could continue the suicidal Kremlin-directed policies of the nation.

Now I'm not going to give you a speech tonight. Tonight I'm a lawyer giving you the facts on the evidence in the case of Stevenson vs. Stevenson.

Let me make it clear that I'm only covering his history in so far as it deals with his aid to the Communist cause and the extent, the extent to which he is part and parcel of the Acheson-Hiss-Lattimore group. Now I perform the unpleasant task because the American people are entitled to have the coldly-documented history of this man who says, "I want to be your President." . . .

I shall now try to fit together the jigsaw puzzle of the man who wants to be President on the Truman-Acheson ticket. And I don't call it Democratic ticket because it would be a great insult to all the good Democrats in this nation. . . .

Now these facts, my good friends, cannot be answered—cannot be answered by screams of smears and lies. These facts can only be answered by facts. And we call upon Adlai of Illinois to so answer those facts.

[6] *The New York Times*, October 28, 1952, p. 26. Editor's title. Copyright © 1952 by The New York Times Company. Reprinted by permission.

The time is short, so let me get about the task of looking at his record. The Democratic candidate has said, and I quote him verbatim. He said, "As evidence of my direction I have established my headquarters here in Springfield with people of my own choosing." In other words he says, judge me, judge me by the advisers whom I have selected. Good, let's do that. Let's examine a few of those advisers first.

First is Wilson Wyatt, his personal manager. Now Wilson Wyatt is a former head of the left-winger A.D.A., the Americans for Democratic Action. The A.D.A. has five major points in its program. Listen to these and remember them if you will.

> Point No. 1. Repeal of the Smith Act, which makes it a crime to conspire to overthrow this Government,
>
> No. 2. Recognition of Red China,
>
> No. 3. Opposition to the loyalty oath,
>
> No. 4. Condemnation of the F.B.I. for exposing traitors like Coplon and Gubitchev, and
>
> No. 5. Continuous all-out opposition to the House Committee on Un-American Activities.

Let me speak to you about that platform. They publish it day after day.

Now, according to an article in *The New York Times,* and I have that which I hold in my hand—the Democratic candidate's campaign manager Wyatt condemns the Government's loyalty program and here's the proof—it condemns the loyalty program in the most vicious terms. Strangely Alger—I mean Adlai—Adlai in 1952, now that he's running for President, says, I will dig out the Communists using as my weapon the loyalty program which my campaign manager damns and condemns.

Next, and perhaps the key figure in the Stevenson camp is his speech writer, Arthur Schlesinger Jr., former vice chairman of the same A.D.A. Now, Schlesinger has been a writer, incidentally, for the New York *Post*—New York *Post* whose editor and his wife admit, admit that they were members of the Young Communist League.

Now in 1946, Stevenson's speech writer wrote that the present system in the United States makes, and I quote. Listen to this, here's his speech writer, he says, "The present system in the United States makes even freedom-loving Americans look wistfully at Russia." I wonder if there's anyone in the audience tonight who's looking wistfully at Russia. And I wonder, also, if some calamity would happen and Stevenson would be elected, what job this man would have.

Perhaps the most revealing article written by Stevenson's speech writer appeared in *The New York Times* on Dec. 11, 1949, on Page 3, and listen to this if you will. I quote, he says, "I happen to believe that the Communist party should be granted the freedom of political action and that Communists should be allowed to teach in universities." . . .

Stevenson says, judge me by the people I choose as my advisers. Here you have the philosophy of his chief adviser, the philosophy of his speech writer, laid bare. This idea of course that religion should be ridiculed is one of the basic principles of the Communist party. Now if you couple—couple [his] ridicule of religion with his statement that Communists should be allowed to teach your children and you have a fairly clear portrait of the man. . . .

Now let us pick up another piece of the jigsaw puzzle of Stevenson's history. On Sept. 23 of this year Admiral Station, who is a holder of the Medal of Honor, signed a statement for us, signed a statement covering his experience with Stevenson after he, Station, had been assigned to the task of enforcing Public Law 151 and removing the Communists from the radios aboard our ships.

Well, Stevenson was a special assistant at that time in the Navy Department. He called Admiral Station to his office and here's the affidavit given to us by Station about that meeting.

It hasn't been used until tonight. Let me read just one paragraph. He says, "On arrival Stevenson told me that he had received six or eight of the Communist cases which my board had recommended for removal and that he wanted to discuss them with me."

Still quoting the Admiral: "Stevenson said that he could not see that we had anything against them and stated that we should not be hard on the Communists. The conference ended with Stevenson disagreeing with our recommendations to fire the Communists."

This was in 1943, my good friends, and two or three days ago Stevenson went on the air and said, but he said, "Oh, in 1943 I was warning about the danger of Communism in the Mediterranean."

Now immediately after, Station appeared at Stevenson's office and said, Mr. Stevenson get rid of those Communists. The law provides you must. And he said no. What happened to Station? He was retired to inactive duty. . . .

But let me go on to another piece of the jigsaw puzzle.

While you think, while you may think that there could be no connection between the debonair Democratic candidate and a dilapidated Massachusetts barn, I want to show you a picture of this barn and explain the connection. Here's the outside of a barn. Give me a picture showing the inside of the barn.

Here's the outside of a barn up at Lee, Mass. Looks like it couldn't house a farmer's cow or goat from the outside. Here's the inside. A beautifully paneled conference room with maps of the Soviet Union. Now in what way does Stevenson tie up with this?

My investigators went up and took pictures of this barn after we had been tipped off about what was in it, tipped off that there was in this barn all of the missing documents from the Communist front I.P.R. [Institute of Pacific Relations], the I.P.R. which has been named by the McCarran Committee, named before the McCarran Committee as a cover shop for Communist espionage. We went up and we found in the room adjoining this conference room 200,000—200,000 of the missing I.P.R. documents. The hidden files showing the vouchers, among other things, showing money from Moscow. Men—a group of Communists.

Now let's take a look at a photostat of a document taken from that Massachusetts barn. One of those documents that was never supposed to see the light of day, rather interesting it is, this is the document that shows that Alger Hiss and Frank Coe recommended Adlai Stevenson to the Mont Tremblant conference which was called for the purpose of establishing foreign policy—post-war foreign policy in Asia.

Now as you know Alger Hiss is a convicted traitor. Frank Coe was the man [named] under oath before Congressional committees seven times as a member of the Communist party. Why, why do Hiss and Coe find that Adlai Stevenson is the man they want representing them at this conference. I don't know, perhaps Adlai knows. . . .

Now I note that the television man is holding up a sign, saying thirty seconds to go—I have much, much more of the documentation here. I'm sorry we can't give it to our television audience and I want our audience to know it was not the fault of the television station— we've only arranged for half an hour and that half an hour's about up.

But with your permission my good friends, when we go off the air I would like to complete for this audience the documentation.

# 3
# McCarthy Takes on Eisenhower

At the beginning of 1953 observers were uncertain about McCarthy's future course. So long as the Democrats had controlled the executive branch, his forays against subversion served the political ends of Republican professionals. But now Dwight Eisenhower was president, and a new hunt for Reds among the bureaucrats could only hurt the first Republican administration in twenty years. In the new Congress McCarthy became chairman of the Senate Committee on Government Operations, where, Senator Taft said, "he can't do any harm." But almost immediately McCarthy used his new authority to harass the administration. No longer the servant of Republican purposes, McCarthy became a political renegade.

Throughout 1953 McCarthy probed for Communists in government agencies. The Senator exposed the Government Printing Office, threatened the CIA, and investigated the army's Signal Corps at Fort Monmouth. But McCarthy's favorite target was still the State Department. He examined departmental procedures in handling loyalty files. He sought traitors in the Voice of America and communist books in America's overseas libraries. He caused anguish in the State Department by negotiating a private agreement with Greek shipowners to cut off their commerce with communist nations. And he opposed Eisenhower's nominee for ambassador to Russia, Charles ("Chip") Bohlen.

## "WE MUST PUT COUNTRY ABOVE PARTY"

Present at Tehran and Yalta, Bohlen in the eyes of the right wing was a holdover from the hated Acheson regime. McCarthy not only attacked Bohlen's diplomatic record; he charged that Bohlen was a bad security risk. When Secretary of State John Foster Dulles testified that security files contained "no substantial evidence" to justify doubts about Bohlen, McCarthy stated, "what Dulles said . . . is untrue." But Senators Robert Taft and John Sparkman examined Bohlen's security file for the Senate and personally cleared him. On the vote to confirm Bohlen, McCarthy

65

*carried only twelve senators with him into opposition. Parts of McCarthy's speech on Bohlen, March 25, 1953, follow.[1]*

*Mr. McCarthy:* Mr. President, for 20 years the American people have been tasting nothing but the dregs of defeat—the defeat of such fundamental concepts as loyalty, honor, and duty.

We have passed through two black decades, and history will write large the names of those who sold out this country at the diplomatic tables at home and abroad.

Where statesmen should have been working for us, traitors and their dupes connived against us. Where patriots should have fought, cowards fled the enemy or joined his camp.

The names of Hiss, Lattimore, and Acheson have become synonymous with defeat, disgrace, and dishonor.

But there is such a thing as victory.

*Mr. Lehman:* Mr. President, will the Senator yield?

*Mr. McCarthy:* I will not yield until I finish. I shall be glad to yield then.

Finally last fall the Amercian people became so sick of the entire sorry mess that they voted by an overwhelming majority that we clean out Washington lock, stock, and barrel.

During last fall's campaign, I spoke to perhaps more people than any other man in the United States—with the exception of President Eisenhower and Vice President Nixon. Over a period of 2 months I spoke in practically every State in the Union—sometimes speaking as often as 3 or 4 times in 1 day. I listened to the speeches of President Eisenhower and Vice President Nixon, as well as to the speeches of a great number of other Republicans. We promised the American people that if they would elect Eisenhower and Nixon and a Republican Congress three major things would be accomplished.

> No. 1. We would bring an honorable end to the Korean war.
> No. 2. We would work toward a financially solvent America—toward a balanced budget and lower taxes.
> No. 3. We would clean out the mess in Washington, especially in the State Department and get rid of all of Acheson's architects for disaster. . . .

As to point No. 3—the task of scrubbing, flushing, and washing clean the foul mess that the Truman-Acheson crowd left in Washington—some considerable progress is being made. The new Secretary of State,

---

[1] U.S., Congress, Senate, *Congressional Record,* 83d Cong., 1st sess., 1953, 99, 2291, 2292, 2293, 2295.

John Foster Dulles, has turned his back upon a sizable number of the Acheson gang who have been found at every time and place where disaster struck America and success came to Communist Russia. . . .

I do not relish the task which I must perform today—the task of calling attention to what I think is a grave and inexcusable mistake on the part of our Secretary of State—the selection of Charles Bohlen as our Ambassador to Russia.

I would dishonor the confidence of people who elected me and the 31,000,000 Americans who put the Republican Party in power if I did not speak out and oppose the nomination of Bohlen—if I did not put together the history of the part Bohlen played in formulating that foreign policy which played directly into the hands of international communism—that foreign policy which was so overwhelmingly rejected by the American people.

In 1950 and again in 1952 I spent a great deal of time campaigning against Senators who placed party above country and who took the position that no matter what Truman did and no matter how wrong or how bad for this country his decisions were, they had to back him up because he happened to belong to their political party.

I campaigned against those New Deal-Truman Senators who felt that regardless of the cost to the Nation they had to blind the eyes and close the ears of the American people to the fact that we were rapidly getting a government of, by, and for Communists, crooks, and cronies. If the day comes that we, the Republican Party, follow that same course which we so vigorously condemned, then it will indeed be a black day for America and the world.

We want no Lattimores in our Republican Party. But what is more important, if any are found, we want no Tydings whitewash of them. We want no Republican Amerasia, but if one is found it must be exposed, regardless of how much our own party may bleed because of the exposure.

We must put country above party, and if we make a mistake we Republicans must admit it and rectify it as soon as possible.

Such a mistake was the nomination of Bohlen as Ambassador to Moscow.

We have time to correct that mistake and show the American people that we will never keep in power men who played an important role in selling out the people of Europe and Asia to the Soviet dictatorship.

President Eisenhower, burdened with work and pressed for time, has had little opportunity to study the complete record of Bohlen. I am sure that President Eisenhower who campaigned against the treason of Yalta is not aware of the fact that Bohlen within the past few days has stated before the committee that the Yalta agreement was "the best attempt that could have been made under the circumstances"—

page 113, hearings before the Committee on Foreign Relations. . . .
Only last week Bohlen still played coy regarding his own role in
the diplomatic intrigues of the New Deal gang. Before the Senate
Foreign Relations Committee Bohlen said:

> Senator, I have testified and I repeat again, that my primary function
> there (at Yalta) was that of an interpreter for the President. I think
> you will find that in Secretary Stettinius' book on the conference.

Mr. Dulles also has said that Bohlen was only an interpreter of the
Russian language meekly chattering on the sidelines at Yalta as mil-
lions of human beings were placed on the auction block and sold to
Stalin.

In an executive session of the Senate Foreign Relations Committee
on March 18, Senator Mansfield asked the Secretary of State:

> Would you say that Mr. Bohlen was a policymaker at Yalta and
> Teheran or just an interpreter?

Secretary Dulles replied:

> My understanding is that he was only an interpreter. I was not there,
> but he was still only an interpreter when I first met him later and he
> did not emerge into what I regard as a policymaking position until, I
> would say, some time about 1946.

Mr. President, I do not accuse Secretary Dulles of knowingly falsify-
ing the record. He is an extremely busy man, having taken over a
tremendously important task; but, when he is in error, I think we
must call it to the attention of the Senate. I may say I am sure the
error was an honest one on his part, but I think we should turn to the
book by Mr. Stettinius to see what Stettinius had to say about Bohlen,
and as to whether Bohlen was merely an interpreter.

I quote from the book *Roosevelt and the Russians,* written by the
late Mr. Stettinius. On page 103, the Secretary of State wrote of Bohlen
at Yalta:

> Bohlen, however, was more than a professional interpreter. He was
> an expert, as well, on substantive matters.

\*     \*     \*

Today we want no part of a man who was part of the Acheson betrayal team.

We want no part of this "chip" off the old block of Yalta.

Aside from the fact that Bohlen can speak Russian, I can find no reason why he should be sent to Moscow to represent Americans. The reason, simply stated, why he should not be sent to Moscow is that he has always been a very willing, enthusiastic, and active part and parcel of the Acheson-Vincent-Lattimore-Service clique which was overwhelmingly rejected by 31 million Americans last fall.

## ON THE PROBLEM OF COMMUNIST BOOKS

*As chairman of the Permanent Subcommittee on Investigations of the Committee on Government Operations, McCarthy spent considerable time investigating the State Department's 150 overseas libraries. In the course of his inquiry, McCarthy established that books authored by Communists had found their way onto government library shelves abroad. Responding to McCarthy's pressure, the State Department in the spring of 1953 sent out six secret directives that banned hundreds of books by some forty authors. Dulles soon admitted that at certain overzealous information centers, some of these books had literally been burned. At the commencement of Dartmouth University in June, Eisenhower delivered an extemporaneous denunciation of "book-burners." "Don't be afraid to go to the library and read [Communist] books," the president said. "That's how we will defeat Communism—by knowing what it is." But at his news conference a week later, Eisenhower refused to allow his remarks to be interpreted as an attack on Senator McCarthy. In his capacity as a member of the Senate Appropriations Committee, McCarthy used a hearing on the State Department budget to interrogate Dr. James B. Conant, former president of Harvard and the U.S. High Commissioner for Germany, about his views on communist books in the overseas library program. Parts of the resulting exchange follow.*[2]

*Senator McCarthy:* May I ask you this: Our committee has recently exposed the fact that there are some 30,000 publications by Communist authors on information shelves, many of them in Germany. I am not speaking of the books that explain the workings of the Communist Party; I am not speaking of the books available to the employees of HICOG. We both realize that they must read those Communist

[2] U.S., Congress, Senate, Committee on Appropriations, *Supplemental Appropriation Bill, 1954: Hearings,* 83d Cong., 1st sess., 1953, pp. 25, 26, 57–59.

books to know the Communist objectives. I am referring to the books by Communist authors on our shelves, with our stamp of approval—some 30,000.

May I ask what your attitude toward that is? Do you favor taking those books off the shelves? Would you favor leaving them on the shelves? Would you favor discontinuing the purchase of those books or continuation of that purchase? . . .

*Commissioner Conant:* If I had that responsibility directly—it is clearly one that has to be delegated—I should have to examine each case pretty carefully to see who our Communist author was, what his point of view was, and whether the reading of that book by the Germans would do us more good than harm.

*Senator McCarthy:* Let's see what the point of view of the author is. The Communist is under Communist Party discipline, and the point of view is furthering the Communist conspiracy. There is no doubt about that, is there?

*Commissioner Conant:* With such a man, I would not want his books on the shelves.

*Senator McCarthy:* Such a man, I think—and every Communist—we can agree has the task of furthering the Communist cause; otherwise, he is not a Communist; is that not correct?

*Commissioner Conant:* Quite so.

*Senator McCarthy:* And one of your tasks over there is to fight communism. So, I assume both of us know something about the Communist movement.

Let us get back to the question: Would you favor having on your bookshelves—you are asking for $21 million—would you favor using part of that $21 million to buy the works of Communist authors and put them on your bookshelves?

*Commissioner Conant:* The answer is "No."

*Senator McCarthy:* How about the 30,000 books that are on those bookshelves by Communist authors?

*Commissioner Conant:* I have no information as to that, sir.

*Senator McCarthy:* We will give you the information, then. Our committee has developed that there are some 30,000 by Communist authors, many of them in Germany. Would you favor removing from the bookshelves the works of the Communist authors? . . .

*Commissioner Conant:* Do you mean by "Communist authors" a member of the Communist Party who is under instructions to further its cause?

*Senator McCarthy:* That is right; either a man who has been proved to be a Communist, or a man who says, "I won't tell, because if I told the truth I might go to jail."

*Commissioner Conant:* I would not be in favor of having books by

Communist authors on the shelves. If they are already there, I would be in favor of taking them off.

*Senator McCarthy:* You would not call that book burning if you took them off, would you?

*Commissioner Conant:* I suppose you wouldn't, but I wouldn't suppose that you would burn them.

*Senator McCarthy:* Then we both agree, I think, on that all right. . . .

*Senator McCarthy:* What do you propose to do with those books when they have been removed?

*Commissioner Conant:* I would not have an answer to that. It would seem to me a relatively minor problem whether they were stored somewhere or what was done.

*Senator McCarthy:* What would you store them for? What are you going to save them for?

*Commissioner Conant:* They might be sold as excess property here in the United States.

*Senator McCarthy:* Would you burn them?

*Commissioner Conant:* I certainly wouldn't.

*Senator McCarthy:* You would not burn them?

*Commissioner Conant:* No, I would not burn them.

*Senator McCarthy:* What would you do, pay for storing them?

*Commissioner Conant:* I think I would be able to make a deal by which I could get rid of them as second-hand books for one purpose or another.

*Senator McCarthy:* By second-hand books do you mean for someone to read?

*Commissioner Conant:* Yes; in the United States.

*Senator McCarthy:* In other words, you are trying to sell those 30,000 books so that the people in the United States could read them?

*Commissioner Conant:* I think the people in the United States are perfectly capable of reading books by Communist authors or anyone else.

*Senator McCarthy:* So, then, you propose that we remove the books, 30,000, from the libraries abroad, bring them back to the United States and sell them. Would you sell them to colleges?

*Commissioner Conant:* I think I would sell them through a second-hand bookstore.

*Senator McCarthy:* Would you object to having them sold to colleges?

*Commissioner Conant:* I don't see that colleges—you mean—as colleges they would not be interested in buying them probably. But I would not have any objection to their being put in college libraries, certainly not.

*Senator McCarthy:* In other words, you have no objection to Communist works being put in college libraries.

*Commissioner Conant:* Books by Communist authors, certainly not.

*Senator McCarthy:* You understand I am not speaking about books explaining the Communist ideology. I am not speaking about books by authors who say I am a Communist.

*Commissioner Conant:* I understand.

*Senator McCarthy:* I am speaking about books by Communists who claim they are good Americans, who deny they are Communists. You say we should take those out of the libraries and bring them back and sell them to college libraries.

*Commissioner Conant:* No, sir. I said you should sell them. You spoke of selling them to colleges.

*Senator McCarthy:* You say you have no objection to selling them to college libraries.

*Commissioner Conant:* No.

*Senator McCarthy:* As president of your college would you object to buying them and putting them in your library?

*Commissioner Conant:* Undoubtedly, we have all those books in our library. I haven't checked on it, but it would surprise me if we didn't have almost all the books that are published.

*Senator McCarthy:* I would be surprised, too, Professor, if you did not. Now, you realize that when you purchase a book of the Communist author you are putting money into the Communist coffers; do you not?

*Commissioner Conant:* It depends on the contract which the author makes with the publisher. It is the publisher, in my experience, and not the author that gets the money.

*Senator McCarthy:* You know that every member of the party must contribute to the party; do you not?

*Commissioner Conant:* That is what I understand.

*Senator McCarthy:* Then when you buy the books of a Communist author, if he must give a certain percentage of his income to the Communist Party, that means that you are contributing to the party. Right?

*Commissioner Conant:* But I thought the premise of this argument, Senator, was these books have already been bought. The question was trying to recapture some of the taxpayers' money that was spent on them.

*Senator McCarthy:* You were president of the university for some time. I assume that you had Communist books in the library.

*Commissioner Conant:* Yes; I would assume our library had all the books published in the United States when not obscene.

*Senator McCarthy:* You have no objection to that?
*Commissioner Conant:* None whatever.

## VOICE OF AMERICA: "AN INCREDIBLE SITUATION"

*Another of McCarthy's favorite targets in 1953 was the Voice of America. As usual the administration sought to appease McCarthy rather than to protect its agencies. In March McCarthy forced the State Department to rescind a directive to Voice employees permitting them to decide for themselves whether they wished to talk informally with committee staff members in the absence of a senator. Henceforth, employees would be expected to cooperate fully in all of the committee's work. McCarthy also induced the State Department to forbid the Voice of America to quote Communists even if such quotation would serve its purposes. According to his critics, McCarthy permitted embittered Voice personnel to use his committee to vent their animosity against fellow employees. But Senator Taft said that McCarthy's investigation had persuaded him that the Voice was "certainly full of fellow travellers." On January 25, 1954, McCarthy presented the annual report of his committee to the Senate. Portions of that report relating to the Voice of America are reprinted below.*[3]

When our own investigation began, the top policy man for this whole program for the entire International Information Administration was W. Bradley Connors. Mr. Connors came to the attention of the subcommittee when he signed a directive authorizing the use in our anti-Communist information program of some of the works of Howard Fast, one of the top Communist authors in this country. When Fast, some of whose works Connors authorized for use, was called before the subcommittee, he testified as follows:

Testimony at page 98, pt. 2, Voice of America hearings:

> *Mr. Cohn:* Are you Howard Fast, the author?
> *Mr. Fast:* I am.
> *Mr. Cohn:* Mr. Fast, are you now a member of the Communist Party?
> *Mr. Fast:* I will refuse to answer that question, basing my refusal to answer on the rights granted to me by the first amendment to the Con-

[3] U.S., Congress, Senate, Committee on Government Operations, *Annual Report: Report No. 881,* 83d Cong., 2d sess., 1954, pp. 21–23, 24–25.

stitution, and by the fifth amendment to the Constitution, which guarantees my right against self-incrimination.

*     *     *

*Mr. Cohn:* Were you a member of the Communist Party at the time you wrote any of the books under your authorship which have been published?

*Mr. Fast:* I refuse to answer that question for the same reason I gave before.

Connors was called before the subcommittee to explain this directive authorizing the use of works by this notorious Communist who had been convicted of contempt of Congress, and who invoked the fifth amendment.

Connors exposed a virtually incredible situation by testifying that he, the top policy expert in the anti-Communist program, knew little about communism. He pleaded complete ignorance of the history and methods of the Communist movement, and said he had not read any of the works by the founders and key leaders of the Communist conspiracy.

*The Chairman:* Mr. Connors, how much of an authority are you on the Communist movement?

*Mr. Connors:* I am not.

*The Chairman:* You are not an authority. Have you ever read any of the works of Marx or Lenin, Engels?

*Mr. Connors:* No, sir.

*The Chairman:* Any of the works of Stalin?

*Mr. Connors:* No, sir.

*The Chairman:* Have you ever studied a history of the Communist movement, their methods of operation?

*Mr. Connors:* I have never studied them.

Connors' representative in the Voice of America, as policy adviser for that subdivision of the International Information Administration, was Edwin M. J. Kretzmann. Kretzmann had the responsibility of policy for the Voice of America broadcasts designed to tell millions of people throughout the world about the evils of communism. Mr. Kretzmann's knowledge of communism and his views on it were as dismaying as those of Mr. Connors. Mr. Kretzmann first came to the attention of the subcommittee when Dr. John Cocutz, Acting Chief of the Rumanian Service of the Voice of America, told of how he, Cocutz, took leave as head of the department of philosophy at the University of Georgia and became associated with the Voice of America to "fight against communism."

On arrival at the Voice, Dr. Cocutz conducted a survey of certain personnel of the Voice of America. He testified, "Many of them didn't know what it was all about—what communism was." He added that he immediately drew up a plan to "train our writers and editors to be better equipped to fight communism."

This plan was referred to Mr. Kretzmann, who sent for Dr. Cocutz. Dr. Cocutz described the conversation as follows:

> *Mr. Cohn:* Now, did you have a conversation with Mr. Kretzmann?
> *Dr. Cocutz:* Yes. As soon as I got to his office, Mr. Kretzmann said to me, after he read the memorandum, that I was under the impression that we are there at the Voice of America to fight communism, while we are not. I said to him, "Well, I am surprised, because I left my job at the University of Georgia purposely to come here and fight against communism. There is no business for me to be here, then. I can go back to the university, if I can't fight communism here."
> *The Chairman:* Did I understand you to say, Doctor, that he said you apparently were under the impression that you were there to fight communism, but actually that was not the function of the Voice?
> *Dr. Cocutz:* Yes.

After a number of similar incidents involving Mr. Kretzmann were described to the subcommittee, Mr. Kretzmann appeared before it. The testimony of this policy adviser for the Voice of America showed that apparently he chose to use the Voice of America to send broadcasts into South Korea attacking its strongly anti-Communist President Syngman Rhee at the vital time that Rhee was fighting for his political life. The testimony showed that Kretzmann in effect was using the Voice of America in an attempt to bring about the defeat of Rhee in the elections at the very moment that American soldiers were fighting alongside of Rhee's soldiers against the common Communist enemy in Korea.

> *The Chairman:* Let us try to get one clearance today. There is no question but what your broadcasts beamed to South Korea over the Voice's facilities was material extremely critical of Syngman Rhee, you say of his methods, just at a time shortly before the elections were held? There is no question about that, is there?
> *Mr. Kretzmann:* That is right, sir.
> *The Chairman:* And as a result of that, the South Korean Government denied facilities of the South Korean radios to the Voice; is that correct?
> *Mr. Kretzmann:* That is correct.
> *The Chairman:* Did you carry any favorable comment on Syngman Rhee?
> *Mr. Kretzmann:* We were asked to balance it.

*The Chairman:* Did you carry any favorable comment on those broadcasts about Syngman Rhee?

*Mr. Kretzmann:* We did not, because we could not find any in either the American press or the European press at the time.

The testimony disclosed that the Government of South Korea immediately denied all further facilities to the Voice of America in South Korea.

Mr. Kretzmann did not consider it pertinent to inquire of the head of the religious desk whether he was an atheist.

With this view of the policy chief for the entire hundred million dollar International Information Administration, and his representative as policy adviser for the Voice of America, the subcommittee directed attention to the type product that was being turned out under their supervision.

### Conditions in Voice of America Operation

Many Voice of America scripts were studied by the subcommittee. Some of them, particularly those from branches under the direction of such knowledgable anti-Communists as Alexander Barmine of the Russian Division and Gerald F. P. Dooher of the Near East, South Asian Division, were most impressive.

However, the influence of Mr. Connors and Mr. Kretzmann apparently permeated far too large a number of products turned out by the Voice. In a program called Inside Wall Street from a feature of September 13, 1952, Wall Street was referred to as "the den of wretchedness."

In a broadcast of December 2, 1952, concerning Edna Ferber's book, *The Giant,* Texans were portrayed as men who "drink bourbon by the gallon," and the "women are nitwits who talk but say practically nothing."

Senator Dirksen, a member of the subcommittee, had personal experience with the peculiar approach to some of these matters when he was invited to narrate a Lincoln Day program for the Voice and discovered it centered around a letter written by Karl Marx. Senator Dirksen declined to appear on the program.

The hearings developed the fact that an attempt was made to shut down the Hebrew broadcast of the Voice of America just at a time when maximum advantage could have been taken of the open anti-Semitic actions of the Soviet Union.

Reed Harris, the Deputy Administrator of the International Information Administration, was questioned on this and other matters. It developed that Mr. Harris had a background of association with Communist organizations; that he had written pro-Communist material, some of which was reprinted in the Daily Worker; he had been the advocate for a suspended Communist professor, and had made a statement to the subcommittee under oath which was directly contradicted by a person of such standing as General Alexander Barmine. . . .

### Conditions in International Information Administration Field Offices

Field offices around the world, with approximately 8,000 personnel, were under the direction of Dr. William Johnstone, Jr., when the subcommittee commenced its probe. Dr. Johnstone was well known to congressional committees. He was listed by the Senate Internal Security Subcommittee in 1952 as one of the 59 individuals, identified by witnesses before it, as "having been affiliated with one or more Communist-controlled organizations." Dr. Johnstone, the Internal Security Subcommittee records showed, was the major domo at a luncheon which brought together Vladimir Rogov, an agent of Soviet Military Intelligence, and such noted figures as Owen Lattimore and John Carter Vincent.

Dr. Johnstone's contribution did not end with arranging this meeting. In a writing, he echoed the old Communist chant that the main objective of the Chinese Communists was "agrarian reform."

> Chinese Communists were also Nationalists and their main objectives were agrarian reform and an economic democracy that they practiced as well as preached.

This is the man who, until the subcommittee held hearings, had charge of the thousands of State Department officials throughout the world who were part of a program to fight communism through the International Information Administration.

The chief counsel and the chief consultant for the subcommittee investigated certain specific items concerning the activities of the information program in these field offices abroad. A few of the facts developed were:

> 1. A lecturer, echoing the Communist line, describing Malenkov as a "lover of peace," and praising the Communist educational system, had been used in the State Department information center in Munich, Germany, as part of our program to fight communism. The shocked officials of that information center entered written protest concerning this lecturer, but Lowell Clucas, the public-affairs officer in Munich, refused to prevent future appearances of this lecturer in our anti-Communist program. The lecturer was thus permitted to appear on nine subsequent occasions. The subcommittee is advised that Clucas still holds his position.
> 2. Millions of dollars were being expended by the United States in a revolving fund to subsidize hundreds of German newspapers—

(a) Some of this American money, given as a subsidy to a German newspaper, was used to print pamphlets and literature for the Communists.

(b) The United States was spending additional millions of dollars each year, in running its own newspaper in Germany in competition with these German newspapers which it was helping to support. Since the time of this exposure, the expenditures on this American-owned newspaper in Germany have been drastically curtailed.

3. Theodore Kaghan, the deputy director of our entire public-affairs program in Germany, had been the author of a number of pro-Communist plays hailed in the *Daily Worker* and produced by a Communist front group, and had signed a petition pledging support to Communist Party candidates during the Hitler-Stalin Pact.

4. A history book to be subsidized by funds for the United States information program was printed in Germany echoing the Communist line.

5. A publication of the information program in Vienna, Austria, was actually being printed in a Communist-owned printshop in the Communist zone with funds contributed by the American taxpayers, thus furnishing revenue to the Communists, and also giving them a preview of what form our attack against them would take, by seeing proofs of our material well before it was to be made public.

### "McCARTHYISM IS THE ISSUE IN THIS CAMPAIGN"

*In November, 1953, McCarthy shouldered his way into a bitter argument between Attorney General Herbert Brownell and former President Truman. Brownell had accused Truman of knowingly appointing a Communist agent, Harry Dexter White, to the International Monetary Fund in 1946. Truman went on television to accuse Brownell of distorting the facts and practicing "McCarthyism." McCarthy then demanded and received equal time on television to reply to this "attack upon me." More interesting than McCarthy's reply to Truman, however, was the criticism of the Eisenhower administration that he managed to work into his address. Excerpts from McCarthy's speech, November 24, 1953, follow.[4]*

Well, my good friends, this gives you some of the picture why the Communists, the fellow-travelers, the Truman-type Democrats, who place party above country, scream so loudly about McCarthyism, why their hatred and venom knows no bounds.

Now, a few days ago—a few days ago, I read that President Eisen-

[4] *The New York Times*, November 25, 1953, p. 5. Editor's title. Copyright © 1953 by the New York Times Company. Reprinted by permission.

hower expressed the hope that by election time in 1954 the subject of Communism would be a dead and forgotten issue. The raw, harsh, unpleasant fact is that Communism is an issue and will be an issue in 1954.

Truman's diatribe against those who expose Communists is the best proof of that. . . .

Now Democrat office-seekers from the Atlantic to the Pacific have been proclaiming that McCarthyism is the issue in this campaign. In a way, I guess, it is, because Republican control of the Senate determines whether I shall continue as chairman of the investigating committee.

Therefore, if the American people agree with Truman, they have a chance to get rid of me as chairman of the investigating committee next fall by defeating any Republican up for election.

If the American people, on the other hand, believe in the necessity of digging out and getting rid of the type of Communists who have been before our committee; if they believe, as I do, that treason, dishonesty and stupidity should be exposed wherever and whenever found, regardless of the party label, then their answer is to keep the Republicans in power so we may continue to clean out the Augean stables.

But now, now let's take a look at the Republican party. Unfortunately, in some cases, our batting average has not been too good. Before looking at some of the cases in which our batting average is zero, let me make it clear that I think that the new Administration is doing a job so infinitely better than the Truman-Acheson regime that there is absolutely no comparison.

For example, the new Administration in the first ten months in office has gotten rid of 1,456 Truman holdovers who were all security risks. And over 90 per cent of the 1,456 security risks were gotten rid of because of Communist connections and activities or perversion. Fourteen hundred and fifty-six, I would say: an excellent record for the time President Eisenhower has been in office.

However, let us glance at a few cases where we struck out. For example, we still have John Paton Davies on the payroll after eleven months of the Eisenhower Administration.

And who is John Paton Davies? John Paton Davies was (1) part and parcel of the old Acheson-Lattimore-Vincent-White-Hiss group which did so much toward delivering our Chinese friends into Communist hands; (2) he was unanimously referred by the McCarran Committee to the Justice Department in connection with a proposed indictment because he lied under oath about his activities in trying to put—listen to this—in trying to put Communists and espionage agents in key spots in the Central Intelligence Agency.

A question which we ask is: Why is this man still a high official in our department after eleven months of Republican Administration?

Now let us examine the failure of my party, if we may, to liquidate the foulest bankruptcy of the Democrat Administration.

On September 12, 1953, the Chinese Communists announced that they would not treat as prisoners of war American fliers who were shot down during the Korean war over Manchuria. On September 10, 1953, the Army announced that some 100 American young men known to have been prisoners of the Communists in Korea were still unaccounted for. Unaccounted for as of tonight, my good friends.

Well, why do I bring this situation up tonight in telling about the Republican party? The Republican party did not create the situation, I admit. We inherited it. But we are responsible for the proper handling of the situation as of tonight. Now what are we going to do about it? Are we going to continue to send perfumed notes, following the style of the Truman-Acheson regime?

Or are we going to take the only position that an honorable nation can take—namely, that every uniformed American packs the pride and the honor and the power of this nation on his shoulder.

Millions of people in my radio and television audience tonight will recall that even in grade school your hearts beat a bit faster and you felt a great surge of pride when you heard in song this was the land of the free and the home of the brave.

But let me ask you, how free are we? How free are we when American aviators fighting under the American flag at this very moment, on November 24, 1953, are being brainwashed, starved or murdered behind an Iron or Bamboo Curtain? How brave are we—how brave are we when we do not use all the power of this nation to rescue those airmen and the 900 other military men who have been unaccounted for for months?

I realize, of course, the low ebb to which our honor has sunk over the past twenty years. But it is time that we, the Republican party, liquidate this blood-stained blunder of the Acheson-Truman regime. We promised the American people something different. It is up to us now to deliver—not next year, next month—let us deliver now, my good friends.

How are we going to do it? Once a nation has allowed itself to be reduced to a state of whining, whimpering appeasement, the cost of regaining national honor may be very high. But we must regain our national honor regardless of what it costs. Now I know it is easy to talk in general terms about what can be done. Let us be specific.

As you know, we have been voting billions of dollars each year to help our allies build up their military and economic strength, so that they can help in this day-to-day struggle between the free half of the world and the Communist slave half. If that money we give them is being used for that purpose, then it is well spent. If not, then those allies are defrauding us.

How does that affect you? As of today, some money was taken out of your paycheck and sent to Britain. As of today, Britain used that money from your paycheck to pay for the shipment of the sinews of war to Red China.

What can we do about that? We can deal a death blow to the war-making power of Communist China. We can, without firing a single shot, force the Communists in China to open their filthy Communist dungeons and release every American. We can blockade the coast of China, without using a single ship, a single sailor or a single gun.

In this connection I want to point out that Lloyds of London, the outfit that keeps track of shipping, according to their records the shipments to Red China for this year have increased over 1,500 per cent over what they were last year.

Now what can we do about it? We can handle this by saying this to our Allies: If you continue to ship to Red China, while they are imprisoning and torturing American men, you will get not one cent of American money.

If we do that, my good friends, this trading in blood-money will cease. No question about that.

Now, I see time is running out. Let me remind you that when the smoke-screen of false political righteousness is raised against McCarthyism by Harry Truman, or anyone else singing in his choir of defeat, remember that he, Truman, stands on his record as an individual and as a President. He promoted Harry Dexter White, Russian spy. He fired General Douglas MacArthur, one of the greatest living Americans.

In conclusion I would like to quote as well as I can remember Abraham Lincoln, who when discussing the only way this nation could ever be destroyed said: "All the armies in Europe, all the armies of Europe and Asia combined, with all the wealth of the world in their military chests, with a Bonaparte for a commander, in a trial of a thousand years, could not place one foot upon the Blue Ridge Mountains; could not take one drink from the Ohio River."

As Lincoln said: "From whence then will danger come? If this nation is to be destroyed, it will be destroyed from within, if it is not destroyed from within, it will live for all time to come."

# 4
## Downfall of a Senator

### WHO PROMOTED PERESS?

*In January, 1954, McCarthy was at the height of his influence. In the Senate the Republican leadership gave Mc-Carthy a seat on the powerful Rules Committee, and his fellow legislators voted him ample funds to pursue his investigations. According to a Gallup poll, 50 percent of the public had a favorable opinion of the senator, and only 29 percent opposed him. But in a few months, as a result of reckless attacks that McCarthy launched on the U.S. Army, his fortunes began to ebb.*

*The circumstances that brought McCarthy's downfall were, to understate the matter, implausible. In 1953 McCarthy chose for chief counsel of his committee twenty-six-year-old Roy M. Cohn, who had been a government lawyer active in prosecuting Communists for the Truman administration. Cohn was brilliant, abrasive, and a driving force behind McCarthy's investigations. In 1952, before his career became linked with McCarthy's, Cohn struck up a friendship with G. David Schine, heir of a hotel fortune and author of one brief essay on communism. Cohn subsequently made Schine an unpaid consultant of Mc-Carthy's committee and in April, 1953, took him along on an uproarious and widely publicized eighteen-day trip to Europe to uncover communist influence in the government's information program. In July, 1953, the U.S. Army interrupted the good times of Cohn and Schine by informing Schine of his imminent induction into the armed services. Cohn immediately began harassing the army on Schine's behalf. He sought a commission for Schine, and when that failed, he asked the army to assign Schine to Mc-Carthy's committee. Although McCarthy secretly informed the army that he was glad to get rid of Schine, the army nevertheless sought to appease Cohn and permitted its rules to be rather flexibly applied where Schine was concerned. But on one point the army held firm: Private Schine, in his own peculiar fashion, would have to take basic training.*

*In the army's view Cohn now began to use the threat of investigation to blackmail the Pentagon into doing more for*

*Schine. And, indeed, in October, 1953, McCarthy opened hearings on the Army Signal Corps at Fort Monmouth. McCarthy demonstrated that Communists had infiltrated the installation during World War II and charged that spies were still at work there. (Although McCarthy uncovered no current espionage at Fort Monmouth, his investigation hastened army suspension of a number of "security risks," some of whom were later reinstated.) When John G. Adams, Department of the Army Counsellor, informed Cohn in January, 1954, that Schine might eventually be shipped overseas, Cohn threatened to "wreck the army" and drive Secretary of the Army Robert Stevens from the government. McCarthy, meanwhile, moved his investigation from Fort Monmouth to other army matters. There was, for instance, the case of Major Irving Peress.*

*Irving Peress was a dentist who, in October, 1952, was commissioned a captain in the U.S. Army. Until February, 1953, no one in the army noticed that Peress had refused on constitutional grounds to answer a questionnaire about possible subversive affiliations. In October, 1953, as his case was making its slow way through bureaucratic channels, Peress was routinely promoted to the rank of major. In December, 1953, an army personnel board finally completed its investigation of Peress and recommended his separation on security grounds from the service. Lacking a simple procedure for getting rid of him, the army decided to issue Peress an honorable discharge. But before Peress received his discharge papers, McCarthy summoned him to testify before his committee, demanded that Peress' honorable discharge be withheld, and called for his court-martial. The army ignored McCarthy's demands and permitted the discharge to stand. McCarthy then sought an answer to the question, who promoted Peress?*

*In the course of his inquiry, McCarthy's committee interrogated Brigadier General Ralph Zwicker, commanding officer at Fort Kilmer, where Peress was stationed. In McCarthy's view Zwicker's responses to the committee's questions were evasive. In the army's view McCarthy's treatment of Zwicker was intolerably abusive. When Secretary of the Army Stevens heard that McCarthy had insulted Zwicker, he announced, "I intend to support the loyal men and women of our army," and he ordered Zwicker not to appear again before McCarthy's committee. But a few days later, on February 24, 1954, at a secret luncheon with McCarthy, Stevens agreed to a "Memorandum of Understanding" that the press regarded as an abject surrender by the secretary to the senator. Eisenhower at last decided*

*that the prestige of his administration was now at stake. Stevens
was soon announcing from the White House, "I shall never
accede to the abuse of army personnel [or] to their being brow-
beaten or humiliated." Zwicker's testimony (February 18, 1954),
parts of which follow,[1] is important not only because it brought
Eisenhower into the struggle against McCarthy, but also because
it later played a prominent role in the Senate's eventual censure
of McCarthy.*

*The Chairman:* You know that somebody signed or authorized an
honorable discharge for this man, knowing that he was a fifth amendment Communist, do you not?

*General Zwicker:* I know that an honorable discharge was signed
for the man.

*The Chairman:* The day the honorable discharge was signed, were
you aware of the fact that he had appeared before our committee?

*General Zwicker:* I was.

*The Chairman:* And had refused to answer certain questions?

*General Zwicker:* No, sir, not specifically on answering any questions. I knew that he had appeared before your committee.

*The Chairman:* Didn't you read the news?

*General Zwicker:* I read the news releases.

*The Chairman:* And the news releases were to the effect that he
had refused to tell whether he was a Communist, and that there was
evidence that he had attended Communist leadership schools. It was
on all the wire service stories, was it not? You knew generally what
he was here for, did you not?

*General Zwicker:* Yes; indeed.

*The Chairman:* And you knew generally that he had refused to tell
whether he was a Communist, did you not?

*General Zwicker:* I don't recall whether he refused to tell whether
he was a Communist.

*The Chairman:* Are you the commanding officer there?

*General Zwicker:* I am the commanding general.

*The Chairman:* When an officer appears before a committee and
refuses to answer, would you not read that story rather carefully?

*General Zwicker:* I read the press releases.

*The Chairman:* Then, General, you knew, did you not, that he
appeared before the committee and refused, on the grounds of the

[1] U.S., Congress, Senate, Permanent Subcommittee on Investigations of Com-
mittee on Government Operations, *Communist Infiltration in the Army,* 83d
Cong., 2d sess., 1954, pp. 146–48, 149, 152–53. The Chairman in this exchange is
Senator McCarthy.

fifth amendment, to tell about all of his Communist activities? You knew that, did you not?

*General Zwicker:* I knew everthing that was in the press.

*The Chairman:* Don't be coy with me, General.

*General Zwicker:* I am not being coy, sir.

*The Chairman:* Did you have that general picture?

*General Zwicker:* I believe I remember reading in the paper that he had taken refuge in the fifth amendment to avoid answering questions before the committee.

*The Chairman:* About communism?

*General Zwicker:* I am not too certain about that.

*The Chairman:* Do you mean that you did not have enough interest in the case, General, the case of this major who was in your command, to get some idea of what questions he had refused to answer? Is that correct?

*General Zwicker:* I think that is not putting it quite right, Mr. Chairman.

*The Chairman:* You put it right, then.

*General Zwicker:* I have great interest in all of the officers of my command, with whatever they do.

*The Chairman:* Let's stick to fifth-amendment Communists, now. Let's stick to him. You told us you read the press releases.

*General Zwicker:* I did.

*The Chairman:* But now you indicate that you did not know that he refused to tell about his Communist activities. Is that correct?

*General Zwicker:* I know that he refused to answer questions for the committee.

*The Chairman:* Did you know that he refused to answer questions about his Communist activities?

*General Zwicker:* Specifically, I don't believe so.

*The Chairman:* Did you have any idea?

*General Zwicker:* Of course I had an idea.

*The Chairman:* What do you think he was called down here for?

*General Zwicker:* For that specific purpose.

*The Chairman:* Then you knew that those were the questions he was asked, did you not? General, let's try and be truthful. I am going to keep you here as long as you keep hedging and hemming.

*General Zwicker:* I am not hedging.

*The Chairman:* Or hawing.

*General Zwicker:* I am not hawing, and I don't like to have anyone impugn my honesty, which you just about did.

*The Chairman:* Either your honesty or your intelligence; I can't help impugning one or the other, when you tell us that a major in your command who was known to you to have been before a Senate

committee, and of whom you read the press releases very carefully—
to now have you sit here and tell us that you did not know whether
he refused to answer questions about Communist activities. I had
seen all the press releases, and they all dealt with that. So when you
do that, General, if you will pardon me, I cannot help but question
either your honesty or your intelligence, one or the other. I want to
be frank with you on that.

Now, is it your testimony now that at the time you read the stories
about Major Peress, that you did not know that he had refused to
answer questions before this committee about his Communist activities?

*General Zwicker:* I am sure I had that impression. . . .

*The Chairman:* Will you tell me whether or not you were at all
concerned about the fact that this man was getting an honorable discharge after the chairman of the Senate Investigating Committee
had suggested to the Department of the Army that he be court-
martialed? Did that give you any concern?

*General Zwicker:* It may have concerned me, but it could not have
changed anything that was done in carrying out this order.

*The Chairman:* Did you take any steps to have him retained until
the Secretary of the Army could decide whether he should be court-
martialed?

*General Zwicker:* No, sir.

*The Chairman:* Did it occur to you that you should?

*General Zwicker:* No, sir.

*The Chairman:* Could you have taken such steps?

*General Zwicker:* No, sir.

*The Chairman:* In other words, there is nothing you could have
done; is that your statement?

*General Zwicker:* That is my opinion. . . .

*The Chairman:* Do you think, General, that anyone who is responsible for giving an honorable discharge to a man who has been named
under oath as a member of the Communist conspiracy should himself be removed from the military?

*General Zwicker:* You are speaking of generalities now, and not on
specifics—is that right, sir, not mentioning about any one particular
person?

*The Chairman:* That is right.

*General Zwicker:* I have no brief for that kind of person, and if
there exists or has existed something in the system that permits that,
I say that that is wrong.

*The Chairman:* I am not talking about the system. I am asking
you this question, General, a very simple question: Let us assume that
John Jones, who is a major in the United States Army——

*General Zwicker:* A what, sir?

*The Chairman:* Let us assume that John Jones is a major in the United States Army. Let us assume that there is sworn testimony to the effect that he is part of the Communist conspiracy, has attended Communist leadership schools. Let us assume that Major John Jones is under oath before a committee and says, "I cannot tell you the truth about these charges because, if I did, I fear that might tend to incriminate me." Then let us say that General Smith was responsible for this man receiving an honorable discharge, knowing these facts. Do you think that General Smith should be removed from the military, or do you think he should be kept on in it?

*General Zwicker:* He should be by all means kept if he were acting under competent orders to separate that man.

*The Chairman:* Let us say he is the man who signed the orders. Let us say General Smith is the man who originated the order.

*General Zwicker:* Originated the order directing his separation?

*The Chairman:* Directing his honorable discharge.

*General Zwicker:* Well, that is pretty hypothetical.

*The Chairman:* It is pretty real, General.

*General Zwicker:* Sir, on one point, yes. I mean, on an individual, yes. But you know that there are thousands and thousands of people being separated daily from our Army.

*The Chairman:* General, you understand my question——

*General Zwicker:* Maybe not.

*The Chairman:* And you are going to answer it.

*General Zwicker:* Repeat it.

*The Chairman:* The reporter will repeat it.

(The question referred to was read by the reporter.)

*General Zwicker:* That is not a question for me to decide, Senator.

*The Chairman:* You are ordered to answer it, General. You are an employee of the people.

*General Zwicker:* Yes, sir.

*The Chairman:* You have a rather important job. I want to know how you feel about getting rid of Communists.

*General Zwicker:* I am all for it.

*The Chairman:* All right. You will answer that question, unless you take the fifth amendment. I do not care how long we stay here, you are going to answer it.

*General Zwicker:* Do you mean how I feel toward Communists?

*The Chairman:* I mean exactly what I asked you, General; nothing else. And anyone with the brains of a five-year-old child can understand that question.

The reporter will read it to you as often as you need to hear it so that you can answer it, and then you will answer it.

*General Zwicker:* Start it over, please.

(The question was reread by the reporter.)

*General Zwicker:* I do not think he should be removed from the military.

*The Chairman:* Then, General, you should be removed from any command. Any man who has been given the honor of being promoted to general and who says, "I will protect another general who protected Communists," is not fit to wear that uniform, General. I think it is a tremendous disgrace to the Army to have this sort of thing given to the public. I intend to give it to them. I have a duty to do that. I intend to repeat to the press exactly what you said. So you know that. You will be back here, General.

### "TO WHAT PARTY DOES HE BELONG?"

*McCarthy's conflict with the army, which enjoyed wide public respect, put him on the defensive and emboldened other senators to speak out against him. On March 9, 1953, seventy-three-year-old Ralph Flanders, Republican of Vermont, delivered a stinging attack on McCarthy.[2] Flanders was a respected moderate and his speech received wide notice.*

Mr. President, this brief talk is in the nature of advice to the junior Senator from Wisconsin [Mr. McCarthy]. I had hoped that he would be present. I do not feel constrained to put off the talk in his absence. I find that he is to be in New York today. Not knowing when he can be present, I proceed.

Mr. President, the junior Senator from Wisconsin [Mr. McCarthy] interests us all—there can be no doubt about that—but also he puzzles some of us. To what party does he belong? Is he a hidden satellite of the Democratic Party, to which he is furnishing so much material for quiet mirth? It does not seem that his Republican label can be stuck on very tightly, when, by intention or through ignorance he is doing his best to shatter the party whose label he wears. He no longer claims or wants any support from the Communist fringe. What is his party affiliation?

One must conclude that his is a one-man party, and that its name is "McCarthyism," a title which he has proudly accepted.

The junior Senator from Vermont finds much to praise and much to deplore in McCarthyism, as he sees it displayed on the national

[2] U.S., Congress, Senate, *Congressional Record,* 83d Cong., 2d sess., 1953, **100,** 2886.

stage. That which is praiseworthy is the vigorous and effective house-cleaning which it undertakes.

In January of last year the Republican family moved into quarters which had been occupied by another family for 20 long years. The outgoing family did not clean up before it left. The premises were dirty indeed.

Into these dirty premises the junior Senator from Wisconsin charged with all the energy and enthusiasm of a natural-born housekeeper. He found dirt under the rug. He found dirt behind the chiffonier. He found dirt in all the corners. He found cobwebs and spiders in the cellarway. All this dirt he found and displayed, and the clean-up he personally superintended.

Of course it was not done quietly. In the long years of my life I have come to the conclusion that natural-born housewives seldom work quietly—particularly when cleaning premises left by someone else. There is much clatter and hullabaloo. The neighbors across the backyard fence are apprised of each newly discovered deposit of grime. Much of this in his long life has the junior Senator from Vermont seen and heard, but he has never seen or heard anything to match the dust and racket of this particular job of housecleaning. Perhaps these extremes are necessary if a one-man party is to be kept in the headlines and in the limelight.

Now the question before the Nation is this: Is the necessary house-cleaning the great task before the United States, or do we face far more dangerous problems, from the serious consideration of which we are being diverted by the dust and the racket? It is the deep con-viction of the junior Senator from Vermont that we are being di-verted, and to an extent dangerous to our future as a nation. He feels called upon to say to the junior Senator from Wisconsin, "Right about face." Having looked inward so long, let him now look out-ward. . . .

In very truth the world seems to be mobilizing for the great battle of Armageddon. Now is a crisis in the agelong warfare between God and the Devil for the souls of men.

In this battle of the agelong war, what is the part played by the junior Senator from Wisconsin? He dons his war paint. He goes into his war dance. He emits his war whoops. He goes forth to battle and proudly returns with the scalp of a pink Army dentist. We may assume that this presents the depth and seriousness of Communist penetration in this country at this time.

If he cannot view the larger scene and the real danger, let him return to his housecleaning. Let him sweep out all the dirt that is under the rugs, back of the furniture and in the remotest corners. After he has done all this, let him take a clean pocket handkerchief and rub over the tops of the doors and window frames. He may find a little dust there too. But let him not so work as to conceal mortal danger in which our country finds itself from the external enemies of mankind.

Let me appeal to him in the words of a great hymn, written by St. Andrew of Crete about the year of our Lord 700:

> Christian, dost thou see them
> On the holy ground,
> How the hosts of darkness
> Compass thee around?
> Christian, up and smite them,
> Counting gain but loss;
> Smite them, Christ is with thee,
> Soldier of the cross.

## "HAVE YOU LEFT NO SENSE OF DECENCY?"

*In March, 1954, the army took the offensive against McCarthy. Conveniently, the army's thirty-four-page report detailing its incredible dealing with Cohn, Schine, and McCarthy was leaked to the press. As public opinion rallied behind the army, McCarthy and Cohn began a counterattack. The army, they announced, was holding Schine "hostage" as part of its attempt to dissuade McCarthy from pursuing his investigations. With McCarthy agreeing to step aside temporarily as chairman, the rest of his Government Operations sub-committee reluctantly undertook to examine the whole controversy. On March 16, 1954, the committee opened its famous Army-McCarthy hearings, a television spectacular that ran for two months and commanded an audience of millions.*

*Narrowly viewed, the hearings showed that Cohn had indeed exerted improper pressure on the army and that the army had compromised itself to appease Cohn. But the real importance of the hearings, as numerous commentators observed then and later, was to permit the nation a prolonged view of McCarthy in action. His crude tactics and bad manners alienated great numbers who before had been indifferent or friendly. The man at the hearings who did most to make McCarthy look bad was Joseph Welch, a gentle and witty lawyer brought down from Boston to argue the army's case. It was Welch who provided the hearings with a dramatic climax that, more than any other episode in McCarthy's career, damaged his public standing. It happened in the course of Welch's cross-examination of Roy Cohn.*[3]

*Mr. Welch:* I want to come back, Mr. Cohn, to the item that we were talking about this morning. I gathered, to sum it up a little, that as early as the spring, which must mean March or April, you knew about this situation of possible subversives and security risks, and even spies at Fort Monmouth, is that right?

*Mr. Cohn:* Yes, sir. . . .

*Mr. Welch:* Mr. Cohn, if I told you now that we had a bad situation at Monmouth, you would want to cure it by sundown, if you could, wouldn't you?

*Mr. Cohn:* I am sure I couldn't, sir.

*Mr. Welch:* But you would like to, if you could?

*Mr. Cohn:* Sir——

*Mr. Welch:* Isn't that right?

*Mr. Cohn:* No, what I want——

*Mr. Welch:* Answer me. That must be right. It has to be right.

*Mr. Cohn:* What I would like to do and what can be done are two different things.

*Mr. Welch:* Well, if you could be God and do anything you wished, you would cure it by sundown, wouldn't you?

*Mr. Cohn:* Yes, sir.

*Mr. Welch:* And you were that alarmed about Monmouth?

*Mr. Cohn:* It doesn't go that way.

*Mr. Welch:* I am just asking how it does go. When you find there are Communists and possible spies in a place like Monmouth, you must be alarmed, aren't you?

*Mr. Cohn:* Now you have asked me how it goes, and I am going to tell you.

*Mr. Welch:* No; I didn't ask you how it goes. I said aren't you alarmed when you find it is there?

*Mr. Cohn:* Whenever I hear that people have been failing to act on FBI information about Communists, I do think it is alarming, I would like the Communists out, and I would like to be able to advise this committee of why people who have the responsibility for getting them out haven't carried out their responsibility. . . .

*Mr. Welch:* Mr. Cohn, tell me once more: Every time you learn of a Communist or a spy anywhere, is it your policy to get them out as fast as possible?

[3] U.S., Congress, Senate, Special Subcommittee on Investigation of Committee on Government Operations, *Special Investigation,* 83d Cong., 2d sess., 1954, pp. 2424, 2425, 2426–30.

*Mr. Cohn:* Surely, we want them out as fast as possible, sir.

*Mr. Welch:* And whenever you learn of one from now on, Mr. Cohn, I beg of you, will you tell somebody about them quick?

*Mr. Cohn:* Mr. Welch, with great respect, I work for the committee here. They know how we go about handling situations of Communist infiltration and failure to act on FBI information about Communist infiltration. If they are displeased with the speed with which I and the group of men who work with me proceed, if they are displeased with the order in which we move, I am sure they will give me appropriate instructions along those lines, and I will follow any which they give me.

*Mr. Welch:* May I add my small voice, sir, and say whenever you know about a subversive or a Communist or a spy, please hurry. Will you remember those words?

*Senator McCarthy:* Mr. Chairman.

*Mr. Cohn:* Mr. Welch, I can assure you, sir, as far as I am concerned, and certainly as far as the chairman of this committee and the members, and the members of the staff, are concerned, we are a small group, but we proceed as expeditiously as is humanly possible to get out Communists and traitors and to bring to light the mechanism by which they have been permitted to remain where they were for so long a period of time.

*Senator McCarthy:* Mr. Chairman, in view of that question——

*Senator Mundt:* Have you a point of order?

*Senator McCarthy:* Not exactly, Mr. Chairman, but in view of Mr. Welch's request that the information be given once we know of anyone who might be performing any work for the Communist Party, I think we should tell him that he has in his law firm a young man named Fisher whom he recommended, incidentally, to do work on this committee, who has been for a number of years a member of an organization which was named, oh, years and years ago, as the legal bulwark of the Communist Party, an organization which always swings to the defense of anyone who dares to expose Communists. I certainly assume that Mr. Welch did not know of this young man at the time he recommended him as the assistant counsel for this committee, but he has such terror and such a great desire to know where anyone is located who may be serving the Communist cause, Mr. Welch, that I thought we should just call to your attention the fact that your Mr. Fisher, who is still in your law firm today, whom you asked to have down here looking over the secret and classified material, is a member of an organization, not named by me but named by various committees, named by the Attorney General, as I recall, and I think I quote this verbatim, as "the legal bulwark of the Communist Party." He belonged to that for a sizable number of years, according to his own admission, and he belonged to it long after it had been exposed as the legal arm of the Communist Party.

Knowing that, Mr. Welch, I just felt that I had a duty to respond to your urgent request that before sundown, when we know of anyone serving the Communist cause, we let the agency know. We are now letting you know that your man did belong to this organization for either 3 or 4 years, belonged to it long after he was out of law school.

I don't think you can find anyplace, anywhere, an organization which has done more to defend Communists—I am again quoting the report—to defend Communists, to defend espionage agents, and to aid the Communist cause, than the man whom you originally wanted down here at your right hand instead of Mr. St. Clair.

I have hesitated bringing that up, but I have been rather bored with your phony requests to Mr. Cohn here that he personally get every Communist out of government before sundown. Therefore, we will give you information about the young man in your own organization.

I am not asking you at this time to explain why you tried to foist him on this committee. Whether you knew he was a member of that Communist organization or not, I don't know. I assume you did not, Mr. Welch, because I get the impression that, while you are quite an actor, you play for a laugh, I don't think you have any conception of the danger of the Communist Party. I don't think you yourself would ever knowingly aid the Communist cause. I think you are unknowingly aiding it when you try to burlesque this hearing in which we are attempting to bring out the facts, however.

*Mr. Welch:* Mr. Chairman.

*Senator Mundt:* Mr. Welch, the Chair should say he has no recognition or no memory of Mr. Welch's recommending either Mr. Fisher or anybody else as counsel for this committee.

I will recognize Mr. Welch.

*Senator McCarthy:* Mr. Chairman, I will give you the news story on that.

*Mr. Welch:* Mr. Chairman, under these circumstances I must have something approaching a personal privilege.

*Senator Mundt:* You may have it, sir. It will not be taken out of your time.

*Mr. Welch:* Senator McCarthy, I did not know—Senator, sometimes you say "May I have your attention?"

*Senator McCarthy:* I am listening to you. I can listen with one ear.

*Mr. Welch:* This time I want you to listen with both.

*Senator McCarthy:* Yes.

*Mr. Welch:* Senator McCarthy, I think until this moment——

*Senator McCarthy:* Jim, will you get the news story to the effect that this man belonged to this Communist-front organization? Will you get the citations showing that this was the legal arm of the Communist Party, and the length of time that he belonged, and the fact that he was recommended by Mr. Welch? I think that should be in the record.

*Mr. Welch:* You won't need anything in the record when I have finished telling you this.

Until this moment, Senator, I think I never really gaged your cruelty or your recklessness. Fred Fisher is a young man who went to the Harvard Law School and came into my firm and is starting what looks to be a brilliant career with us.

When I decided to work for this committee I asked Jim St. Clair, who sits on my right, to be my first assistant. I said to Jim, "Pick somebody in the firm who works under you that you would like." He chose Fred Fisher and they came down on an afternoon plane. That night, when he had taken a little stab at trying to see what the case was about, Fred Fisher and Jim St. Clair and I went to dinner together. I then said to these two young men, "Boys, I don't know anything about you except I have always liked you, but if there is anything funny in the life of either one of you that would hurt anybody in this case you speak up quick."

Fred Fisher said, "Mr. Welch, when I was in law school and for a period of months after, I belonged to the Lawyers Guild," as you have suggested, Senator. He went on to say, "I am secretary of the Young Republicans League in Newton with the son of Massachusetts' Governor, and I have the respect and admiration of my community and I am sure I have the respect and admiration of the 25 lawyers or so in Hale & Dorr."

I said, "Fred, I just don't think I am going to ask you to work on the case. If I do, one of these days that will come out and go over national television and it will just hurt like the dickens."

So, Senator, I asked him to go back to Boston.

Little did I dream you could be so reckless and so cruel as to do an injury to that lad. It is true he is still with Hale & Dorr. It is true that he will continue to be with Hale & Dorr. It is, I regret to say, equally true that I fear he shall always bear a scar needlessly inflicted by you. If it were in my power to forgive you for your reckless cruelty, I will do so. I like to think I am a gentleman, but your forgiveness will have to come from someone other than me.

*Senator McCarthy:* Mr. Chairman.

*Senator Mundt:* Senator McCarthy?

*Senator McCarthy:* May I say that Mr. Welch talks about this being cruel and reckless. He was just baiting; he has been baiting Mr. Cohn here for hours, requesting that Mr. Cohn, before sundown, get out of any department of Government anyone who is serving the Communist cause.

I just give this man's record, and I want to say, Mr. Welch, that it has been labeled long before he became a member, as early as 1944——

*Mr. Welch:* Senator, may we not drop this? We know he belonged to the Lawyers Guild, and Mr. Cohn nods his head at me. I did you, I think, no personal injury, Mr. Cohn.

*Mr. Cohn:* No, sir.

*Mr. Welch:* I meant to do you no personal injury, and if I did, I beg your pardon.

Let us not assassinate this lad further, Senator. You have done enough. Have you no sense of decency, sir, at long last? Have you left no sense of decency?

*Senator McCarthy:* I know this hurts you, Mr. Welch. But I may say, Mr. Chairman, on a point of personal privilege, and I would like to finish it——

*Mr. Welch:* Senator, I think it hurts you, too, sir.

*Senator McCarthy:* I would like to finish this.

Mr. Welch has been filibustering this hearing, he has been talking day after day about how he wants to get anyone tainted with communism out before sundown. I know Mr. Cohn would rather not have me go into this. I intend to, however. Mr. Welch talks about any sense of decency. If I say anything which is not the truth, then I would like to know about it.

> The foremost legal bulwark of the Communist Party, its front organizations, and controlled unions, and which, since its inception, has never failed to rally to the legal defense of the Communist Party, and individual members thereof, including known espionage agents.

Now, that is not the language of Senator McCarthy. That is the language of the Un-American Activities Committee. And I can go on with many more citations. It seems that Mr. Welch is pained so deeply he thinks it is improper for me to give the record, the Communist-front record, of the man whom he wanted to foist upon this committee. But it doesn't pain him at all—there is no pain in his chest about the unfounded charges against Mr. Frank Carr; there is no pain there about the attempt to destroy the reputation and take the jobs away from the young men who were working in my committee.

And, Mr. Welch, if I have said anything here which is untrue, then tell me. I have heard you and everyone else talk so much about laying the truth upon the table that when I hear—and it is completely phony, Mr. Welch, I have listened to you for a long time—when you say "Now, before sundown, you must get these people out of Government," I want to have it very clear, very clear that you were not so serious about that when you tried to recommend this man for this committee.

And may I say, Mr. Welch, in fairness to you, I have reason to believe that you did not know about his Communist-front record at the time you recommended him. I don't think you would have recommended him to the committee if you knew that.

I think it is entirely possible you learned that after you recommended him.

*Senator Mundt:* The Chair would like to say again that he does not believe that Mr. Welch recommended Mr. Fisher as counsel for this committee, because he has through his office all the recommendations that were made. He does not recall any that came from Mr. Welch, and that would include Mr. Fisher.

*Senator McCarthy:* Let me ask Mr. Welch. You brought him down, did you not, to act as your assistant?

*Mr. Welch:* Mr. McCarthy, I will not discuss this with you further. You have sat within 6 feet of me, and could have asked me about Fred Fisher. You have brought it out. If there is a God in heaven, it will do neither you nor your cause any good. I will not discuss it further. I will not ask Mr. Cohn any more questions. You, Mr. Chairman, may, if you will, call the next witness.

*Senator Mundt:* Are there any questions?

*Mr. Jenkins:* No further questions, Mr. Chairman.

### THE WATKINS COMMITTEE: COMMUNISM'S "UNWITTING HANDMAIDEN"

*McCarthy's bout with the army left him vulnerable, and his enemies now moved to finish him. On July 30, 1954, Senator Flanders introduced a resolution stating "that the conduct of the Senator from Wisconsin is unbecoming a Member of the United States Senate, is contrary to senatorial traditions, and tends to bring the Senate into disrepute, and such conduct is hereby condemned." Flanders told the Senate that he was prepared to support his resolution with a lengthy list of McCarthy's transgressions. A few days later the Senate leadership chose six respected but inconspicuous members to form a select committee to consider Flanders' resolution. The committee chairman, Arthur Watkins, Republican of Utah, barred television from the hearings and ruled with such a firm hand that Mc-Carthy found no chance to employ his customary tactics. On*

*November 8, 1954, Watkins submitted a unanimous committee report to the Senate. The report recommended McCarthy's censure on two counts: (1) that he had shown contempt for the Senate by refusing to testify in 1951–1952 before a Senate committee examining his finances and by saying of one of this committee's members, Senator Robert Hendrickson of New Jersey, "he is a living miracle in that he is without question the only man in the world who has lived so long with neither brains nor guts"; (2) that McCarthy's conduct toward General Zwicker at their famous encounter was "reprehensible."*

*McCarthy's friends in the Senate consulted Republican leaders and worked out the terms of compromise. The Senate, it was agreed, would table the censure motion and replace it with one criticizing McCarthy's methods but praising his fight against communism. For his part McCarthy would have to apologize for his insult to Senator Hendrickson. But McCarthy was not in a mood to compromise, and he refused to apologize. The Senate learned how intransigent McCarthy had become when on November 10, 1954, he put his defense into the* Congressional Record. *His intemperate remarks, portions of which follow, assured his censure.*[4]

This week the United States Senate convened in special session to debate Senator Flanders' resolution to censure me. I take it, judging from declarations of individual Senators—made in most cases without bothering to study the Watkins committee record—that the resolution will be approved. I will be censured.

Today I want to discuss with you the implications, as I see them, of the censure vote.

There are two things about censure that the American people should understand. There is one thing that censure unquestionably does mean. It does mean that those who are leading the fight against subversion have been slowed down, and that others who might otherwise have been enlisted in the fight will be discouraged from joining us by the now-established hazards of such a course. It thus does mean that the Communist Party has achieved a major victory.

But there is another thing that the censure votes does not mean. It does not mean that the Communists have achieved a permanent success; it does not mean that either the will or the ultimate ability of the American people to ferret out traitors and security risks has

[4] U.S., Congress, Senate, *Congressional Record*, 83d Cong., 2d sess., 1954 **100**, 15952, 15953, 15954.

been destroyed—or that their present leaders in this fight have been intimidated.

Let me say, incidentally, that it is not easy for a man to assert that he is the symbol of resistance to Communist subversion—that the Nation's fate is in some respects tied to his own fate. It is much easier, I assure you, to be coy—to play down one's personal role in this struggle for freedom. Self-effacement is always a comfortable posture.

But I take it that you would rather I be frank than coy; that you would rather I acknowledge and accept the fact that McCarthyism is a household word for describing a way of dealing with treason and the threat of treason; and so I shall.

I am saying that the censure vote is to be understood primarily in terms of its bearing on the Communist issue. During the course of the Senate debate, I shall have occasion to discuss in some detail the specific charges considered by the Watkins group. I shall be comparing that committee's report with both the written and unwritten record of its hearings. I shall point out the discrepancies, the inaccuracies, the misrepresentations. Of course, in criticizing a Senate committee, I will run the risk of someone reactivating Senator Flanders and setting him agoing with a new censure resolution. So be it. I shall also call attention to the blatant prejudice of some of the Watkins committee members. I shall discuss these things just to keep the record straight.

But I would be missing the point entirely and I would be guilty of misleading you if I were to suggest that the Senate has made up its mind, or that the Watkins group made up its mind, on the basis of the petty charges contained in the Flanders resolution. Even my bitterest enemy will admit, if he is honest, that these matters would not have been given a second thought if someone other than McCarthy were involved.

"Abuse" of General Zwicker? Why, within the last months several committee members have used much stronger language toward witnesses. No censure resolution has been offered in these instances, and none will be.

Denouncing a Senate committee and its members? Why, Senators have done this with varying degrees of gusto from time immemorial —sometimes (as I believe to be the case with the Gillette committee) with justification, sometimes without it—but always with impunity, inasmuch as this is a land of free speech.

My colleagues are perfectly well aware that they would not be in Washington this month were it not for the fact that I have been prominently involved in the fight against Communist subversion. That being the case, let us not pretend otherwise.

If I lose on the censure vote, it follows, of course, that someone else wins. Now, I ask the American people to consider carefully: Who is it that wins? And then, having answered that question, I ask them to contemplate the shocking truth revealed by the fact that the victors have been able to win.

There is one group that is pretty sure about who has won.

When the Watkins committee announced its recommendation of censure, the Communists made no attempt to conceal their joy. The *Daily Worker*'s headline that day read, "Throw the Bum Out" (that's me). And the story beneath said, and I quote: "America is catching up with McCarthy. * * * It is good news for America—for its free speech, its right to speak out for peace, co-existence, and the abolition of H-bomb war."

Now, the *Daily Worker* was not just applauding a committee of the United States Senate. Its cry was primarily one of self-congratulation, of smug jubilation over the success of the Communists' own efforts to rebuke me. The Communists could point with justifiable pride to the campaign they have waged vigorously and unceasingly long before Senator Flanders was taken out of mothballs and persuaded to advance his censure motion last July.

No sooner had the Flanders resolution been moved than the *Daily Worker* called to party members in flaming headlines, "Aid Senate Fight on McCarthy." The *Daily Worker*'s story that day read, and I quote it: "We urge all New Yorkers to write to Ives insisting he support the Flanders resolution. We urge New Yorkers to write to Senator Herbert Lehman suggesting he put the heat on the Democrat Senate leadership to line up behind the resolution. We urge readers everywhere to line up behind the resolution. We urge readers everywhere to take similar action in connection with their Senators." In this vein the campaign continued, gaining momentum day by day; and even as I speak to you now a new story denouncing me is rolling off the *Daily Worker* presses.

There is, of course, nothing remarkable in the fact that the Communists have mobilized their strength behind the Flanders resolution. This was to be expected. From the moment I entered the fight against subversion back in 1950 at Wheeling, West Virginia, the Communists have said that the destruction of me and what I stand for is their No. 1 objective in this country.

Now it does not follow necessarily that an objective of the Communist Party is, ipso facto, contrary to the interests of the United States. But surely the strongest sort of presumption lies in this direction. And I beg the American people in every instance to have cogent, airtight reasons for disregarding this presumption before they embrace the objectives of those who have sworn to destroy this country.

Perhaps the Communists are mistaken in believing that McCarthyism is the greatest obstacle to their success. But I know of no better judge of what helps and what hurts communism than the Communist Party itself.

There is another group that regards my destruction as its chief political goal and that will claim a victory if censure is voted. This group has been well characterized as the anti-anti-Communists—persons who profess opposition to communism but who spend most of their time attempting to discredit those who hurt the Communists. For some years now this group has played the theme—in the press and on the radio, from public lecture platforms and in the classroom —that hard anticommunism somehow represents a greater threat to America than communism itself. They have chosen to call hard anti-communism, "McCarthyism." I accept their nomenclature and I am, of course, honored by it.

This group is as powerful as it is ruthless. It has at its beck and call the greater part of the opinion-molding machinery of the United States. It dominates the Nation's literature. It has enlisted a majority of the press. It manages the Luce empire which long ago abandoned any pretext of objective reporting in its newssheets.

After censure has been voted, the anti-anti-Communists will indeed deserve a large share of the credit. For they contributed mightily to the campaign to get McCarthy. But who benefits from such a victory? Is the Communist gain any the less because it has been brought about by the cooperation of non-Communists? Whenever the advocates of softness toward communism get their way, the only real victor is the Communist Party.

Now, my fellow Americans, is not all of this eloquent testimony to the great danger confronting our country? If I succeed in nothing else during the rest of my life, I would like to impress upon you the immense and awesome power of the Communist Party in this country.

Nothing is more frightening to me than that some Americans have apparently accepted the shabby dictum that the Communist Party is a small, ineffectual group whose strength is measured only by its several thousand members.

The real strength of the Communist Party is measured by the extent to which Communist objectives have been embraced by loyal Americans. It is measured by the Communists' ability to influence the American mind—to persuade large numbers of otherwise sound-thinking Americans that our Government is wise to let up in its efforts to clean out the subversives and to attack, instead, those who have hurt the Communists. I would have the American people recognize, and contemplate in dread, the fact that the Communist Party—a relatively small group of deadly conspirators—has now extended its tentacles to that most respected of American bodies, the United States Senate; that it has made a committee of the Senate its unwitting handmaiden.

Let me be very clear about this. I am not saying, as I am confident the opposition press will have me saying tomorrow, that the Watkins committee knowingly did the work of the Communist Party. I am saying it was the victim of a Communist campaign; and having been victimized, it became the Communist Party's involuntary agent.

I am aware that many of you listening to me regard this as an unpalatable proposition. I have made similar statements before, in other contexts. Such statements never fail to exasperate a good number of loyal Americans. But said they must be if we are to survive, and said they will be.

I regard as the most disturbing phenomenon in America today the fact that so many Americans still refuse to acknowledge the ability of Communists to persuade loyal Americans to do their work for them. In the course of the Senate debate I shall demonstrate that the Watkins committee has done the work of the Communist Party, that it not only cooperated in the achievement of Communist goals, but that in writing its report it imitated Communist methods—that it distorted, misrepresented, and omitted in its effort to manufacture a plausible rationalization for advising the Senate to accede to the clamor for my scalp.

But perhaps more important than explaining how the Watkins committee did the work of the Communist Party is the job of alerting the American people to the fact that this vast conspiracy possesses the power to turn their most trusted servants into its attorneys-in-fact.

We must not underestimate our enemy. . . .

There is nothing remarkable in the fact that the Communists sought to discredit me in 1950 when I first charged that Communists had managed to infiltrate the State Department in force. It is remarkable, however, that they were successful in preventing even an investigation of those charges. The Tydings committee was given this job, but instead of investigating the State Department, it investigated me. Paying not the slightest attention to the evidence I presented, it labeled my charges a "fraud and a hoax." This success of the Communists is indeed startling in the light of the fact that over a score of the cases I gave the Tydings committee were later discharged on loyalty grounds.

It is not surprising that after my Tydings charges were vindicated the Communists supported the efforts of Senator Benton to have me expelled from the Senate. But it is very significant that the Gillette committee spent a year and a half trying to put some substance into Benton's trumped-up charges.

It is neither significant nor newsworthy that the Communist Party has attempted to discredit the Senate Permanent Subcommittee on Investigations ever since I became its chairman. It is significant, however, that they have to a large extent succeeded in discrediting it.

It is not significant that the Communists claimed my committee's investigation of the State Department's Information Service was a failure. But it is significant that large numbers of Americans really believe that nothing was accomplished—despite the fact that as a result of the committee's work the State Department in the person of Secretary Dulles reversed its policy of subsidizing Communist books with the money of American taxpayers.

It is not significant that the Communists claimed the committee's investigation at Fort Monmouth was a failure. But it is very significant that the majority of the press, many of our national leaders, and so many individual Americans have bought this lie—in the teeth of the uncontrovertible fact that 33 security risks at Fort Monmouth were suspended after the committee got on the job.

It is not significant that the Communists should want members of the military who are acquainted with the Fort Monmouth situation to be silenced. But it is frighteningly significant that they have succeeded in this—that General Lawton to this day is still forbidden by his superiors in the Pentagon to tell the story of his own long and unsuccessful attempts to get rid of security risks at Fort Monmouth, attempts that bore fruit only after the Investigations Subcommittee arrived on the scene.

It is surely not significant that the Communists desire that the names of the Pentagon officials who were responsible for the promotion and honorable discharge of Major Peress be kept secret. But it is most significant that as a matter of fact these names have never been disclosed.

It is hardly significant that the Communists should have wanted to divert an investigation of the friends of Major Peress to an investigation of those who have exposed Major Peress. But it absolutely beggars belief that they have managed to do so.

In view of this pattern of Communist success—in view of the Communists' uncanny ability to strike back just when it would appear that their strength has dissipated—can anyone doubt that the security of this country is still in great danger?

But while I would never have you underestimate the Communist threat, neither would I have you believe that this thing is unbeatable. I haven't the slightest doubt that one day, and perhaps soon, the American people will rise up in righteous fury and, once and for all, extinguish the Communist menace. As for me, I will be around for some time and I will continue to serve the cause to which I have dedicated my life.

The Communists have now managed to have me investigated five times. If they fail to silence me this time—and make no mistake about it, they will fail—I will be investigated a sixth time and a seventh. But, in a sense, a new investigation of me is good news. It means that the Communists have been hurt again.

Since the Democrat Party will, next January, organize the Senate, I will no longer be in a position to direct a formal committee investigation of communism. Therefore, I shall proceed as I proceeded before when the Democrats controlled the Senate. I shall take to the people what evidence I have of Communists and other security risks in positions where they can endanger this Nation. Unfortunately, a substantial volume of such evidence exists.

But in this effort I will, as before, need your cooperation. The shouts that America is in no real danger from Communist infiltration will become louder before they grow softer. It will be said with increased frequency that more important than making America strong is getting the approval of Europeans for our system of security enforcement. If the American people should succumb to these views I truly fear for civilization.

I have, in conclusion, a word for my Senate colleagues. Many of you have either already declared yourselves or have agreed to follow a party policy. It is probably too late to turn back. It is not easy to ignore the clamor of the mob. But as you vote "aye" on this resolution I urge you to weigh carefully the question: Who has really won by this vote of censure? Perhaps the answer will encourage you to wage purposeful, yes, vengeful battles against communism in the future. And perhaps the answer will constrain some of you, at not a too distant date, to say with Representative O'Connor: "The pack got the smell of blood and tracked down the prey * * * in our hearts we knew the plot was not idle gossip and we lunged at the discloser to appease our consciences."

### "SUCH CONDUCT IS HEREBY CONDEMNED"

*In the course of the Senate's debate on the censure resolution, the charge that McCarthy had abused General Zwicker was dropped and a new one put in its place. On December 2, 1954, the Senate voted 67 to 22 to make McCarthy only the fourth senator in American history to be condemned by his peers. It was a blow from which McCarthy never recovered. Though he remained a senator until his death in 1957, he never again ex-*

*ercised influence in the Senate, and his career as the nation's
foremost anti-Communist was over. The final text of the censure resolution follows.*[5]

*Resolved,* That the Senator from Wisconsin, Mr. McCarthy, failed
to cooperate with the Subcommittee on Privileges and Elections of
the Senate Committee on Rules and Administration in clearing up
matters referred to that subcommittee which concerned his conduct
as a Senator and affected the honor of the Senate and, instead, repeatedly abused the subcommittee and its members who were trying
to carry out assigned duties, thereby obstructing the constitutional
processes of the Senate, and that this conduct of the Senator from
Wisconsin, Mr. McCarthy, is contrary to senatorial traditions and is
hereby condemned. . . .

The Senator from Wisconsin, Mr. McCarthy, in writing to the
chairman of the Select Committee To Study Censure Charges (Mr.
Watkins) after the select committee had issued its report and before
the report was presented to the Senate charging three members of the
select committee with "deliberate deception" and "fraud" for failure
to disqualify themselves; in stating to the press on November 4, 1954,
that the special Senate session that was to begin November 8, 1954,
was a "lynch party"; in repeatedly describing this special Senate session as a "lynch bee" in a nationwide television and radio show on
November 7, 1954; in stating to the public press on November 13,
1954, that the chairman of the select committee (Mr. Watkins) was
guilty of "the most unusual, most cowardly thing I've heard of" and
stating further: "I expected he would be afraid to answer the questions, but didn't think he'd be stupid enough to make a public statement"; and in characterizing the said committee as the "unwitting
handmaiden," "involuntary agent," and "attorneys-in-fact" of the
Communist Party and in charging that the said committee in writing
its report "imitated Communist methods—that it distorted, misrepresented, and omitted in its effort to manufacture a plausible rationalization" in support of its recommendations to the Senate, which char-
acterizations and charges were contained in a statement released to
the press and inserted in the *Congressional Record* of November 10,
1954, acted contrary to senatorial ethics and tended to bring the
Senate into dishonor and disrepute, to obstruct the constitutional
processes of the Senate, and to impair its dignity; and such conduct
is hereby condemned.

[5] U.S., Congress, Senate, *Congressional Record,* 83d Cong., 2d sess., 1954, **100,**
16392.

# McCARTHY APPRAISED

*From February, 1950, until his censure nearly five years later, Senator McCarthy was probably the most controversial politician in America. Because he had a genius for arousing deep feelings, few who wrote of him, then or later, proved able to render dispassionate judgment. There quickly developed a repetitive character to the literature on McCarthy. To liberal commentators he was a reckless subverter of civil liberties, a practitioner of the Multiple Untruth, a destroyer of reputations, an advocate of thought control, a seditionist, a fascist. To a small group of conservative publicists McCarthy was a lovable bear of a man whom history had called to do what no one before had done—to awaken the American people to the threat of treason in high places. This section offers a sampling of appraisals of McCarthy and his work.*

# Richard Rovere: "He Was In Some Meaningful Sense Aberrant"

*As a correspondent for the* New Yorker *Richard Rovere, a veteran liberal writer, followed McCarthy's career. In 1959 he published* Senator Joe McCarthy, *a piece of literate journalism that made no pretense to objectivity. Excerpts from Rovere's memorable analysis of McCarthy's character follow.*[1]

This sovereign of the assemblies was "foul-mouthed," all right, and "a low mean fellow," and he wanted no one to think otherwise of him. He was a master of the scabrous and the scatological; his talk was laced with obscenity. He was a vulgarian by method as well as, probably, by instinct. He belched and burped in public. If he did not dissemble much, if he did little to hide from the world the sort of human being he was, it was because he had the shrewdness to see that this was not in his case necessary. He seemed to understand, as no other politician of his stature ever has, the perverse appeal of the bum, the mucker, the Dead End kid, the James Jones–Nelson Algren–Jack Kerouac hero to a nation uneasy in its growing order and stability and not altogether happy about the vast leveling process in which everyone appeared to be sliding, from one direction or another, into middle-class commonplaceness and respectability. (I am not altogether satisfied that this appeal is strongest in these circumstances. But one can observe, I think, that the seditionists in societies that are rank with inequality and injustice tend toward austerity and asceticism, *e.g.,* Robespierre and Lenin, Gandhi and Fidel Castro; in circumstances more nearly resembling ours, one finds Hitlers and Mussolinis. Where the powers that be are relatively decent, the indecent makes a large appeal.) Sometimes, when he found himself among Gold Star Mothers or before a Catholic Youth Organization, he would get a shave, perfume his breath, scrub up his language, slick down what remained of his hair, and lay on the particular kind of charm that in my youth and his was identified by respectable ladies of a certain class as that of "a nice Catholic boy." But there was always a note of self-mockery, a

---

[1] Abridged from Richard Rovere, *Senator Joe McCarthy* (New York, 1959), pp. 48–49, 52, 57, 64–65, 69–71, 73–74. Copyright © 1959 by Richard Rovere. Reprinted by permission of Harcourt, Brace & World, Inc.

kind of hamming of this part. In general, the thing he valued was his reputation for toughness, ruthlessness, even brutality. He didn't mind at all having it get around Washington that he had threatened to "kick the brains out" of Robert Stevens if the Secretary of the Army didn't get in line on the Zwicker case. He once said to a Wisconsin crowd, "If you will get me a slippery-elm club and put me aboard Adlai Stevenson's campaign train, I will use it on some of his advisers, and perhaps I can make a good American of him." He boasted of how he had been instructed by some old North Woods scamp named Indian Charlie to go straight for an adversary's groin whenever he was in serious trouble.

And this sort of thing was always well received by his followers. They were pleased with the thought that their leader had had so sage a mentor; those who might have suspected that Indian Charlie was pure fiction and that McCarthy had never needed instruction in going for the groin would have been pleased with the turn his inventive gifts took. . . .

Where other politicians would seek to conceal a weakness for liquor or wenching or gambling, McCarthy tended to exploit, even to exaggerate, these wayward tastes. He was glad to have everyone believe that he was a drinker of heroic attainments, a passionate lover of horse-flesh, a Clausewitz of the poker table, and a man to whom everything presentable in skirts was catnip. (When a good-looking woman appeared as committee witness, McCarthy, leering, would instruct counsel to "get her telephone number for me" as well as the address for the record.) His drinking prowess, until the last year of his life, was in fact notable. He could "belt a fifth," as it was put in his set, between midnight and five A.M., catch a couple of hours of sleep, and be at his office at eight or nine, ready for a hard day's work leading the populace to mischief with empty words. His devotion to horse racing was real; he was a fixture at Pimlico and Laurel and Bowie during the season, and one often saw him, during slow moments in hearings, running over the day's form sheet while Roy Cohn confounded and crushed the generals and commanders. He was said to be a brilliant poker player, and was, in any case, a frequent one. And if the sexual aggressiveness he displayed at social gatherings was a true measure of his prowess, it, too, was notable. . . .

"That fighting Irish marine," Welker once said of McCarthy, "would give the shirt off his back to anyone who needs it—except a dirty, lying, stinking Communist. That guy he'd kill." Welker was capable of more hate than McCarthy, as well as of more ideology. McCarthy had no wish to kill Communists, and he might very well, in certain circumstances, have given one the shirt off his back. There is a case on record of a proffered act of charity to a man he had just handled brutally in a hearing. Having learned that his victim not only bled from the wounds he had inflicted but was also desperately in need of money, McCarthy sought the man out and said that he might be able to give him a hand with his financial problems. The man of course refused—no doubt thinking that McCarthy sought to rob him of his pride as well as of his good name. In fact, McCarthy wanted neither; he wanted only the tumult occasioned by the session on the witness stand, and that he already had. . . .

McCarthy's particular style, I have often thought, owed a great deal to that of a certain kind of American athlete: the kind who earns and revels in such sobriquets as Killer and Slugger; who looks ugly and talks ugly and wants to deceive no one on this score; who attaches enough importance to winning the Goddamned game to throw spitballs and rabbit punches and do a little Indian Charlie work with elbows and knees in the clinches and pileups. It was not, I imagine, without some such image in mind that he acquired his swaggering, shoulder-heaving walk and his ballplayer's slouch; that he cultivated a five-o'clock shadow with almost cosmetic care; and even that, in 1951, he changed his signature and all his listings from "Joseph R. McCarthy" to "Joe McCarthy." (The name, as it happened, was that of a former manager of the New York Yankees; there is no reason to believe, though, that he sought a specific identification with this particular Joe McCarthy.) He liked to be known as a politician who used his thumbs, his teeth, and his knees, and I suspect he understood that there is a place for a few such men in our moral universe. Our ideas and ideals of sportsmanship may be no lower than those of most people, but they exist in an ambiance with our ideas and ideals of success, and they thus include an appreciation of Leo Durocher's famous maxim, "Nice guys finish last," and a certain tolerance—particularly in the ninth inning and the fourth quarter and maybe even in the eighth chukker—for mean, low-down bastards who win. Senator John Bricker, a former Y.M.C.A. official and for many long years the plumed knight of Ohio conservatism, was not being in the least un-American when he told McCarthy in the Senate cloakroom in 1950, "Joe, you're a dirty son of a bitch, but there are times when you've got to have a son of a bitch around, and this is one of them." McCarthy, it was said at the time, was mightily pleased. . . .

There is no doubt about McCarthy's self-preoccupation; whether or not it was obsessive, it was surely excessive. There was a gorgeous instance of its excessiveness once on the Senate floor when a speech on a subject of large importance to him was being delivered and listened to attentively by most of his colleagues. It was a moment for him to take with high seriousness. What he took seriously, though, was an envelope that had reached his office without anything on it but the necessary postage and a picture of him clipped from a newspaper and pasted to the envelope. While the speech was in progress, he moved from desk to desk, putting a hand on the shoulder of each seated colleague and displaying this new evidence of the celebrity he had attained.

And there was no doubt that he was full of bodily afflictions commonly associated with an afflicted psyche. He was a mass of allergies. His hands trembled incessantly. His stomach ailments were unending. "He had a flaming belly all the time," one of his closest friends said. He had bursitis, troubled sinuses, and was accident prone.

Certainly no one who tried to see McCarthy whole could doubt that he was in some meaningful sense aberrant, even if he seemed in no meaningful way disabled or out of touch with the realities he needed (as a demagogue leading a flight from reality) to be in touch with. It would be hard to maintain a faith, even one heavily salted with skepticism, in the values of our civilization if we did not regard a wholly contemptuous and destructive attitude as somehow psychopathic. Yet to many of us who watched him in Washington over the years, the extraordinary thing about his behavior was his composure. He was prodded, he was goaded, he was taunted, and he never really went to pieces, though he sometimes pretended to do so. Whatever he did he did for an effect that he seemed either to have calculated or intuitively to have appraised with soundness. My own view was that whatever the wellsprings of his behavior and whatever tributaries fed them, he could be described as a true cynic and a true hypocrite. This seemed to me to make him a rather special case. True cynics—"those canine philosophers," as St. Augustine called them—are very rare, and true hypocrites are even rarer. Cynicism requires a disbelief in the possibility of sincerity, and most men, at least in our kind of society, find it necessary to insist upon their own sincerity. As for hypocrisy, one cannot practice it without acknowledging the fact to oneself; to be a hypocrite, a man must *see* a hypocrite whenever he faces a mirror. And such is the human capacity for self-deception that almost every sinner born of woman has some device for convincing himself that his base acts serve in some perspective some sort of good. . . .

A. C. Bradley, the Shakespearean scholar, once wrote of Macbeth that "He has never . . . accepted as the principle of his own conduct the morality which takes shape in his imaginative fears." Putting aside the question of fear, McCarthy's imagination was surely full of the shapes of the morality he rejected. He said that "mud, slime, filth, and moral squalor" characterized his opponents in 1952. It could be argued, of course, that his appeals to this alien morality were pure rhetoric—that when he spoke of the monitoring of telephone calls, a common practice in his own office, as "the most indecent and dishonest thing I have heard of," he was simply playing tricks of a debasing nature upon the language. But the same words turned up with suspicious regularity: "completely indecent and improper," "indecent and illegal under the laws," "vicious," "dishonest and vile," "dishonest, grossly dishonest," "vile and scurrilous"—all of this in an outburst over the use by others, against him, of a technique he used every day, against others. And he was always making demands upon others "in common decency, in common honesty"—in the instant case, a demand that Senator Symington take the witness stand at the Army-McCarthy hearings. Offended, he was always "sick, Mr. Chairman, sick deep down inside."

# Roy Cohn: "He Was Right in Essentials"

*No man knew McCarthy better or played a more prominent role in the Senator's affairs than Roy Cohn. In 1968, removed from politics but now a controversial figure in the world of finance, Cohn published his recollections of McCarthy and the great days that the two of them knew together. Near the end of his book Cohn discussed McCarthy's character.[2]*

This was the man McCarthy as I knew him.

He was rough-hewn, never managing to throw off his country-boy origins. He was warm and friendly. He took his job seriously but never himself. He would go to great lengths to help those he knew who were in trouble. He had more real personal courage than almost any man I ever knew.

To his enemies he was something else entirely. He was the "Prince of Nihilists," a man with a "total disregard for normal ethical standards" who got "an enormous pleasure out of kicking people" (Professor John P. Roche). He was bestial and fiendish (Tommy McIntyre, former press aide to Senator Charles Potter).

That I saw him differently is hardly surprising, because I knew him intimately and the others did not. Let me recount a few incidents recalled from my association with him over the years that may shed light on the kind of person Joe McCarthy really was. Let me also try to analyze his behavior and answer, as candidly as I can, some of the charges leveled against him, on the basis of my own knowledge of the facts.

This "ruthless" man was unable to hurt anyone's feelings by telling him he didn't want to speak to him on the telephone. Instead of instructing Mary Driscoll, his secretary, to tell an unwelcome caller he wasn't in or wouldn't be available for the call, McCarthy would fabricate a long explanation: "Tell him I just received a call from Senator Dirksen, who wants to discuss a very special matter that just came up, and after that say I have an appointment with Senator Symington in the Senate dining room, and I'll be there until two,

[2] Abridged from Roy Cohn, *McCarthy* (New York, 1968), pp. 267–71, 275–76, 277, 279. Copyright © 1968 by Roy Cohn. Reprinted by permission of The New American Library, Inc. and The Foley Agency.

111

then I've got to be on the floor and will probably stay there until four. Get that? Now repeat it to me to make sure you've got it." Even persons quite unimportant in the Washington hierarchy would receive this kind of special consideration. Often I thought it would have been easier for him to have taken the call.

McCarthy genuinely liked people. Once in New York several of us were walking up Park Avenue with him toward the Waldorf-Astoria. Passersby hailed him: "Good work, Joe," and "Keep at it, Joe." The Senator did more than smile and accept the good wishes—he stopped and got into earnest conversation with every greeter until Frank Carr had to take him firmly by the elbow and drag him away. It was also in New York that Carr became edgy one morning because the Senator, who was flying up from Washington, was late for the start of a hearing. Carr left the hearing room in the Federal Court House and went out into Foley Square to look for McCarthy. He was anxiously pacing the top of the Court House steps when finally a taxicab drew up and McCarthy stepped out. With him were a young man and a pretty girl, the three of them chatting animatedly. Carr ran down the steps to pull Joe inside. "Frank," the Senator said, "I want you to meet Bob and Ruth, wonderful young couple. I invited them to listen in at the hearings." On the way inside, Carr asked about Bob and Ruth. Who were they? Were they related to important constituents back home? "Gee, I don't know," McCarthy answered. "I just met them on the plane—they were going to lower Broadway and there was just this one cab so I gave them a ride. Awfully nice people."

McCarthy never protected himself from press critics. He should have known his enemies were scrutinizing every move and listening intently to every word, waiting for the exploitable opening. Joe talked freely to all journalists, friendly or not. During the Army-McCarthy hearings, Richard Harkness broadcast an especially lacerating criticism. Next day, Harkness approached the Senator with some trepidation. "Joe," he said, "I need a line for tonight. Have you got an angle?" McCarthy, who had heard the broadcast, willingly conferred with him while we seethed. I told Joe, "You know how far he would have gotten with me." He replied, "Oh well, it's his job. He's got a living to make and the easiest way to do it these days is to blast me."

Once a reporter for *Time* wrote an account in *Time*-style sarcasm at its worst. This man, too, came to McCarthy a few days later and asked for an interview. Joe was rushing to fly to Wisconsin and offered to take the reporter along in a private plane he was using. The Senator talked to him at length during the flight. The *Time* reporter wrote another vicious story.

Actions such as these have been misinterpreted by critics who postulate either that McCarthy was too thick-skinned to realize he was being insulted or that he couldn't understand how others felt about him. Richard Rovere, whose biographical hymn of hate about McCarthy is a classic example of frothing-at-the-mouth reportage, says "this ogrish creature" was unable to "comprehend true outrage, true indignation, true anything." Another interpretation is that he didn't care what was said about him so long as his name continued to appear before the public.

The actual explanation, in my view, could be found in McCarthy's simple friendliness. He was a hard, tough fighter, but he was not a devious man, not a plotter, not a shrewd calculator of the odds, not a manipulator. Everything he did was done openly. The question must be asked, if Joe McCarthy sought political power for himself, as many insist, would he have left himself so foolishly vulnerable? Wouldn't he have taken care to get the best possible press on every occasion?

I am not suggesting that McCarthy was unaware of his position and importance. Actually, he liked being Senator and he enjoyed importance. I cannot see that this sets him apart from fellow mortals. Someone told him a story he liked so much he repeated it many times. It is somewhat inelegant, but then, as I have indicated, McCarthy lacked Ciceronian polish. And it did make a point.

Acheson, the story goes, died and went to heaven to find St. Peter barring the gate. "You can't come in here. Go through the door at the end of the corridor." Acheson went, opened a door, and fell up to his neck into a ditch filled with excrement. In the distance, he spotted Owen Lattimore, another McCarthy target. "We're sure in trouble," Acheson called out to Lattimore. The latter replied, "This is nothing. Wait till Joe McCarthy comes through in his speedboat!"

McCarthy was never pompous; he had simple tastes and a horror of the fancy life. He was miserable in a salon and rarely went to the parties for which Washington is famous. In all the time I knew him, I can only recall two formal Washington functions he attended. He had a miserable time at each. He preferred to stay home and relax with a western story, or play gin rummy, at which he was expert. He knew little about art and music; his entertainment tastes ran to exciting movies. He hated cold weather and liked to swim and water-ski and would occasionally play golf. I don't think Joe ever ate a full-course meal in his life. In restaurants, while others in the party would begin at the top of the menu and work down, McCarthy ordered cheeseburgers and tea, occasionally roast beef or steak. He would never have made the list of best-dressed men: he paid little attention to clothes and before he was married, his ties and socks would match his suit only on a lucky day.

When he wasn't working, McCarthy could always be found at home. He was once described by a woman journalist as "home-loving, wife-loving, baby-loving," which may sound sticky but isn't far from the mark. One Christmas, a staff assistant brought four of his children to visit the McCarthys. The day before, Joe had gone out and bought toys—four dozen of them—and hidden them all over the house. Then, all through the day, he would suddenly "discover" toys and present them to the delighted children. Each kid went home at the day's end clutching a dozen packages. Overdoing it, perhaps? But that was Joe McCarthy.

Money did not concern him. He could have become wealthy by exploiting his name, but he never did. He bought no clothes beyond the basic necessities. He never owned an expensive watch, boat, or car, and altogether lived on a more modest scale than anyone I have ever known in a similar position.

While devoted to his wife, he never bought her any luxuries. I arranged for his engagement ring for Jean at wholesale. It was a very small diamond and cost about 10 per cent of what he could afford. But she didn't care either. It would not have occurred to either of them that some people might measure his love by the size of the ring he bought her.

Anyone who tries to fault McCarthy on profit-seeking grounds comes up against a blank wall, yet it is surprising how many have tried it. Various biographers have accused him of trying to make big money through investments. The truth is he made little investments all the time, but he played around the way the average man would play gin rummy. He would come up with a "sensational" idea upon which he would proceed to place a small bet in the form of an investment. Then he'd forget about it. He dabbled in the stock and the commodities markets. He was in and out all the time I knew him; it was a form of relaxation, without much common sense or judgment or even real interest.

But of course it is the public senator, not the private Joe McCarthy who is important. The fact that Joe McCarthy lived well within his means did not prevent his enemies from accusing him of trying to line his pockets out of hours. The chief harassment along these lines was led by former Senator William Benton, Democrat of Connecticut, who launched an investigation into his income-tax payments and occasional sources of outside income. This grew into a campaign that plagued McCarthy for years, even after the charges were dropped. Benton's opening gambit was a politically explosive resolution before the Senate on August 6, 1951, which called for McCarthy's impeachment and charged that the Wisconsin senator had accepted ten thousand dollars in "influence money" from the Lustron Corporation, manufacturers of prefabricated homes.

I am acquainted with the facts in this case and can say that they were disgracefully distorted. The Lustron case actually dated back to 1947, when the housing shortage was acute and returning veterans were unable to find homes for their new families. McCarthy proposed to the Joint Housing Committee that laws should be enacted making it possible for veterans to build or buy a house. He further suggested that the committee draw up a simple explanation free of legal jargon telling veterans how they could take advantage of these laws.

When the committee, while agreeing that the project was a worthy one, declined to act, McCarthy forgot he was a very junior senator and proceeded on his own. In 1948, with the help of a staff of researchers and writers, the Senator issued a pamphlet entitled *A Dollar's Worth of Housing for Every Dollar Spent.*

McCarthy told me some time later that he first approached the Henry Luce publications and offered them the book free, since *Time, Life,* and *Fortune* had published a good deal about deplorable housing conditions. The Senator said they rejected his offer on the ground that it would not sell.

Casting about for some way to finance publication of the pamphlet, McCarthy finally turned to Lustron, which agreed to distribute the booklet at ten cents a copy, paying the Senator a royalty on the understanding he keep the book up-to-date. Shortly after he sold the booklet to Lustron, McCarthy called a press conference and related the details of the transaction and the ten-thousand-dollar royalty, adding that "I have to split it with ten people who helped me."

The incident might have ended there had not Lustron gone into bankruptcy in 1950, offering McCarthy's critics an unexpected chance. The first rumbling of trouble was a statement by Clyde Foraker of Cleveland, receiver in bankruptcy for Lustron: "I'll bet he couldn't have gotten it [the ten thousand dollars] if he weren't a senator."

The Luce magazines chimed in, deploring McCarthy's "ethics" in giving the rights for his booklet to a company making prefabricated houses and accepting money for it. In 1951, Benton put in his impeachment resolution, and the lawmakers tossed it to a subcommittee of low-seniority senators headed by Guy Gillette, Democrat of Iowa. . . .

I was fully aware of McCarthy's faults, which were neither few nor minor. He was impatient, overly aggressive, overly dramatic. He acted on impulse. He tended to sensationalize the evidence he had— in order to draw attention to the rock-bottom seriousness of the situation. He would neglect to do important homework and consequently would, on occasion, make challengeable statements.

His impatience with detail sometimes caused minor explosions at executive sessions of the subcommittee. Much of a senatorial committee's work consists of tedious and often uninteresting detail, so that whenever McCarthy knew that a meeting was to be devoted to ratification of appointments, promotions, and what he called "office manager stuff" he would deputize an assistant to act for him. Once, when he could not dodge such a session, I watched him grow more and more irritated. When two senators actually quarreled over the promotion of a girl on the staff, McCarthy banged with an ashtray—he never used a gavel—and shouted: "Look, I'm trying to get my appropriation for the year so that I can get Communists out of Government. I'm not going to sit here all afternoon listening to you two arguing over whether Mary is going up to grade eleven or not. I don't want to hear about it. Fight it out later."

Ultimately, this inattention to detail, this failure to check and recheck every point he made, enabled his enemies to divert attention from the main thrust of his attack to the details—which, in too many cases, did not bear close scrutiny.

But it must be understood that in an important sense McCarthy was a salesman. He was selling the story of America's peril. He knew that he could never hope to convince anybody by delivering a dry, general-accounting-office type of presentation. In consequence, he stepped up circumstances a notch or two.

Did the urgent need to get the story across excuse a broad-brush approach? I can understand why he did it, as I can realize that his dramatizations hurt him in many quarters. I quarreled with him frequently on this score and stressed that by using this technique he sometimes placed himself in an indefensible position. But I never disagreed with the substance of his thesis.

This controversial technique was evident in the very first speech that launched McCarthy upon the great issue of his career. He was planning a nationwide series of talks, beginning at Wheeling, on an explosive subject he hoped would arouse the country. Surely this called for careful advance preparation. The speech should have been written out beforehand and copies distributed. And surely, precise information on the number of individuals concerned was essential. But because the speech was not prepared in advance, and because he really wasn't certain exactly how many persons were Communists and how many security risks, he gave his enemies a perfect opportunity to throw up a smoke screen. Thus the so-called numbers game began.

A great controversy arose after McCarthy's Wheeling speech. McCarthy's critics claimed that whereas he said there that 205 Communists were working in the State Department, later in Reno he whittled the number down to 57. Still later he spoke of "81 cases." They demanded to know what he really meant. Didn't his confusion over the figures reveal that he didn't know what he was talking about? . . .

But let us never forget that the substance of his charges was true. There *were* persons working in the State Department whose activities and associations indicated they had pro-Communist leanings. Could any American rest easily, knowing pro-Communists may have been helping to shape our foreign policy?

McCarthy's broad-brush technique was again illustrated by his charge that the Democratic party was guilty of "twenty years of treason." This is nonsense if taken literally. Frederick Woltman, the late Scripps-Howard journalist, pointed out that this statement pinned the label of traitor on the 26,898,281 Americans who voted the Democratic ticket in 1952.

Certainly McCarthy did not intend the statement to be accepted at face value. He meant to shock, to awaken. He singled out the New Deal era, during which Communism in Government flourished with impunity. This attack on the Democrats made McCarthy many powerful enemies and accounted for the solid Democratic vote for censure in 1954. . . .

Looking back with whatever objectivity I can muster, I believe that even after all the excesses and mistakes are counted up, Senator McCarthy used the best methods available to him to fight a battle that needed to be fought. The methods were far from perfect, but they were not nearly as imperfect as uninformed critics suggest. The use of Executive sessions to protect witnesses from publicity until they had an opportunity to explain adverse evidence; the respect of the constitutional privilege; the right given each witness to have counsel beside him at all times—these compare favorably not only with methods of other investigating committees but with methods of certain prosecutors. The "methods" attack on McCarthy suffers from a credibility gap because of the double standard of many critics, particularly the press, radio, and television. To them, anything McCarthy did was wrong, but the excesses and outrageous methods of those not investigating subversion are often overlooked or excused.

He may have been wrong in details, but he was right in essentials. Certainly few can deny that the Government of the United States had in it enough Communist sympathizers and pro-Soviet advisers to twist and pervert American foreign policy for close to two decades.

He was a man of a peculiar time: the Cold War. His particular "package" would not have been deliverable in the depressed but exhilarating thirties. But he came forward at the time of Communist aggression in Korea and the triumph of Mao's revolution. The job he felt he had to do could hardly have been done by a gentle, tolerant spirit who could see all around a problem.

What is indisputable is that he was a courageous man who fought a monumental evil. He did so against opposition as determined as was his own attack—an opposition that spent far more time, money, and print seeking to expose *him* than Communism.

Since his day, Cuba has fallen to the Communists. The free world was rocked in 1967 by the Harold Philby revelation of Communist infiltration in high Government security posts. Nuclear explosions echo over China and the Soviet Union. American men are defending the borders of South Vietnam against Communist aggressors. North Korea has laid down the gauntlet to us.

Has not history already begun his vindication?

# Arthur Eisenhower: "I Automatically Think of Hitler"

*McCarthy aroused the indignation of others besides liberals and Democrats. The following report of an interview with Arthur Eisenhower, brother of the president, is reprinted from the* Progressive, *April, 1954, a famous issue devoted to a documented attack on McCarthy's career.*[3]

Arthur Eisenhower, brother of the President and vice-president of the Commerce Trust Company, in Kansas City, was quoted by the Associated Press in a dispatch from Las Vegas, Nevada, July 24, 1953, as saying: "It is a horrible shame that McCarthy is a Republican for he has done the party no credit. He is the most dangerous menace to America.

"When I think of McCarthy, I automatically think of Hitler. I would believe anything about him."

Asked if he thought the Wisconsin Senator had an ultimate objective, Eisenhower was quoted as saying:

"Of course he has. He wants to keep his name in the papers at all costs. He follows the old political game which is 'whose name is mentioned the most in politics is often selected for the highest office.'

"McCarthy is a throwback to the Spanish inquisition. He calls in people and proceeds to make fools of them by twisting their answers. What chance do they have? They have no rebuttal because they have no recourse to the press, radio, and magazines. It is Nazi-like and what makes it all so much more of a fiasco is that he has never been responsible for the conviction of one—of one, mind you—Communist."

[3] "Arthur Eisenhower Compares McCarthy to Hitler," *Progressive*, 18 (April, 1954), 53. Editor's title. Reprinted by permission of the *Progressive*.

# Will Herberg: "No Idea, No Cause, No Program, Nothing"

*Will Herberg, a noted observer of the American religious scene, wrote an article for the* New Republic *in 1954 taking liberals to task for their tendency to characterize McCarthy as a fascist. His sensible discussion is reprinted in its entirety.*[4]

Senator Ralph E. Flanders' denunciation of Senator McCarthy early in June, and again the address accompanying his motion of censure five weeks later, gave explicit expression to a theme that had been running through liberal polemics against "McCarthyism" for some time and had begun to acquire the status of an article of faith in most liberal circles. In both of these statements, Mr. Flanders likened McCarthy to Hitler and professed to find in McCarthyism a resurgence of the characteristic features of Nazism. The junior Senator from Vermont based what he called the "parallelism with Hitler" on the charge that like Hitler, McCarthy has "exploited the issue of Communism," has stirred up trouble for Jews, Catholics, and Protestants, has set up his "private police force and spy system," and has received "his financial support from wealthy businessmen." "Each of these features [of Hitlerism]," Mr. Flanders contended, "finds its parallel, though it must be admitted to a weaker degree, in the career of the junior Senator from Wisconsin." For good measure, the Vermonter added a reference to McCarthy's part in the Baldwin investigation of the Malmédy massacre and clinched his case by noting that many of the letters he received denouncing him and supporting McCarthy were "fanatically anti-Semitic in content." He generously admitted that perhaps McCarthy wasn't actually copying Hitler; perhaps "he [was] just naturally going that way."

Not long after Senator Flanders had broached the subject in his June address, Marquis Childs devoted one of his columns to a schematic presentation of the parallel. In the manner of columnists, he did not speak directly in his own name, but in the name of certain anonymous "Europeans," whom Mr. Childs pictured as deeply disturbed at the course of events in America. These Europeans, Mr. Childs reported,

[4] Will Herberg, "McCarthy and Hitler: A Delusive Parallel," *New Republic,* 131 (August 23, 1954), 13–15. Editor's title. Reprinted by permission of *The New Republic,* © 1954, Harrison–Blaine of New Jersey, Inc.

were asking "if America was going Fascist." Proceeding to answer his own question, one of these disturbed Europeans, who, we are told, had been reading Wheeler-Bennett's *The Nemesis of Power*, outlined to Mr. Childs the "important parallels" between Hitler and McCarthy. Curiously, this anonymous European mentioned none of Mr. Flanders' points, but added four of his own: (1) the "struggle for the loyalty of the armed services," (2) the "stab-in-the-back myth," (3) the "breakdown of legal and constitutional procedures," and (4) "a deep and disturbing suspicion of psychopathic forces at work behind the political façade." By this time the picture was complete: McCarthy was a Hitler *redivivus;* McCarthyism was an American version of Nazism in incipient form; the United States was going Fascist! Many American liberals, who had been thinking very much the same all along, eagerly took up the refrain, and the analogy between Hitler and McCarthy, between Nazism and McCarthyism, soon became almost official liberal doctrine, to be repeated in the halls of Congress, in the columns of respectable journals and newspapers, and in the dicussions of McCarthyism that seem to have become obsessive with liberals in this country and abroad.

And yet it is surely obvious how flimsy this parallel between Hitler and McCarthy really is and how utterly irresponsible is the line of argument leading to it. If "exploiting" the issue of Communism makes one a Hitler because "Hitler exploited the issue of Communism and on it rode to power," then McCarthy is not the only "Hitler" in American politics and the Communists are right in maintaining that anti-Communism is equivalent to Fascism.

Even more ludicrous is the indictment of McCarthy as a Hitler because he has received financial support from wealthy businessmen; where does Mr. Flanders think the leading candidates of his party get their financial support? McCarthy, as far as I know, does not yet possess a private army or police force, as did Hitler on his way to power, and his "spy system" (his contacts in the various government agencies) is something not altogether new in American political history.

But what shall we say of Mr. Flanders' allegation that, like Hitler, McCarthy is stirring up anti-Semitism along with other racial and religious hatreds? If one thing is clear in this whole murky business of McCarthy and McCarthyism, it is that Joe McCarthy has never shown the least inclination to racial or religious discrimination, let alone anti-Semitism. Senator Flanders ought to be particularly careful in such matters, for was it not Senator Flanders himself who introduced the so-called "Flanders Amendment" to the Constitution calling for the acknowledgement by the nation of "the authority and law of Jesus Christ, Saviour and Ruler of Nations . . ."? And is not this amendment precisely what a number of anti-Semitic "Christian Front" organizations have been agitating for these many years? What would Mr. Flanders say if the tactics he employs against McCarthy were turned against himself? Anti-Semitism, and charges of anti-Semitism, are dangerous things to play around with.

Nor is the indictment drawn up by Mr. Childs' "European" any more impressive. "Legal and constitutional procedures" have not broken down in the United States, McCarthy notwithstanding. The nasty insinuations about "psychopathic forces" should be brought out in the open or not made at all; is not resort to insinuation and innuendo something McCarthy is constantly being accused of? In so far as McCarthy employs the "stab-in-the-back myth" by blaming the disasters of recent years exclusively on "treason" in high places, he is merely following the example of eminently respectable statesmen; did not Senator Flanders himself declare, after his first blast at McCarthy, that all would be forgiven if only Joe stopped attacking the Republican Administration and reverted to his "twenty years of treason" theme? As for the allegation that there is going on in this country a "struggle for the loyalty of the armed forces" of the kind that disrupted pre-Hitler Germany, it is too fantastic to require refutation.

The fact is that the entire enterprise of trying to turn McCarthy into another Hitler and McCarthyism into an American brand of Fascism is not only utterly false in terms of American reality; it is, as *The Commonweal* at the time pointed out in rebuking Senator Flanders, a venture into "McCarthyism against McCarthy." That's what it is even though those who indulge in it proclaim themselves to be the most uncompromising foes of the junior Senator from Wisconsin.

But the crucial question remains: What is this McCarthy who has so distracted the American people, bedeviled the liberals, and driven even his opponents to resort to devices known by his name? In some way, he does indeed seem to recall the totalitarian demagogue fighting for power; and yet he and what he stands for appear to me to represent something essentially different from the totalitarian movements that have become so characteristic of the political life of our time.

Like Lenin, Hitler, Mussolini or Huey Long, this Joe McCarthy is a demagogue. His one aim is to arouse masses, to stir them up, to dominate them, to incite them to action outside of and against the established channels of constitutional government. To do so, he naturally employs many of the familiar devices of the demagogue, and a few of his own invention. That is what induces so many people to think of him as in the line of Hitler and Huey Long.

But the totalitarian demagogue is not just a demagogue; he is a rabble-rouser all right, and usually adept in all the arts of rabble-rousing; but he also stands for something, for something positive—an idea, a cause, a program, which becomes the spearhead of his mass appeal. Lenin stood for "socialism" (which in 1917 he translated into "peace, land, and bread"); Hitler stirred millions of lost, disoriented souls with his vision of genuine "folk community"; Huey Long worked his rabble-rousing magic through the power of his "Share-the-Wealth" idea. Operating in this way, the totalitarian demagogue is able to rouse the masses and build a movement, an organization, a party, by providing expression for the numberless fears, hatreds, aggressions and frustrations that beset a society in crisis; but these dark and obscure passions he is also able to focus on his positive program, transforming them into something very like idealism. The totalitarian gospel is a demonic perversion and corruption of the ideals it embodies, but the ideals are there. "It was their ideals, as well as their unconscious aggressions, that were betraying them," David Riesman points out with reference to the Nazi youth during the rise of the Hitler movement.

The totalitarian demagogue operates with something positive, with some idea or cause, which he himself believes in, yet perverts and exploits for his purposes. The totalitarian demagogue is concerned with building a movement and organization, with arousing and rallying masses against the existing order. The power with which he operates is fundamentally the power of the positive idea he stands for.

Joe McCarthy is obviously something very different. He operates with no positive ideas; he stands *for* no cause, no program. He rallies his support by exploiting the country's fears, anxieties, and frustrations, and the incredible blunders of the men in power. He is *against* Communism and fights it in a way that has won him the allegiance of many who are deeply disturbed over the Communist peril, as well as of many others for whom "Communism" is actually the surrogate of inner threatening forces on the unconscious level. But he is not *for* anything, not even for the familiar brand of "one hundred per cent Americanism": his harangues include practically nothing but diatribes against Communism and against those whom he accuses of protecting or "coddling" Communism. McCarthyism is thus the very apotheosis of negativity: it is a conglomeration of oppositions and resentments clinging around a vacuum.

Nor is Joe McCarthy out to build a movement or organization. Observers have been puzzled by his apparent neglect of these essentials. He has no machine, no party, no press, no agitators, no organization-builders, and he doesn't seem to want any. He operates with himself alone, and while he has many friends and volunteer assistants, he has properly no associates or subordinates (except the staff of his investigating committee, which is a governmental agency). If McCarthyism stands for any kind of "ism," it is certainly an "ism" that is neither idea, movement, nor organization.

For the truth is, Joe McCarthy is a free-swinging soldier of fortune who has hit upon a good thing, anti-Communism. He is *against* Communism and *for*—Joe McCarthy. He is, in a way, a genius at it, but he has neither the talent nor the interest for the kind of thing the building of a totalitarian mass movement requires. He exploits and utilizes many of the sinister forces that go into the making of totalitarianism, but he does not seem to be interested in organizing them into a cohesive political force. He addresses vast crowds, gets enthusiastic ovations, but leaves his people as he found them, all for McCarthy and against Communism, but not involved in any movement or organization, and certainly not stirred up to insurgency and disaffection, as Fascist or Communist mobs are. It is not in the nature of McCarthyism, nor in the purpose of Joe McCarthy, to desire or encourage such things.

There are liberals who tell us that Joe McCarthy is their notion of the devil in politics. But they forget that the devil is a fallen angel, that the demonic is the perversion and corruption of something positive, something creative, and acquires its demonic power from that fact. Despite all appearances, Joe McCarthy does not possess this demonic power because, as I have pointed out, there is nothing but emptiness at the heart of McCarthyism, no idea, no cause, no program, nothing. This basic fact makes McCarthyism in the long run far less dangerous than it would be were it genuinely an "idea" movement. I do not mean to suggest that Joe McCarthy is through, but one must be blind to recent events not to recognize that he is by no means the invincible, all-devouring Juggernaut liberals have pictured him as being. He has his difficulties and limitations of a kind a genuine Hitler or Lenin, or even a Huey Long, would never be confronted with. Imagine Huey Long vulnerable to a Senate vote of censure, or a Hitler or Stalin dependent on a place in Congress!

The fact of the matter is, as Frederick Woltman has pointed out, that Joe McCarthy is to a large extent the "creature of his enemies." They—the former and present Administrations, the liberals, the intellectuals, the respectable people generally—have helped greatly to endow him with the power and prestige he enjoys today. From the very beginning, each of these groups, for its own reasons, has acted as if driven by some inner compulsion to build up McCarthy and McCarthyism as a force in the land. Automatically, they have rushed to the defense of everyone Joe McCarthy has attacked, apparently on the principle that if Joe McCarthy attacks anyone he must be innocent; and in case after case, they have had to backtrack most ingloriously, discrediting themselves and leaving the field to their hated enemy.

They coined the word "McCarthyism" and began to employ it as a self-exculpating, self-justifying projective device. Before long, they were seeing everything in terms of an Omnipotent Joe, the ubiquitous devil, credited with responsibility for every atrocity, real or imagined, at home and abroad. But most absurd and self-defeating has been the way the press, the anti-McCarthyite section in particular, has made Joe McCarthy into the best known American, next to President Eisenhower, throughout the world. It's got so that if Joe McCarthy is *not* present somewhere, or is *not* denounced on some occasion, that fact too is proclaimed in the press under appropriate headlines and captions! It would be interesting to inquire just what it is that has made anti-McCarthyites act in this strangely compulsive manner, as though hypnotized by the evil genius from Wisconsin.

It is about time someone challenged the McCarthy myth. Joe McCarthy is not the superman of the anti-McCarthyite imagination; he is not the Hitler of American Fascism, he is not a sinister fanatic plotting a totalitarian revolution. He is just a political swashbuckler from Wisconsin who—almost accidentally—struck it rich and is determined to exploit his strike to the utmost. Those who prize American freedom and sanity in politics ought to be able to see him for what he is and deal with him in a way that such demagogues can be dealt with—by cutting them down to size, by taking away whatever legitimate issues they may be exploiting through coping more effectively with the evils out of which these issues arise, and by exposing the utter nothingness that lies at the heart of the big noise they make. The first step in ending McCarthyism is to understand just who and what Joe McCarthy really is.

# William S. Schlamm: "He Had Seen the Truth—and It Killed Him

*William S. Schlamm, a reformed leftist, was an editor of the conservative* National Review. *In the issue that took sad note of McCarthy's death Schlamm paid McCarthy a final tribute.*[5]

There was no roof from which to jump and so there were no editorials bewailing an innocent man's annihilation by the hound-dogs of malice. There was only a young man of forty-eight, a young mountain of a man, but fatigued to the bone, fatigued and harassed and greatly astonished. It seems that Joe McCarthy never fully understood what had happened to him. When a stupid virus struck, a tired young body gave up. At the wake, Mr. Acheson said *"de mortuis nil nisi bonum,"* which is a certified gentleman's and Harvard overseer's way of saying that the deceased was a son of a bitch.

But the deceased was a good man, and I have come here to bear this witness. I knew him, not too well, but well enough to testify. And about the hound-dogs that kept snapping at him until he fell prostrate, I know everything there is to know. So here I am to deposit testimony, for a certain tomorrow of trial, on an epoch of insane guile, an epoch in which Joe McCarthy was tarred and feathered by genteel Ivy Leaguers, by gracious ladies of Women Voters Clubs and by noble princes of the press.

Joe McCarthy became the center of the century's most scandalous fracas because he had the strength and the defects of organic innocence. When his day of destiny came, he looked around, innocently, saw the gargoyles of Anti-Christ staring and sneering at him from everywhere, and innocently he reached out to crush them. Now others had seen the gargoyles before him, and some had even visibly shuddered. But, at mid-century, everyone who spoke or wrote or emoted before the public had gone through the post-graduate school of relativism (which is the insolent denial of the free will that chooses

[5] William S. Schlamm, "Across McCarthy's Grave," *National Review*, 3 (May 18, 1957), 469–70. Editor's title. Reprinted by permission of *National Review*.

between right and wrong). And so the speakers and the writers and the emoters, who among them are the true rulers of our society, kept constantly changing the subject. To them, the sneering gargoyles were artifacts, morally neutral, esthetically interesting, intellectually provocative and, of course, not really serious. But Joe McCarthy, once he had caught sight of them, could never again speak of anything else. The subject had taken possession of the speaker. For the subject was deadly serious. And so was the speaker.

Joe McCarthy must have had many defects, and I know some of them, but I will admit none—not because he is dead (Mr. Acheson speaks, in Latin as well as in English, sheer cant), but because he was hated and hunted for his virtues. He was hated, above all, for his impregnable innocence. What the learned frauds could not stand about McCarthy was his certainty: he knew what he knew, he believed what he believed, and there were no two ways about it. But the learned ass balks with invincible stubbornness when there are no two ways on which to move at the same time. And then, Joe McCarthy just could not be lukewarm. This, in the catechism of modernity, is the gravest of all mortal sins—not to be lukewarm. Let your word be *never* Yea, Yea and Nay, Nay! The hot and the cold will be spewed out of the Establishment's mouth, but the lukewarm shall be forever accepted. For the Establishment lives according to this blasphemous perversion of the Apocalypse.

Joe McCarthy could not have conformed with it if his life had depended on it. (It did.) And as I was not born in this country, I might be clearly seeing something that native Americans so easily forget: that there is no greater American virtue, in fact no other, than the American's natural revulsion against cynicism. Which is why Progressive Education proves so much more pernicious in America than anywhere else: it corrodes the native resistance to cynicism and so deprives the American of his one formative trait. Joe McCarthy, who would have politely put up with, but secretly yawned over, such an abstraction, was its ideal test case and evidence. He, so often and so stupidly accused of cynical crudeness by the Liberal falsificators, was physically incapable of a cynical act. He said and he thought and he did what he said and thought and did for the one unheard-of reason only: to him, it seemed the thing to say and to think and to do. All his defeats and all his blunders were due to the fact that he was incapable of the clever maneuver, of the professional's prudent opportunism. He had seen the truth—and it killed him.

When McCarthy proceeded to uncover the immense Communist infiltration of free government and society, this was his activating premise: that man is responsible for the choices he has made in an exercise of his free will; and that, until a man is proven an irresponsible fool, he must be presumed to have made his choices in earnest. McCarthy's rationale was invariably the same: certain people are dedicated to certain ideas—*ergo,* whatever they do in positions they have obtained must have been determined by, and serve, these ideas. It is the obscene joke of the age that this ultimate compliment to the supremacy of the mind has been taken by the Liberal intelligentsia as the supreme affront against the intellect, a sordid assault of Know-Nothingism on Reason.

The huge intellectual scandal around McCarthy has always been the frightening frivolousness of his opposition which holds that man's choices signify nothing; that on his walks through the valley of decisions man picks and then discards commitments the same way Peter Pan picks and discards daisies. That Caliban, McCarthy, insisted that man must be taken seriously. The intelligentsia tarred and feathered him because it insists that man is intellectually an eternal child and morally a vegetable. In short, at the heart of what McCarthy said and did was the very essence of Western civilization; while his postgraduate opposition lost its mind on a savage binge of irrelevancy.

There he came, from the heartland of America, a tenacious and quite ordinary politician; and, in a sudden and lasting moment of recognition, he saw the central truth of his age: that his country, his faith, his civilization was at war with Communism, war pure and simple. "This war will not end except by either victory or death for this civilization," he said again and again. And it was this hot sense of urgency which distinguished him from all jovial practitioners of the political trade. It is this hot sense of urgency which he, for a short moment of truth, forced upon his country. But the automobiles were much too sleek, prosperity much too tepid, Eisenhower much too nice, TV much too amusing; and so the country grew tired of the truth and of the man who kept shouting it, redundantly and, at the end, hoarsely. The country went to sleep again. And the man lay down and died.

Then they gave him a funeral in the same Senate chamber in which the world's most exclusive club had gathered, only two years before, to ostracize the young member who had had the temerity to see and to say the truth. The mourning Senators looked, almost all of them, as if they all had drafted Mr. Eisenhower's message of condolence— ill at ease, confused, and rather exasperating. The black suits looked rented and the miens of mourning borrowed. Never before had an outlaw been so honored by the posse. Was he honored for having died in time?

Yet there was a weird feeling in the air on that day, a tremor of urgency throughout the nation, a sudden fearsome shock. This, some-how, was an unnatural death. A man had died in bed, but the coun-try felt that he had been stoned unto death. This, in spite of its slick communicators and ruling hucksters, is an inarticulate nation. Too often it expresses its truest feelings by reflexes rather than in orderly prose. And, last Friday, I felt violent shocks contort the well-fed body of the nation.

Last Friday morning, when the TV networks were finally ready to exploit the death notice of the night before, they found no better climax to the McCarthy story than the allegedly unforgettable TV shots of his collision with the eloquence of Mr. Joseph N. Welch, the attorney from Boston. I for one had forgotten Mr. Welch's act, but when I saw it again I felt, again, the painful shame of the badinage of what Professor Max Lerner called, the very same Friday, "a part of the history of great utterance." The last time I had witnessed Mr. Welch utter greatly on TV was when he performed, also for a fee (Ford Foundation), as actor-narrator of Lizzie Borden's ax-murder story; and though the greasy old juggler was here much more in his element than in the chambers of statecraft, there was still that phony sanctimonious creak in his voice even when he considered the forty whacks.

Indeed, I can conceive of no better casting for the role of the Anti-McCarthyite than that clown from Boston. He, more than any other figure from the comic strip of our age, personifies the Establishment. He reeks of gentility. He is as eloquent as a Cicero who has gone to school at Dale Carnegie's. He is as witty as Georgie Jessel himself, as urbane as any one of the Brooks Brothers, almost as sophisticated as the whiz who composes *Time's* promotion letters, and keen enough a legal mind to fill several pages of close-ups in *Life*. He is cute. But a century ago, a personality of his dimensions would hardly have qualified its possessor to seek employment as a gentleman's gentleman. Today, it assures for a supernumerary much fame and respect and a more than comfortable living in the employ of an entertainment in-dustry which, let's face it, runs our government as surely as it runs our television. For Jack London (another organic innocent from the heart-land of America) was foolishly wrong when he suspected that the "Iron Heel" of a ruthless gang rules the modern state. It is ruled by the soft-spoken and the soft-brained, the well-mannered and the luke-warm, the genteel and half-educated asses. And Mr. Joseph N. Welch is properly their attorney and clown.

I shall be perfectly satisfied to be called for the rest of my life a McCarthyite, provided Messrs. Welch and Lerner shall be known as Anti-McCarthyites. The dividing line is acutely drawn and quite precisely marked. A McCarthyite is a person who is instructed, either by organic innocence or by true sophistication, to fight for his life and his verities—those "simple" verities which only organic innocence or true sophistication can fathom. An Anti-McCarthyite is a person who, for the sake of godlessness, puts the genteel rules of a vulgar game above life itself, above life and the verities which, to an Anti-Mc-Carthyite, are only figments of a superstitious imagination.

This, then, shall be the dividing line, and it is drawn across a fresh grave. In this grave we have put, for whatever future God has in His mind, a young man who, in five gruesome years, was stoned by the genteel into an ultimate fatigue. We do not crave his fate. We dread it. But we are ready to face it. We, too, have seen the gargoyles stare and sneer at us. We, too, are reaching out to crush them. We mean it. We are McCarthyites.

## PART THREE

# WHO WERE THE McCARTHYITES?

*Long after McCarthy ceased to dominate the head-
lines, analysts of his career continued to speculate about the
causes of his wide appeal. Assuming, as most scholars did, that
McCarthyism was an irrational movement, who were his followers and why did they rally to his cause? The answers to these
questions have been bewildering in their variety. At one time or
another McCarthy has been viewed as the spokesman for wealthy
new businessmen, frustrated small businessmen, German isolationists, traditional conservative Republicans, Irish Catholics
resentful of the Yankee establishment, and Midwestern heirs of
Populism suffering from status anxiety. Each of these explanations, and others less notable, has been subjected to criticisms
of varying effectiveness, and research has yet to yield a definitive
solution to the problem.*

*In the mid-1950s, analysis of McCarthyism in terms of status
resentment achieved the widest influence. A book of essays edited
by Daniel Bell and entitled* The New American Right *(1955)
popularized this concept. Working independently, an impressive
list of contributors—including Richard Hofstadter, David Reis-
man, Nathan Glazer, Seymour Martin Lipset, and Talcott Par-
sons—argued that insecure groups (rural Midwesterners, for instance, or lower-class Catholics in Eastern cities) had become
sufficiently prosperous to ignore economic issues and were now
using politics, especially McCarthyism, to express their "status
resentment" against the social elites that had always snubbed
them. McCarthy's real targets, in this view, had not really been
Communists but respectable, upper-class Americans, and this
was the true source of the Senator's popularity.*

*Aside from its worth as an explanation of McCarthyism, this
hypothesis is historically significant because of its effects on contemporary political theory. The groups accused of status anxiety
and of practicing McCarthyism (e.g., urban Catholics and midwestern farmers) belonged to the same "masses" whom the intellectuals had romanticized in the 1930s. Traumatized by Mc-
Carthyism, many intellectuals began to reasses the assumptions
that had once supported their faith in these masses and in pop-*

ular democracy. *The result of their reflections was the so-called New Conservatism, or as political theorists called it, pluralism. New Conservatism was perhaps the most significant consequence of McCarthyism. Citing the* Federalist Papers, *Burke, Tocqueville, and even Calhoun, the pluralists argued that "direct democracy," whose spokesman McCarthy had been, was a threat to individual liberty. To keep the masses from rising against traditional liberties, power must be distributed among existing institutions and interest groups. Since the masses had proved untrustworthy by rallying to McCarthy, the intellectuals, or at least a vocal and important group of them, placed their confidence in elites, who, the polls showed, had a greater appreciation for tradition, procedure, and liberty. As this section will illustrate, both the status resentment hypothesis and the New Conservatism in time met serious challenges.*

# Nathan Glazer: McCarthyism as Isolationism

*Writing in* Commentary *in March, 1953, Nathan Glazer, a well-known sociologist, attempted to locate McCarthy's support among ethnic isolationists, especially Midwestern Germans. Glazer found the clue to McCarthy's career in the role that he had played in 1949 as defender of the German soldiers charged with the Malmédy Massacre. Glazer believed that the convicted Germans had no real case to make against American justice, that McCarthy took up the issue only to appeal to his pro-German constituency in Wisconsin, and that during the Senate's hearings on Malmédy McCarthy revealed the demagogic qualities that would later make him famous. In the section from his article reprinted below, Glazer explained why McCarthy's later anti-Communist crusade allegedly appealed to the same constituents whom he had already courted in his defense of the Malmédy Germans.[1]*

But why had Senator McCarthy taken on the job of clearing convicted German war criminals in the first place? Why, indeed, did he take a position that was perilously close—for a politician with large hopes—to being pro-Nazi and anti-American, not to speak of lending ammunition, as Mr. Perl suggested, to one of the main lines of Communist propaganda? For this is just what he did. To speak of a concern for victims of possible injustice would be, in his case, farcical. It would be equally unreal to think that Senator McCarthy was angling for the votes of civil libertarians. If he had, he would have found it unnecessary to use his peculiar talents in defense of Ernst von Weizsäcker, who, as State Secretary in the German Foreign Office under Hitler, had signed orders for Jewish deportations. Nor would such a concern have led him to concentrate from the very beginning, as we saw from the question addressed to Secretary Royall, on seeking punishment for the army investigators and prosecutors, rather than on the prior question of whether there had really been any abuse of prisoners. Nor would such a concern explain his harping on the fact

[1] Nathan Glazer, "The Methods of Senator McCarthy," *Commentary*, 15 (March, 1953), 252–54. Editor's title. Copyright © 1953 by the American Jewish Committee. Reprinted by permission of the author and *Commentary*.

—as if it were itself a crime—that refugees from Nazism were "disproportionately" represented among the Americans who prepared the war crime trials:

> Senator McCarthy: I think we should find out who is responsible for hiring refugees from Hitler, men whose wives were in concentration camps, men who had every reason to dislike the German race and dislike them intensely, and the prosecution goes out and hires those individuals and gives them complete charge of the job of getting confessions. The prosecution or whoever was responsible for doing that should be asked to resign from the Army immediately.
>
> Mr. Chairman, as we go along this picture becomes more and more gruesome. That is worse than anything we have ever accused the Russians of doing. (p. 188.)

And finally, the desire to clear the convicted men could not conceivably have led to his continual comparing of America's behavior with Russia's to our own disadvantage, a comparison repeated again and again in these hearings, and whose unjustness could only serve to infuriate American officers and officials, as it did infuriate Secretary Royall. This comparison obviously had a political point: one could almost hear, under "This is worse than anything the Russians have done," the real meaning: "This is worse than anything the Germans did," and the intended effect: "Not the Germans, but the Americans, committed atrocities."

In any case, this was the net effect of everything Senator McCarthy did at the Malmédy hearings. He was not appealing to Nazi sympathizers, but he was appealing to that whole broad spectrum in American opinion of which pro-Nazism formed an extreme wing. It is this element that has been Senator McCarthy's strongest support since the Malmédy case; it was with this element that Senator McCarthy decided, in the Malmédy hearings, to identify himself.

Many Americans, as we know, did not support the war against the Axis with enthusiasm. This element was not an *ad hoc* amalgamation, but a permanent grouping of some size and influence in American politics. As Samuel Lubell has shown, the "isolationists" were made up primarily of Americans of German descent, uncomfortable at going to war against Germany, and Americans of Irish descent whose hatred of England had consistently cast them into an isolationist and even directly pro-German position (Germany, after all, had supported the Irish rebels in the First World War). It included others too: there were Socialists, pacifists, and liberals; and there were also industrialists who found fascism for some reason attractive, anti-Semites, and others. But it was persons of German and Irish descent who formed the largest and most stable part of this heterogeneous coalition.

This grouping has had a strange history. Together with other sections of the American electorate, it was responsible for the great Democratic defeat of 1946 that brought Senator McCarthy to the Senate. But in 1948 the war was fading. The old isolationists found their economic interests in conflict with their ethnic emotions, and they returned in good part to the Democratic fold. During this early postwar period, the isolationism that had flared up so fiercely in 1940 and 1941 seemed to have left few political after-effects—Senator McCarthy himself defeated an isolationist leader, Senator Robert M. LaFollette, Jr., in the Republican primary for Senator in 1946, and took a general and ambiguous position in his campaign—by no means a simple isolationist one.

But no body of opinion, once it has come into existence, simply disappears, even though it may be submerged for a while: as Samuel Lubell points out, a given body of opinion offers an irresistible appeal to politicians, who know that the evocation of the slogans that created it may call it to life again and win its support. But more than this, by 1949 many straws in the wind showed that the old isolationist bloc of the early 1940's was reemerging. The growing tension with Russia produced a division that sharply paralleled the old one. On the surface it would appear that the old isolationism, insofar as it was based on a sympathy for Germany, should have been among the strongest supports of a policy to enlist the Germans against the Russian threat. But the pro-Germanism at the bottom of isolationism had been, not only an underground, but even an unconscious, feeling; from the first it had expressed itself negatively rather than positively, and what it expressed was distaste for European "entanglements" that had the unfortunate result, among other things, of putting America in opposition to Germany. This helps explain the old mystery of why the so-called "isolationists" can be quite enthusiastic about overseas involvements so long as they are across the Pacific. They just don't want to *think* about Europe.

Thus, the old isolationists were no friends of European involvement in general, even when directed against Russia alone. But it was a more important factor that helped reconstitute the old isolationist bloc. It had begun to dawn on American public opinion that our sympathy with Russia during the war was fostered by more than considerations of national policy (the Hiss case broke in August 1948), and dissatisfaction began to stir in many Americans with the way the Democrats had handled our wartime and postwar relations with Russia. Those who had wholeheartedly supported the war expressed their dissatisfaction in one way; those who had not, in quite another. The latter saw in revelations of Communist spy rings and infiltration the belated justification for their position: now, they could say, it was not we who dragged our feet who were guilty of disloyalty; quite the contrary, those who were most enthusiastic about pressing the war now turn out to be disloyal—indeed, they may have been traitors.

As soon became clear, the violent anti-Communism of the old isolationists had nothing in common with any realistic policy to check Communist expansion. The isolationists remained uninterested in pacts or military aid programs. What they were, and are, primarily interested in was self-justification. In the early days, indeed, opposition to Communism played so little a role as compared with self-justification, that Senator McCarthy could try to exploit a Communist propaganda line, as we saw, in his effort to discredit our own conduct of the war and occupation. What the isolationist element was really saying, and what Senator McCarthy was intimating to them, was: we were right in being against the war, traitors led us into it.

The reemergence of isolationism explains the role and the line McCarthy adopted at the Malmédy hearings. He was making the first move to define himself as isolationism's contemporary spokesman and apologist. The next target was already in sight: the "Communists," under which label not only could possible Communist sympathizers in the State Department be assailed, but, even more important, all those who had led the war against Germany, from Roosevelt, Marshall, and Eisenhower down. Malmédy was but the prelude. Now the big show opened, and the technique of wholesale distortion was exploited for all it was worth to identify Communism with Roosevelt's and Truman's foreign policy.

This line began to pay off immediately; contributions poured in from friends and strangers. His agitated correspondence with banker Matt Schuh finally comes to a close as a rain of dollars descends on the great Communist-hunter.

# Huberman and Sweezy:
# McCarthyism and the *Parvenus*

*Leo Huberman and Paul M. Sweezy, editors of the socialist periodical* Monthly Review, *devoted most of their January, 1954, issue to McCarthyism. Applying a class analysis, they argued that McCarthy had become the spokesman of new capitalism against the "blue chip corporations" and the social aristocracy.*[2]

## THE ADMINISTRATION'S SOCIO-ECONOMIC BASE

There is no doubt about the socio-economic base of the Eisenhower administration. It can be described in two ways which are related to each other as the two sides of a coin. On the one hand, there are many of the biggest and most powerful corporate monopolies—aggregates of capital which have their roots in the late nineteenth and early twentieth centuries and which have long since established their position among the blue chips of the economic world: Standard Oil, Chase National Bank, General Motors, M. A. Hanna Co., First National Bank of Boston, and so on. . . . On the other hand, there is what might be called the aristocracy of wealth, the well-entrenched families which stand at the top of the social hierarchy both nationally and locally and which have traditionally dominated the Republican Party. Here one might mention such names as Rockefeller, Aldrich, DuPont, Weeks, Lodge; but it is important to remember that every community has its local counterparts and that it is from their ranks that the leading Republican cadres at the state level —which, generally speaking, is the decisive level for the GOP—are recruited. For the sake of convenience, let us refer to this upper stratum of the ruling class as simply "the aristocracy."

That the Eisenhower administration is based upon and represents the blue-chip corporations and the aristocracy can be deduced from various types of evidence. Here we may be content to note that the facts are nowhere more eloquent than in the case of the President himself. After World War I, Bernard Baruch—who, as chairman of

[2] Leo Huberman and Paul M. Sweezy, "The Roots and Prospects of McCarthyism," *Monthly Review*, 5 (January, 1954), 419–25. Editor's title. Copyright © 1954 by Monthly Review, Inc. Reprinted by permission of *Monthly Review*. Footnotes have been omitted for reasons of space.

the War Industries Board, had been a virtual economic dictator in the closing phase of the war—was responsible for the establishment of the Army Industrial College to train leading military and business personnel for cooperation in the next war. Baruch himself gave his time freely to the project, and among the students with whom he came in close contact none seems to have made a greater impression on him than Dwight Eisenhower. This was the beginning of Eisenhower's association with the upper reaches of capitalist society—there is probably no single individual with more prestige and power in the American ruling class than Baruch—and it was an association which was to mature and yield rich fruit.

There seems to be little doubt that it was Baruch's influence that persuaded Roosevelt to jump Eisenhower over the heads of dozens of higher ranking officers into the wartime position of Supreme Allied Commander, and Baruch may well have had a share in grooming him for his present job. At any rate, when Eisenhower was taken in hand by the august Trustees of Columbia University there could no longer be any question that he had made the grade in the fullest sense. His entry into politics under the auspices of Dewey, Brownell, Lodge, and the rest—that is to say, as the candidate of Wall Street and State Street—followed quite naturally. No Republican President of the past, not even McKinley himself, has ever been more openly and obviously the trusty of high finance and high society.

All this is quite clear and hardly needs to be labored at length. The really difficult problem concerns McCarthy's socio-economic base. How is it possible for an upstart like McCarthy, a small-time politician who reached the Senate as just one among many hacks sent there by state Republican machines, to constitute a serious challenge to the entrenched wealth and power of America's aristocracy? And, perhaps even more puzzling, how does it happen that the impeccably conservative Eisenhower administration is challenged, not, as might be expected, from the Left, but from the Right?

Full answers to these questions would, of course, be long and complicated, but we believe that what is really essential can be stated briefly and simply.

### THE PROBLEM OF McCARTHY'S BACKING

First, up to 1950 when he began to get national publicity through skillful manipulation of the Communists-in-government issue, McCarthy's base was in no way remarkable for a United States Senator. He had the usual backing of wealthy capitalists in his own state, and he did a good business with the well-heeled lobbyists who swarm over Capitol Hill. Richard Wilson, chief of *Look's* Washington Bureau, in a revealing article which we shall have occasion to cite again, names Tom Coleman, Madison industrialist and Republican bigwig, and Walter Harnischfeger, Milwaukee manufacturer, as leading figures among McCarthy's early Wisconsin backers. . . . And the well-known Senate Subcommittee report inquiring into McCarthy's financial affairs contains ample evidence of his financial dependence on housing, sugar, and China lobbyists during his first four years in Washington. McCarthy doubtless retains these (or similar) sources of support, but so do a great many Congressmen. There is nothing here that would account for his national power.

The essential *prerequisite* for the emergence of this national power was undoubtedly McCarthy's attraction of a numerous and often fanatically loyal following when he began to exploit the red menace. This is not the place for an analysis of McCarthy's techniques—suffice it to say that they are revealingly set forth in his own book, *McCarthyism: the Fight for America,* which in some respects bears comparison with Hitler's *Mein Kampf*—or for an inquiry into the nature of his appeal. But it is important to note that his following seems to cut across class lines and not by any means to be confined to any particular religious or national minorities. In other words, McCarthy apparently discovered how to exploit certain genuinely national anxieties and neuroses for political ends. And the substantial nature of the achievement was conclusively demonstrated by the 1952 elections in which not only was McCarthy himself re-elected but also he played a large, and perhaps decisive, role in the victory or defeat of quite a number of other senatorial candidates.

It was only after this that the McCarthy movement took on its present formidable shape and strength. Having first acquired the flesh of a popular following, McCarthy soon attracted the bones and muscle of capitalist backing, no longer on a merely local basis but on a genuinely nationwide scale. Without this backing, the movement would have continued, of course, but it would have remained something of a political curiosity which could hardly present a serious challenge to the Eisenhower administration.

The rise of McCarthyism—considered not as a political method but as an actual political movement—presents obvious parallels with the rise of Hitlerism. But there is one crucial difference. In Hitler's case, German Big Business and the German aristocracy transferred their backing to him when he had demonstrated the extent of his popular following. This has not yet happened in the case of McCarthy, or at any rate it has happened only on a relatively minor scale. There is no evidence of any widespread flocking of the American aristocracy to McCarthy's banner: on the whole, it seems to remain loyal to the administration. In this connection, it is surely significant that Taft, very much an aristocrat despite his obvious sympathy for McCarthyite policies and methods, stayed in the administration camp right up to his death and even became one of its main sources of internal strength and cohesion.

Where, then, does McCarthy's formidable capitalist support come from?

## THE NEW MILLIONAIRES

We can answer this question only if we take account of an extremely important, though little noticed and even less studied, development in recent American history. Beginning as early as the mid-thirties, when the American economy was recovering from the depths of the Great Depression, but especially during World War II and the subsequent years of cold war and inflation, the American bourgeoisie has experienced a vast influx of *nouveaux riches* and *parvenus*. It is well known that the last thirteen years have been unprecedentedly profitable for American capitalism as a whole, but it seems not to have been widely remarked that a substantial part of the total take has been, as Veblen might have expressed it, waylaid, ambushed, or otherwise diverted into the pockets and bank balances of ambitious men with few inherited advantages, even fewer scruples, and a resolute eye on the main chance.

The facts in this connection cannot be extensively documented at the present time, which to a certain type of academic mind may mean that they don't exist. But they leave such convincing traces wherever one chooses to look carefully that it is impossible to doubt their reality or importance. Texas oil millionaires of recent vintage—the product of the last decade's enormous expansion in the demand for petroleum products plus a federal tax policy of unbelievable generosity to oilmen—have become almost legendary figures. Within the last few weeks, for example, the newspapers have carried extensive stories about the educational benefactions of Mr. Hugh Roy Cullen, of Houston, who, according to *The New York Times* of November 21st, was so "impressed by the 'great spirit and determination' shown by the University of Houston football team in its upset victory last Saturday over Baylor" that he "gave the university $2,250,000." This, however, is peanuts for Mr. Cullen who had already given the same university $25 million and "a few years ago . . . announced that he and his wife were establishing a $160,000,000 foundation for aid to education and medicine in Texas." Doubtless Mr. Cullen still has something left, but it seems not as much as H. L. Hunt of Dallas whom Dame Rumor has often crowned "the richest man in America." There are plenty of other multimillionaire Texas oilmen—and cattlemen too—who had never been heard of twenty years or so ago when it was widely assumed that the day of the multimillionaire had departed along with the New Era and the Hoover administration.

Texas oilmen are merely the leading species of the genus *nouveau riche Americanus*. Others will be found everywhere, in a great variety of occupations and/or rackets, and of all degrees of affluence. High up in the scale is one to whom we shall call attention again, a certain John Fox of Boston who, as luck would have it, is the subject of an inadequate but still revealing biographical article in the latest (December 5th) *Saturday Evening Post* ("His Time Is Worth $10,000 A Day," by Henry La Cossitt). Born into a poor South Boston Irish family, Fox worked his way through Harvard (class of '29) and made a living as a jazz pianist, security salesman, and small-time operator before entering the Marines during World War II. Released from the armed forces, he launched a meteoric career of borrowing, buying, selling, and liquidating which brought him, among other things, control over Western Union and a fortune now estimated at $18 million. When the somewhat run-down but still politically influential *Boston Post* went on the market last year, Fox snapped it up (though to raise the necessary $4 million cost him control over Western Union), and he is now said to be determined to devote more and more of his time to the newspaper business.

Most of the *nouveaux riches*, of course, are less spectacular as well as less wealthy than the examples so far cited, which is probably why their prevalence has not been the object of more notice and analysis. But the rise of a new bourgeoisie in the South, which was largely responsible for the strong showing made by the Republicans in that region in 1952, was rather extensively commented upon during the election campaign. And we venture to think that any reasonably attentive observer of social conditions will confirm the existence of *parvenu* wealth in his own environment. For example, in one small New England town which we have had an opportunity to inquire about, we were told that one of the wealthiest families—as evidenced by a fine new house, two quality cars, vacations by air to Europe, and so on—had acquired its money entirely in the last decade. The husband and father was a wage-earning mechanic before the war who set up a small shop with one of his fellow workers to handle a subcontracting job on torpedoes at a time when facilities for their production were desperately short. The enterprise prospered, profits were plowed back, a tool-making business was bought and moved from a neighboring state, and today the man owns a small factory which, to judge from the cars parked outside on a working day, must employ at least a hundred workers. This story must be typical rather than exceptional: We can hardly go wrong in assuming that the phenomenon of new wealth is nationwide in scope and impressive in proportions.

The important thing from our present point of view is that this new wealth provides a "natural" base for a fascist movement such as has not existed in the United States before—at least not since fascist movements have become fashionable in the "free world." The characteristic qualities and attitudes of the *nouveau riche* dispose him toward fascism in the present-day capitalist environment. He tends to be aggressive, unscrupulous, vain; he develops feelings of jealousy and even hatred for the aristocracy which refuses to accept him as an equal. Self-important and yet frustrated, craving power and prestige commensurate with his wealth, longing to humiliate the snobs who don't appreciate his true value, the *nouveau riche* finds a natural outlet in political support of a movement which is simultaneously reactionary, brutal, vulgar—and shows signs of succeeding.

McCarthyism has always been reactionary, brutal, and vulgar; and since the 1952 elections it has shown definite signs of succeeding. Small wonder, then, that it has attracted enthusiastic backing from the *nouveau riche* element, and especially from the Texas multimillionaires who are as rich as the Rockefellers and DuPonts but trail way behind in fame and power.

The public first got wind of McCarthy's Texas connections about a year ago when H. L. Hunt sponsored the Senator's appearance on a TV program. According to the *Look* article cited above, "some say that Hunt will eventually back him in a series of reports to the nation on his activities." And the author adds the following highly relevant information:

> Lately, McCarthy has widened his circle of associates in Texas. He recently stayed at the home of Douglas Marshall, son-in-law of H. R. Cullen, the oil multimillionaire, who has a keen interest in McCarthy.
>
> Cullen contributed $5,000, the legal limit, to Joe's campaign for re-election in 1952. . . . Cullen put up $48,000, in addition, to help other candidates for Congress in 1952.
>
> The backers and associates of McCarthy in Texas include another of the present-day miracle men of oil finance, Clint Murchison, who owns Henry Holt & Company, book publishers in New York. Like Joe's other big Texas friend, Hunt, Murchison is interested in influencing public opinion.
>
> Austin Hancock, former San Antonio insurance executive, is a friend of McCarthy. Hancock heads an organization called the American Heritage Protective Association. He has said that he hopes to get the Republican presidential nomination for McCarthy.

Meanwhile, Joe's Texas supporters found an opportunity to express their admiration in a quite tangible way when they presented Mr. and Mrs. McCarthy with a Cadillac for a wedding present. (Some press reports, incidentally, placed the total value of wedding presents at $100,000.)

The support which McCarthy gets from John Fox of Boston seems to be of a different, but hardly less important, kind. No evidence of direct personal or financial relations between Fox and McCarthy has come to our notice, but there is no doubt that the *Boston Post* under Fox's ownership has become a rabid journalistic supporter of the Senator's witch-hunting activities. The *Saturday Evening Post* article to which we have already referred, reports that "Fox bought the [Boston] *Post* to give direction to his rage against Communism, a philosophy he has hated since his Harvard days." (The rage seems to take in Harvard too: at any rate when McCarthy recently denounced America's oldest university as a hotbed of Communism, he had the enthusiastic applause of Fox who eagerly joined in the attack on his alma mater.)

The foregoing analysis indicates that the real socio-economic base of McCarthy and McCarthyism is the new wealth of the past ten years or so. It is this that makes the movement vastly more solid and powerful (both actually and potentially) than earlier fascist movements under the leadership of such figures as Huey Long, Father Coughlin, Gerald L. K. Smith, and so on. Unlike them, McCarthy has virtually unlimited financial support to draw upon, and his publicity and propaganda channels are assured. These are the indispensable weapons of large-scale political warfare: for the first time in the United States a fascist movement is well provided with them. Let no one underestimate the ominous significance of this fact.

# Peter Viereck: McCarthy and *Ressentiment*

*One of the leading publicists of the New Conservatism was Peter Viereck, poet, critic, and social commentator. Though undisciplined and wholly speculative, his writings on politics are sometimes perceptive and always interesting. In his book* The Unadjusted Man *Viereck attacked direct democracy and especially its chief practitioner in the 1950's, Joe McCarthy. In the selections reprinted here from that book, Viereck, who was one of the contributors to* The New American Right, *offered his explanation of McCarthy's support.*[4]

The year 1954 witnessed two magnificent defeats of "the people": the Senate censure of McCarthy, the Supreme Court ban on Negro segregation in schools. Neither triumph of liberty would have been won in a direct democracy, a government settling issues only by majority vote. Senator Watkins frankly admitted that the count of telegrams ran against censuring McCarthy but declared his censure Committee would instead be guided by ethics and the Constitution.

By twice placing ethics and law above majority bigotry in 1954, the Senate and Supreme Court justified the insistence of Madison, Adams, Hamilton, Jay during 1787 on two undemocratic institutions to preserve liberty: the Supreme Court, the Senate. The Supreme Court is neither elective nor subject to popular recall. The Senate until 1918 was elected only indirectly through State legislatures; even today, not being based on population statistics, it remains less democratic than the House. In contrast, many Jeffersonian liberals of 1787 had preferred (fortunately foiled by the Federalists) a more direct democracy, no aristocratic veto power for the judiciary, and only one House of Congress, elected directly and democratically—no Senate.

The refutation of McCarthy's slanders by the rational logic of liberals had failed to dent the popularity of this now almost forgotten demagogue. What, then, did eliminate most of his following? America still retained enough respect for the aristocratic, Constitutional traditions, established during 1787–1800 by Washington, Adams, and the Federal-

---

[4] Abridged from Peter Viereck, *The Unadjusted Man* (Boston, 1956), pp. 146–47, 166–68, 170, 171, 172. Editor's title. Copyright © 1956 by Beacon Press. Reprinted by permission of the Beacon Press.

ist party, to drop McCarthy permanently after a committee of non-liberal Senate traditionalists censured him. When the Senate appointed the Watkins committee in 1954, liberal magazines and the author's liberal friends predicted unanimously that it would "whitewash Mc-Carthy" because its members were "outdated fuddy-duddies, too conservative and élite-minded." Just because they were "too conservative," too steeped in the "outdated" undemocratic concept of the Senate as a clubby élite, the fuddy-duddies rose up and stopped McCarthy, at a time when the egalitarian masses were still supporting him overwhelmingly in the plebiscite of telegrams. . . .

Eastern liberals and radicals today often forget how much anti-intellectualism (prelude to thought control) and Anglophobia (prelude to isolationist or pro-fascist foreign policies) were present in western liberals and radicals: the pre-1914 Populist and Progressive parties. Not always but often, these earlier orators distrusted eastern intellectuals and "perfessors" as alien, un-American city-slickers, whether as the "Harvard plutocrats" hated by the Populist farmer or the "Harvard Reds" hated by his Republican grandson today. In either case, behind that hate is the same instinct, whether verbalized in Populist radicalism or in Republican anti-communism.

Untroubled by subtle moral dilemmas of means versus ends, the old western frontier-instinct trusts the rough-and-ready means of a plebeian "Indian Charlie," not the finicky, legalistic means of non-earthy cosmopolitans with an educated ("alien British") accent. Hence, the disproportionate intensity of the hate for Dean Acheson and all who resemble him in Yale-Harvard mannerism and in educational and social status. Acheson's initial complacency and initial negligence toward the monstrous Red menace in China do not suffice to explain the intensity of the movement against him and why it picked him out as a single scapegoat for a negligence and a complacency so widely diffused among leaders of both parties. And he did at least help stop communism in western Europe; this is more than Republican isolationists, with their hate of the Marshall Plan, would have done. The real Acheson is a fairly conservative Wall Street financier, a symbol of civilized privilege and undemocratic reserve. He would have been denounced with betraying China to communism. In a parodying pile-up of clubby veneers, not one but three or four Brahmin schoolings have sleeked several of the State Department officials most associated with these political vices in the tabloid-fed popular mind. Thus ex-Secretary of State Acheson was schooled successively in Groton, Yale, Harvard Law, Wall Street—a quadruple provocation to the out-group majority! Equally provocative, and more frequent in the State Department and academic world, is the gamut of at least two or three such veneers. That gamut cannot help but condition the mannerisms and diction-patterns of its graduates;

thereby it unintentionally goads beyond endurance, at some deep half-aware level, the egalitarian direct democracy of old Populists and new rightists.

But the above musical-comedy farce changed to potential tragedy when it became the unconscious "depth psychology" behind attacks in the early 1950's on academic freedom at Yale and Harvard and ultimately on the Constitutional liberties of all Americans of whatever status. Subsequently most of these atacks on academic freedom and civil liberties have failed or declined. Their failure or decline, though not justifying a complacent relaxation of vigilance, is the most reassuring aspect of American life today. Their failure or decline reflects forces still deeper and stronger than the above "depth psychology" of direct democracy, namely the underground forces of America's tacit Federalist-party heritage, America's permanent traditionalism beneath our overpublicized innovating flux, in short America's unlabeled, unaware conservatism.

Yet even the decline of the rightist out-group still leaves the public with a downright morbid overawareness of ivied schooling in government service. Whether a toadying pro or a sour-grapes con, any such emotion-charged overawareness distracts from the obvious duty of judging the government servant on his individual merits. . . .

The entire status-resentment thesis of the present interpretation is frankly borrowed—elaborated—from Nietzsche. . . . He defined a sublimated *"ressentiment"* (he preferred the French term) as the basic, half-unconscious motivation of mass politics. Thereby he was the foremost of those making possible for America today that whole new branch of social psychology. Other early authorities who also helped make it possible, by their explorations of status-resentment, include Tocqueville (*Ancien Régime and the Revolution*), Henri de Man (*Psychology of Socialism*), Vilfredo Pareto (doctrine of circulating élites).

Nietzsche in *Genealogy of Morals,* 1887: "That most dangerous explosive, *ressentiment.* . . . The slave-insurrection in morals begins when *ressentiment* itself becomes a creator of values. . . . Slave morality says 'no' to everything outside [the conformist mass], everything different. . . ." In other words, the resentment of the quantity-minded Overadjusted Man is forever trying to crush, beneath the weight of mass mediocrity, everything private, unadjusted, quality-minded, whether as "too aristocratic" (in the traditional terminology of resentment) or as "too leftist" (in the inaccurate terminology—a drugstore "conservatism"—of the new American right).

Resentment, to be sure, takes varying forms. Owing to the physical priority of bread over culture, the form is often economic during depressions (also during all other times in the case of the cash-nexus commercialism analyzed in Part II). But in prosperous contemporary America, the rebel plebeian impulse behind the would-be anti-radicalism of the new right is not the usual, familiar resentment against economic exploitation but a resentment against social, educational, and sectional aristocracy. This resentment is a part of the Overadjusted Man's preference for new stereotypes over traditional archetypes, for conforming over conserving. The Old Guard huckster-type of Republican differs from his merely expedient and temporary ally, the nationalist-agitator type, in motivation; the former's motivation is economic and complacent, the latter's psychological and resentful. . . .

In the west, that resentment has been sufficiently emotional to unite a poor, business-baiting wing with a rich, big-business wing. That is, to unite the down-with-everybody left of the Populists (barn-burners from way back and distrusters of Anglicized city highbrows) with the pro-industrialist right of the *Chicago Tribune* nationalists. Both these western groups are mainly Protestant, not Catholic. Both resent the east as internationalist, overeducated, highfalutin'.

The east likewise has its status-resenters. Their characteristic emotion is the resentment felt by lower-middleclass Celtic South Boston against institutions like Harvard and Yale, alleged symbols simultaneously of communism and plutocracy. Each resentment, western and eastern, was relatively powerless when by itself. It was only when an unrich Catholic South Boston became allied, via the new American right, with newly-rich Protestant Texans (excluded from the *chicté* of Wall Street) and with flag-waving Chicago isolationists that the old American seaboard aristocracy was seriously threatened in its domination of both governmental and intellectual opinion and in its special old-school-tie preserve, the Foreign Service. Against the Foreign Service, the old Populist weapon of "you internationlist Anglophile snob" was replaced by the deadlier weapon of "you egghead security-risk"— meaning either atheist, subversive, or homosexual, allegations made for centuries in any society by wholesome peasants against "effete" noblemen.

# Nelson Polsby: McCarthyism as a Republican Phenomenon

*In 1960 the political scientist Nelson W. Polsby tested the status anxiety hypothesis against available quantitative evidence and found only "relatively meager empirical confirmation." Using Gallup polls, Polsby then offered his own explanation: McCarthy's supporters were primarily Republicans behaving for political rather than psychological reasons.[5] While valuable, Polsby's argument is not invulnerable. In table X of his article, for instance, who were the 21 per cent of those favorable to McCarthy who also voted for the Democratic nominee for president in 1952? If most of these McCarthy Democrats were urban Catholics, then the status hypothesis can still claim viability. Also, if McCarthy found acceptance primarily because he was a Republican, why did he attain his greatest popularity in 1953 and early 1954, when he was attacking the Eisenhower administration?*

*In his article, before he examines the status anxiety hypothesis, Polsby disposes of two lesser explanations of McCarthyism offered by previous scholarship. The first stresses the unhealthy postwar atmosphere created by the Korean War, the fall of China, atom spies, and entangling alliances. Since this atmosphere was presumably the same for everyone, Polsby contends, the atmospheric hypothesis cannot explain why only some groups supported McCarthy. The second explanation argued that McCarthy's appeal was primarily to so-called authoritarian personalities. While some confirmation of this view exists, says Polsby, "contrary evidence suggests the need for more precise specification of the personality characteristics which are supposed to have caused pro-McCarthy sentiments." That brings Polsby to the status anxiety hypothesis, where we join his discussion.*

The authors of *The New American Right* have advanced this hypothesis in its most full-blown and persuasive form. This volume is a collection of essays by a distinguished group of social scientists, all at-

[5] Abridged from Nelson W. Polsby, "Towards an Explanation of McCarthyism," *Political Studies*, 8 (October, 1960), 250–71. Editor's title. Reprinted by permission of the author and the Clarendon Press, Oxford. Footnotes have been omitted for reasons of space.

tempting to explain the social sources and consequences of McCarthyism. The nature of American politics has changed, they say, so as to render the McCarthy movement unintelligible to conventional forms of political analysis. They call for a "new" type of analysis, one that recognizes the significance of the emergence of status groups as entities making important demands upon the rest of American society, through the political system. In times of economic distress demands are made along class lines; economic "interests" divide the nation's wealth and income by putting pressures of various kinds upon one another and on the government, which acts as a mediating and legitimizing agent for society and as a forum for the expression of dissatisfactions and the promulgation of panaceas. In periods of prosperity the continuing adjustments of interests to each other and to the resources of the economy yield the center of political attention to the demands of status groups, which use the arena to insist on the improvement or maintenance of their status position in society. In times of economic well-being the "dynamic of dissent" resides in those status groups who wish to change the *status quo*—and of course consider themselves at a disadvantage in the status hierarchy. The McCarthy movement, the authors agree, expresses a non-economic form of protest which can only mean that those in society who supported McCarthy did so because of status dissatisfactions.

The authors could have predicted from this hypothesis those groups which should be pro-McCarthy and those which should be anti-McCarthy. Secondly, they could have checked these predictions against the available evidence. In fact, they took only one of these steps, deduc-

## TABLE I

### Groups Comprising the New American Right (i.e. McCarthyites)

I. *Named in six out of seven essays:* New rich.

II. *Named in five essays:* Texans, Irish, Germans.

III. *Named in four essays:* Middle class, Catholics, Midwesterners.

IV. *Named in three essays:* Lower middle class, up-mobile, less educated.

V. *Named in two essays:* "Cankered intellectuals," old family Protestant "shabby genteel," recent immigrants, down-mobile, minority ethnics, Old Guard G.O.P., ex-Communists, Midwest isolationists.

VI. *Named in one essay:* Lower class, small town lawyers, auto dealers, oil wildcatters, real estate manipulators, small businessmen, manual workers, elderly and retired, rentier class, youth, Southern Californians, South Bostonians, fringe urbanites in middle-sized cities, transplants to city, Polish Catholics, hick Protestants, patriotic and historical group members (e.g. DAR), Scandinavians, Southern Protestant fundamentalists, soured patricians, small town residents, neo-fascists.

Source: *The New American Right.*

ing who McCarthy's followers might be. It can easily be seen from an inspection of Table I that the "status politics" hypothesis is much too inclusive to have very much explanatory power. Although it may accurately estimate why specific members of each of the groups named may have found McCarthy an attractive political figure (i.e. because of their status anxieties) it neither differentiates successfully among groups, nor provides criteria by which some groups can be excluded from its purview.

A second step would have been to check deductions against facts. Only Lipset, among *The New American Right* essayists, attempted to

## TABLE II

### Groups Comprising the New American Right, According to Empirical Evidence

The vertical axis ranks groups according to the number of essays out of seven in which they are explicitly mentioned in *The New American Right*. The horizontal axis lists sources of empirical data in support of (Yes) or against (No) the listing of groups as nuclei of New American Right sentiment.

| Group | Gallup | Bean | Harris |
|---|---|---|---|
| **5** | | | |
| (1) Germans | — | No | — |
| (2) Irish | — | — | No |
| **4** | | | |
| (3) Catholics | Yes | Yes | — |
| **3** | | | |
| (4) Less educated | Yes | Yes | — |
| **2** | | | |
| (5) Minority ethnics | Yes & No | Yes & No | Yes & No |
| (6) Republicans | Yes | — | — |
| (7) Recent immigrants | Yes & No | Yes & No | — |
| **1** | | | |
| (8) Lower class | Yes | Yes | — |
| (9) Manual workers | Yes | — | — |
| (10) Polish Catholics | — | Yes | — |
| (11) Elderly | Yes | — | — |
| (12) Youth | No | — | No |
| (13) Scandinavians | — | No | — |
| Groups not named in *The New American Right* | | | |
| (1) Farmers | Yes | Yes | — |
| (2) New Englanders | Yes | — | — |

Sources: American Institute of Public Opinion (Gallup Poll), *Influences in the Mid-Term Election*, 1954 (Bean), *Is There A Republican Majority?* (Harris).

do so, and he presents only his conclusions from findings, rather than the findings themselves. At the time of publication of *The New American Right* there were several sources available which might have confirmed at least partially some of the predictions made in these essays. I present the relevant conclusions of these sources in Table II.

As Table II indicates, the "status anxieties" hypothesis yields rather indifferent results, since it apparently fails to account for two groups in the populace found to have been disproportionately pro-McCarthy, yet on the other hand evidence indicates that some groups named as McCarthyite in fact were not. Although there is no reason to be enthusiastic about the quality of the sources on which these conclusions are based, they are very much better than mere surmises about McCarthy's grass roots followers. Given the speculative nature of most writing on McCarthy, attention should be paid to these empirical findings, despite their limitations.

Other criticisms can be made of *The New American Right*. The assertion that "status groups" are at the heart of the McCarthy movement is essentially trivial. The task was to determine *which* status groups were peculiarly situated so as to be especially favorable to McCarthy. And the identification of some of the groups named as McCarthyite is simply implausible. This should weigh heavily in the case of the book under discussion, where the basic argument depends on plausibility rather than more "scientific" demonstrations of truth. For example, it is unclear why members of the DAR should release status anxieties by joining in an attack on the very social groups whose history their organization celebrates. That status anxieties can drive people to attack others—especially the weak—is a reasonable enough argument, but if it is in principle possible to negate *The New American Right* thesis in any way, surely the cases of white Protestant "shabby genteel" McCarthyites succeed in doing so. Finally, it should be noted that the introduction of ethnic and status considerations into political analysis can hardly be said to have originated with the authors of *The New American Right,* as they themselves, aware of the practices of "ticket balancing," the folklore of political "availability," and long-standing academic interest in the group conflict theory of politics, no doubt realize. . . .

### A POLITICAL INTERPRETATION

I want to turn now to a fourth hypothesis, one which attempts to explain McCarthyism as a political phenomenon. It is a surprising fact that analysts have discounted so heavily the purely political aspect of his success. Therefore I want to review now the rather heavy evidence supporting the hypothesis that McCarthy succeeded at the grass roots primarily among Republicans.

TABLE III

*Popularity of Senator Joseph McCarthy*

In general, would you say you have a favorable
or unfavorable opinion of Senator Joseph R.
McCarthy?

|  | $N$ | $\%$ |
|---|---|---|
| Favorable | 456 | 31 |
| Unfavorable | 693 | 46 |
| No opinion | 287 | 19 |
| Don't know him | 41 | 3 |
|  | 1,477 | 99 |

Source: Gallup Survey 529 K, April 6, 1954.

For example, I present immediately above in Table III the results of
a re-analysis of a Gallup survey. In this re-analysis I have attempted to
differentiate between those who were for and those against McCarthy.
Pro- and anti-McCarthy populations were selected by tabulating responses to the following question: "In general, would you say you have
a favorable or unfavorable opinion of Senator Joseph McCarthy?"

The data at hand were limited; none the less they provided an oppor-

TABLE IV

*Sentiment about Germany of Those Favorable and Unfavorable
to Senator J. McCarthy*

Would you, yourself, like to see Germany again
become one of the three or four most powerful
countries?

|  | $F$ (%) | $U$ (%) |
|---|---|---|
| Yes | 29 | 25 |
| No | 56 | 59 |
| No opinion | 7 | 8 |
| Qualified | 8 | 8 |
|  | 100 (N = 454) | 100 (N = 690) |

Source: Gallup Survey 529 K, April 1954.

tunity to test in some approximate way the predictions of each of the hypotheses thus far offered to account for McCarthy's grass roots support.

## TABLE V

### Political Information of Those Favorable and Unfavorable to Senator J. McCarthy

Will you please tell me which of these men you have heard of? And will you tell me what country he is from?

| | Favorable | | | Unfavorable | | |
|---|---|---|---|---|---|---|
| | Chiang (%) | Mao (%) | Nehru (%) | Chiang (%) | Mao (%) | Nehru (%) |
| Yes, correct country | 89 | 34 | 60 | 88 | 42 | 67 |
| Yes, incorrect or don't know country | 6 | 19 | 12 | 8 | 20 | 9 |
| Not heard of, no answer | 5 | 47 | 28 | 4 | 38 | 24 |
| | 100 (N = 458) | 100 (N = 455) | 100 (N = 454) | 100 (N = 700*) | 100 (N = 689) | 100 (N = 690) |

Source: Gallup Survey 529 K, April 1954.

* The fact that the Ns here exceed the total unfavorable population of 693 is perhaps on account of double responses in a small number of cases.

## TABLE VI

### Political Participation of Those Favorable and Unfavorable to Senator J. McCarthy

Question I.  Have you ever voted in any election, or don't you pay any attention to politics?

Question II. In the election in November 1952, did things come up which kept you from voting, or did you happen to vote?

| | Favorable | | Unfavorable | |
|---|---|---|---|---|
| | I (%) | II (%) | I (%) | II (%) |
| Yes | 86 | 77 | 89 | 81 |
| No | 3 | 20 | 2 | 14 |
| Never | 11 | — | 9 | — |
| No, too young | — | 3 | — | 5 |
| | 100 (N = 456) | 100 (N = 455) | 100 (N = 692) | 100 (N = 687) |

Source: Gallup Survey 529 K, April 1954.

The nationwide questionnaire tapped possible pro-German sentiments among respondents, with the results shown in Table IV. The
results, while not extreme, are in the direction indicated by the
"atmospheric" hypothesis.

Authoritarians, it is said, tend to be politically confused and badly
informed. The nationwide survey asked a series of questions designed

### TABLE VII

*Religious Preference of Those Favorable and Unfavorable
to Senator J. McCarthy*

What is your religious preference:—Protestant,
Catholic, or Jewish?

|            | F (%)      | U (%)      |
| ---------- | ---------- | ---------- |
| Protestant | 68         | 71         |
| Catholic   | 28         | 20         |
| Jewish     | 1          | 5          |
| Other      | 2          | 3          |
|            | 99 (N = 452) | 99 (N = 685) |

Source: Gallup Survey 529 K, April 1954.

### TABLE VIII

*Social-economic Rating of Those Favorable and Unfavorable
to Senator J. McCarthy (Rating by Interviewer)*

|               | F (%)        | U (%)        |
| ------------- | ------------ | ------------ |
| Upper         | 3            | 3            |
| Above average | 32           | 34           |
| Average       | 2            | 1            |
| Below average | 47           | 45           |
| Lower         | 11           | 14           |
|               | 95* (N = 433) | 97* (N = 675) |

Source: Gallup Survey 529 K, April 1954.

* Totals are less than 100 per cent apparently
because interviewers failed to rate some respondents.

to elicit political information of various kinds. McCarythites and non-McCarthyites were able to identify Far Eastern political leaders correctly to about the same degree, but, once again, the slight differences recorded were all in the expected direction. This is also true of the questions asking about participation in the last election, and in elections generally (see Tables V, VI).

The same thing happens when crude tests of the "status" hypothesis are applied, the assumption being that a higher proportion of McCarthyites come from the Catholic, lower class, and less educated parts of the population. The tables (VII, VIII, and IX) show, once again, tendencies in the direction of confirmation.

### TABLE IX

*Educational Levels Attained by Those Favorable and Unfavorable to Senator J. McCarthy*

|  | F (%) | U (%) |
|---|---|---|
| No school | 1 | 1 |
| Up to 8 years school | 26 | 21 |
| 9–12 years | 53 | 51 |
| Over 12 years | 17 | 24 |
|  | 97 | 97 |
|  | (N = 441) | (N = 682) |

Source: Gallup Survey 529 K, April 1954.

But this relatively meager empirical confirmation is unimpressive when set against comparable figures describing the two populations by their political affiliations (see Table X).

These findings speak for themselves, but do not stand alone. The distributions of McCarthy's vote in Wisconsin, where, it should be admitted, "The impact [of McCarthyism] on the political and cultural life of the state was not particularly great," indicate strongly that McCarthy ran best in the most heavily Republican areas, and conversely. James G. March has demonstrated this point conclusively with respect to the 1952 primary election. Samuel Lubell has observed that Senator McCarthy in 1952 ran well ahead of his state average in townships populated heavily by people of German extraction, but this also was true of other Republicans, including Senator Taft in the 1952 primary, and Republican Presidential candidates in 1944, 1948, and 1952. Inspection of election returns bears out the thesis that McCarthy ran best

TABLE X

*Party Sympathies and Voting Records of Those Favorable and Unfavorable to Senator J. McCarthy*

Questions
   I. Did you vote for Eisenhower (Republican) or Stevenson (Democratic)?
  II. If the elections for Congress were being held today, which party would you like to see win in this state—the Republican Party or the Democratic Party?
 III. (If undecided)
      As of today, do you lean more to the Republican Party or to the Democratic Party?
  IV. In politics, as of today, do you consider yourself a Democrat, Republican, or Independent?

| Question | Favorable (%) | | | | Unfavorable (%) | | | |
|---|---|---|---|---|---|---|---|---|
| | I | II | III | IV | I | II | III | IV |
| Republican | 76 | 53 | 37 | 46 | 49 | 29 | 28 | 24 |
| Democratic | 21 | 29 | 23 | 30 | 49 | 57 | 38 | 58 |
| Undecided | — | 17 | 27 | — | — | 13 | 26 | — |
| Other | 3 | 1 | 13 | 24 | 2 | 1 | 8 | 24 |
| | 100 | 100 | 100 | 100 | 100 | 100 | 100 | 100 |
| | (N = 350) | (N = 456) | (N = 77) | (N = 456) | (N = 560) | (N = 693) | (N = 88) | (N = 693) |

Source: Gallup Survey 529 K, April 1954.

where the Republican Party was strongest. McCarthy's strongest showing in 1952, for example, generally took place in those counties giving Walter Kohler, Republican candidate for Governor, their heaviest support. Out of the 71 counties in Wisconsin, 30 gave McCarthy a margin of 2–1 or better, and of these 30, 24 were counties in which Governor Kohler beat his opponent by 3–1 or more. In the 29 counties where he made his strongest race, capturing 75 per cent or more of the two-party vote, Kohler received only 28 per cent of his state-wide vote. But in the 30 counties where McCarthy received 65 per cent of the vote or more, fully 35 per cent of McCarthy's state-wide vote was concentrated.

These figures demonstrate that the McCarthy vote was concentrated in areas of Republican strength, and was neither scattered, nor distributed in some pattern unique to McCarthy, nor particularly strong.

# Seymour Martin Lipset:
# McCarthyism and the
# Ethnic Factor

*In 1963 each contributor to* The New American Right *added a second essay to his original, and the expanded volume was published under the title* The Radical Right. *In his 1955 essay Seymour Martin Lipset had relied heavily on status categories to explain McCarthyism. Lipset's 1963 essay, which also examined Father Coughlin's movement and the John Birch Society, made use of polling data unavailable to him in 1955 to evaluate his earlier analysis of McCarthyism. Using more polls than Polsby did, Lipset concluded that the status insecurities of ethnic and religious groups were indeed a factor in McCarthyism and that Polsby had overrated McCarthy's purely political support. Part of Lipset's 1963 essay follows.*[6]

## THE SOCIAL BASE OF McCARTHYISM

It is extremely difficult to ascertain from survey data the proportion of "McCarthyites" in the population during the Senator's heyday. Part of the difficulty arises from the varying meanings that might be attached to the questions posed. Some queries centered on general issue of the prevalence and threat of domestic Communism, while others focused more specifically on Senator McCarthy and approval and disapproval of his tactics. Questions phrased in general terms of whether McCarthy's allegations about Communists in government were largely true or not usually produced a rather large proportion of "pro-McCarthy" replies. But questions implying a more direct evaluation of the Senator himself—e.g., how McCarthy's endorsement of a candidate would affect one's vote—produced a very different pattern of response. When attitude toward the existence of Communists in government was not mentioned, somewhere between 10 and 20 per cent were favorable, while about 30 to 40 per cent were opposed to the Wisconsin Senator. Once in existence, McCarthyism became a much more salient issue to the liberal enemies of the Senator than to his

[6] Seymour Martin Lipset, "Three Decades of the Radical Right," in Daniel Bell, ed., *The Radical Right* (New York, 1955), pp. 391–93, 394–400, 403–7. Editor's title. Reprinted by permission of the author. Some footnotes have been omitted for reasons of space.

conservative or militantly anti-Communist friends. The Communist issue apart, many more people reacted negatively to the mention of his name than positively. His seeming popularity was a result of his riding the existing powerful anti-Communist bandwagon, whose popular influence he may have ultimately reduced rather than enhanced by alienating the militant anti-Communists who believed in due process. This conclusion does not mean that McCarthyism did not exist as a political force. There was a significant minority of Americans who strongly identified with the Senator from Wisconsin, and who approved of any and all methods he used to fight the Communist enemy. Some of them presumably were attracted to, or at least accepted, his attack on the Eastern upper-class elite and on internationalism. But this group of "McCarthyites" was probably always a minority, much smaller than the "anti-McCarthyites," who saw in him and his followers a basic threat to the democratic process once the symbol of McCarthyism had been created as a political issue. . . .

McCarthy differed from other anti-Communist investigators in a number of ways. He was more successful in gaining personal attention through his claims to specific knowledge of numerous Communists in government agencies. His attack on the Eastern elite groups as the major source of Communist infiltration was unique. And he was probably more identified than other anti-Communist politicians with efforts to link Democratic international policies with the growth of international Communism. Consequently, he appealed to the isolationists and other antagonists of American foreign policy. Like Father Coughlin, he was an Irish Catholic and may have also had symbolic significance to the Catholic Irish, and other ethnic groups, which felt resentment in a society dominated by an old American Anglo-Saxon elite. These groups have tended to be isolationist as a result of ethnic identifications with "old-country" issues, and, as Catholics, have been especially sensitive to the Communist issue.

A number of quantitative analyses of the sources of McCarthy's support have been published since the original edition of this book appeared. A summary of the findings of many of these studies is contained in an article by Nelson Polsby.* His report indicates that Mc-

* Nelson W. Polsby, "Towards an Explanation of McCarthyism," *Political Studies*, 8 (1960) [Reprinted above]. Polsby lists as his sources various published Gallup surveys and the results of his own re-analysis of one 1954 Gallup Poll. See also Louis Bean, *Influences in the Mid-Term Election* (Washington, D.C.: Public Affairs Institute, 1954); and Louis Harris, *Is There a Republican Majority?* (New York: Harper & Brothers, 1954). In reporting Harris's findings, Polsby states that Harris found that the Irish were not disproportionately pro-McCarthy. In my judgment, he misinterpreted Harris's finding. Harris reports that the Irish in his 1952 sample divided evenly between support and opposition to McCarthy. Since, however, McCarthy was only supported by a minority of the entire sample, a

Carthy received disproportionate support from Catholics, New Englanders, Republicans, the less educated, the lower class, manual workers, farmers, older people, and the Irish.

These findings coincide, on the whole, with the original assumptions of the authors of these essays, but Polsby suggests that the evidence from these surveys and from an examination of the results of different election campaigns in which McCarthy or McCarthyism were issues indicate that most of McCarthy's support can be attributed to his identification as a Republican fighting Democrats. In other words, the vast bulk of his backing came from regular Republicans, while the large majority of Democrats opposed him. And Polsby notes that while survey results do sustain the original hypotheses, "this relatively meager empirical confirmation is unimpressive when set against comparable figures describing the two populations [pro- and anti-McCarthy] by their political affiliations."

Undoubtedly Polsby is correct in stressing the linkage between party identification and attitude toward McCarthy. Some confirming evidence was reported in a study of the 1954 election by the University of Michigan's Survey Research Center, which showed the positive relationship between degrees of party commitment and attitude toward McCarthy.

TABLE 1

RELATIONSHIP OF PARTY IDENTIFICATION TO ATTITUDE
TOWARD MCCARTHY—OCTOBER, 1954

| | | | | Party Commitment | | | |
| Attitudes to McCarthy | Strong Dem. | Weak Dem. | Ind. Dem. | Ind. | Ind. Rep. | Weak Rep. | Strong Rep. |
| --- | --- | --- | --- | --- | --- | --- | --- |
| Pro-McCarthy | 10% | 9% | 8% | 12% | 12% | 12% | 25% |
| Neutral | 37 | 44 | 42 | 54 | 50 | 47 | 43 |
| Anti-McCarthy | 50 | 40 | 41 | 21 | 32 | 33 | 27 |
| Other Responses | 3 | 7 | 9 | 13 | 6 | 8 | 5 |
| | 100% | 100% | 100% | 100% | 100% | 100% | 100% |
| Excess of Antis Over Pros | 40 | 31 | 33 | 9 | 20 | 21 | 2 |
| N | (248) | (288) | (97) | (82) | (68) | (159) | (146) |

Based on replies to question: "If you knew that Senator McCarthy was supporting a candidate for Congress, would you be more likely to vote for that candidate, or less likely to vote for that candidate, or wouldn't it make any difference to you?"

Angus Campbell and Homer C. Cooper, *Group Differences in Attitudes and Votes* (Ann Arbor: Survey Research Center, University of Michigan, 1956), p. 92.

---

group that was evenly split on him was more *favorable* than most other ethnic groups, and hence Harris should be recorded as finding the Irish disproportionately in favor of McCarthy.

The association between McCarthy support and Republicanism does not, of course, tell us how many former Democrats and Independents may have joined Republican ranks *prior* to 1954, because their social situation of personal values made them sympathetic to McCarthy's version of radical right ideology. As has been noted, a considerable section of Coughlin's 1938 backing came from individuals who had supported Roosevelt in 1936, but had later rejected him. There is no reliable means of demonstrating the extent to which Coughlin or McCarthy contributed to a move away from the Democrats, but the available evidence is at least compatible with the hypothesis that they were to some extent influential. A 1954 study by the International Research Associates (I.N.R.A.) inquired as to the respondent's votes in 1948 and 1952. A comparison of the relationship between 1948 voting, attitude toward McCarthy, and 1952 Presidential vote indicates that over half of those who voted for Truman in 1948 and subsequently favored McCarthy voted for Eisenhower in 1952, while two-thirds of the anti-McCarthy Truman voters favored Stevenson (Table 2). A similar relationship between supporting Mc-

TABLE 2

RELATIONSHIP BETWEEN 1948 AND 1952 PRESIDENTIAL VOTE
AND ATTITUDES TOWARD MCCARTHY
(INRA)

| | *1948 Vote* | | | |
| | *Truman* | | *Dewey* | |
| *1952 Vote* | *Pro-McCarthy* | *Anti-McCarthy* | *Pro-McCarthy* | *Anti-McCarthy* |
|---|---|---|---|---|
| Eisenhower | 53% | 31% | 99% | 95% |
| Stevenson | 47 | 69 | 1 | 5 |
| | (506) | (1381) | (563) | (732) |

Carthy and shifting away from the Democrats is suggested in a study by the Roper public-opinion organization.*

* A 1952 Roper survey that was taken in May, before either party had nominated their Presidential candidates, indicates this clearly:

1952 VOTE INTENTION ACCORDING TO TRADITIONAL
PARTY ALLEGIANCE AND ATTITUDE TOWARD MCCARTHY

| | *Traditional Party Preference* | | | |
| | *Democrat* | | *Republican* | |
| *1952 Vote Intention* | *Pro-McC.* | *Anti-McC.* | *Pro-McC.* | *Anti-McC.* |
|---|---|---|---|---|
| Republican | 28% | 20% | 90% | 85% |
| Democrat | 39 | 45 | 2 | 2 |
| Undecided | 33 | 35 | 8 | 13 |
| N | (389) | (524) | (40) | (344) |

A more detailed analysis of the sources of McCarthy's support, conducted along the lines of the analysis of Coughlin's backing, however, belies the suggestion that party affiliation had more bearing on approval or disapproval of McCarthy than other explanatory variables. The 1952 Roper study and the 1954 I.N.R.A. survey both suggest that the most important single attribute associated with opinion of McCarthy was education, while a 1954 national study conducted by the University of Michigan's Survey Research Center indicated that religious affiliation was of greater significance than party. Table 3 below shows the relationship between education, party identification, and attitude toward McCarthy.

TABLE 3

SUPPORT FOR MCCARTHY BY EDUCATION
AND PARTY PREFERENCE[a]—1954
(INRA)

| Education | Party Identification | | |
| --- | --- | --- | --- |
| | Democrat | Independent | Republican |
| Graduate School | −59 | −44 | −28 |
| College | −44 | −24 | −19 |
| Vocational | −41 | −20 | −19 |
| High School | −27 | −8 | −5 |
| Grammar | −18 | −8 | +6 |

[a] Cell entries refer to percentage differences between approval and disapproval of McCarthy. For example, among grammar-school Republicans, 24 per cent were pro-McCarthy and 18 per cent were anti-McCarthy; among Democrats with graduate education, 8 per cent were pro-McCarthy, 67 per cent anti-McCarthy.

The relationship between less education and support of McCarthy is consistent with what is known about the effect of education on political attitudes in general; higher education often makes for greater tolerance, greater regard for due process, and increased tolerance of ambiguity. The less educated were probably attracted, too, by the anti-elitist, anti-intellectual character of McCarthy's oratory, replete with attacks on the "socially pedigreed."

The findings from the surveys with respect to occupation are what might be anticipated, given the preceding results. Those non-manual occupations that require the highest education—i.e., professional and executive or managerial positions—were the most anti-McCarthy (Table 4). And as was suggested in my original essay, independent businessmen were the most favorable to McCarthy among middle-class or non-manual occupations. Workers (including those engaged in personal service) were more favorable to McCarthy than were those in

TABLE 4

RELATIONSHIP BETWEEN OCCUPATION AND ATTITUDES
TOWARD MCCARTHY

*Per Cent Difference between Approvers and Disapprovers*[a]

| *I.N.R.A.—1954*[b] | | | *Roper—1952*[c] | | |
|---|---|---|---|---|---|
| Professional | −35 | (731) | Prof. & Exec. | −17 | (219) |
| Exec. & Manager | −24 | (511) | Small Bus. | 0 | (123) |
| White Collar | −19 | (1144) | Cler./Sales | −11 | (387) |
| Ind. Bus. | −14 | (583) | Factory Labor | −3 | (317) |
| Supervisor & | | | Non-Fac. Labor | −6 | (235) |
| Foreman | −16 | (405) | Services | −4 | (178) |
| Skilled | −14 | (2823) | Farm Own./Mgr. | −6 | (184) |
| Unskilled | −14 | (1019) | *Gallup—Dec. 1954*[d] | | |
| Personal Serv. | −10 | (677) | Professional | −44 | (163) |
| Farmers | −21 | (824) | Executive | −24 | (154) |
| Retired | −3 | (709) | Cler./Sales | −23 | (188) |
| Students | −34 | (59) | Skilled | −10 | (237) |
| *Michigan—1954*[d] | | | Unskilled | 8 | (286) |
| Prof. & Bus. | −40 | (246) | Labor | 7 | (68) |
| Cler. & Sales | −44 | (102) | Service | −10 | (103) |
| Skilled | −30 | (337) | Farm Owner | −9 | (165) |
| Unskilled | −16 | (144) | | | |
| Farmers | −17 | (104) | | | |

[a] Cell entries represent per cent difference between approval and disapproval of McCarthy. The more negative the entry, the greater the predominance of anti-McCarthy sentiment.

[b] Occupation of respondent recorded, or of chief wage earner if respondent is a housewife.

[c] Occupation of respondent recorded; housewives omitted from table.

[d] Occupation of head of household recorded.

the middle-class occupations, with the exception of independent businessmen.

Farmers were also a pro-McCarthy group, according to three out of the four surveys and the many studies summarized by Polsby. When viewed in occupational categories, McCarthy's main opponents were to be found among professional, managerial, and clerical personnel, while his support was disproportionately located among self-employed businessmen, farmers, and manual workers. . . .

The findings concerning the relation of education and occupational status to support of McCarthy seem to confirm the hypothesis presented in the original essays concerning stratification factors and McCarthyism. Another hypothesis was that McCarthyism also reflected strains inherent in the varying statuses of different ethnic and religious groups in American society. It was assumed that Catholics and other recent immigrant groups with relatively low status, or with ethnic ties to neutral or Axis nations, were disposed to favor Mc-Carthy, while those of high status or with ethnic links to Allied nations opposed the Senator. These generalizations also tend to be supported by survey data. It is clear, as has already been noted, that Catholics as a group were more pro-McCarthy than Protestants, who in turn were somewhat more favorable to him than were Jews. The strong relationship between religious affiliation and attitude toward McCarthy among supporters of the two parties may be seen in Table 5, taken from the University of Michigan study.

TABLE 5

ATTITUDES TOWARD McCARTHY ACCORDING TO RELIGION
AND PARTY IDENTIFICATION—1954
(MICHIGAN SURVEY)

| Attitudes toward McCarthy | Strong Dem. | Protestants Weak Dem. | Ind. | Weak Rep. | Strong Rep. |
|---|---|---|---|---|---|
| Pro | 7% | 6% | 7% | 11% | 23% |
| Anti | 55 | 45 | 35 | 33 | 28 |
| Excess of Anti over Pro | −48 | −39 | −28 | −22 | −5 |
| N | (184) | (213) | (173) | (128) | (123) |

| Attitudes toward McCarthy | Strong Dem. | Catholics Weak Dem. | Ind. | Weak Rep. | Strong Rep. |
|---|---|---|---|---|---|
| Pro | 18% | 23% | 19% | 20% | 39% |
| Anti | 33 | 20 | 21 | 28 | 23 |
| Excess of Anti over Pro | −15 | +3 | −2 | −8 | +16 |
| N | (51) | (58) | (55) | (25) | (18) |

SOURCE: Campbell and Cooper, op. cit., p. 149.

Within the Protestant group, the ranking of the different denominations with respect to sentiment toward McCarthy corresponded on the whole to their socio-economic status. As Table 6 shows, the higher the status of the members of a denomination, the more antagonistic the group was toward the Wisconsin Senator.

Methodists constitute an exception to this generalization: although a relatively low-status group, they were more anti-McCarthy than the Lutherans or Presbyterians. The rank order of denominations in terms of McCarthy support is, with the exception of the Baptists, identical with that reported earlier for Coughlin (see Table 7). Baptists ranked

TABLE 6

PROTESTANT DENOMINATIONAL SUPPORT
FOR MCCARTHY—1952
(ROPER)

*Attitudes toward McCarthy*

| | Per Cent of Group High in SES | Agree | Disagree | Don't Know | Difference between Agrees and Disagrees | N |
|---|---|---|---|---|---|---|
| Episcopalians | 40% | 29% | 44% | 27% | −15% | (157) |
| Congregationalists | 32 | 33 | 44 | 23 | −11 | (89) |
| Methodists | 19 | 29 | 33 | 38 | −4 | (509) |
| Presbyterians | 27 | 37 | 36 | 27 | +1 | (208) |
| Lutherans | 23 | 33 | 31 | 36 | +2 | (207) |
| Baptists | 12 | 28 | 24 | 49 | +4 | (471) |

TABLE 7

RANK ORDER OF DIFFERENT PROTESTANT DENOMINATIONS
IN SUPPORT OF COUGHLIN AND MCCARTHY

| | *Coughlin—1938* | *McCarthy—1952* |
|---|---|---|
| *High Support* | Lutherans | Baptists |
| | Presbyterians | Lutherans |
| | Methodists | Presbyterians |
| | Baptists | Methodists |
| | Congregationalists | Congregationalists |
| *Low Support* | Episcopalians | Episcopalians |

relatively high in opposition to Coughlin and in support for Mc-
Carthy. It is difficult to suggest any plausible explanation for this
change in the position of the Baptists other than that they may have
been particularly antagonistic to the Catholic Church, and hence un-
willing to approve the political activities of a priest, yet not deterred
from supporting a Catholic Senator.

Both the I.N.R.A. and Roper surveys contain information concerning the ethnic origins of respondents which permits an elaboration of
the relationship between ethnic and religious identification and Mc-
Carthy support (see Table 8). Unfortunately, the two studies differed
greatly in the wording of questions on ethnicity. Because I.N.R.A.
asked for the country of ancestors, while Roper asked for the country
of the respondents' grandparents, the Roper survey reported many
more Protestants as simply "American" in background. Among Catholics, too, the Roper survey reported a smaller proportion with German

TABLE 8

RELATIONSHIP BETWEEN RELIGION AND ETHNIC BACK-
GROUND AND ATTITUDES TO McCARTHY

Per Cent Difference between Approvers and Disapprovers

| Roper—1952 | | | I.N.R.A.—1954 | | |
|---|---|---|---|---|---|
| Catholics | (N) | | Catholics | (N) | |
| 4th Generation Amer. | (198) | −11 | No Answer | (252) | −2 |
| Ireland | (81) | +18 | Ireland | (545) | +5 |
| Italy | (61) | +16 | Italy | (393) | +8 |
| Germany | (54) | +13 | Germany & Austria | (424) | −6 |
| Great Britain | (13) | * | Great Britain | (272) | +4 |
| Poland | (36) | −6 | Poland | (246) | −2 |
| | | | | | |
| Protestants | | | Protestants | | |
| 4th Generation Amer. | (1190) | −2 | No Answer | (1037) | −22 |
| Ireland | (29) | +7 | Ireland | (487) | −21 |
| Germany | (172) | +2 | Germany & Austria | (1266) | −19 |
| Great Britain | (102) | −8 | Great Britain | (1814) | −25 |
| Scandinavia | (68) | −3 | Scand. & Holl. | (851) | −25 |
| Jews | (96) | −6 | Jews | (245) | −54 |
| Negroes | (252) | −7 | Negroes | (438) | −13 |

* Too few cases for stable estimates.

or British ancestry than did the I.N.R.A. survey. On the other hand, I.N.R.A.'s request for country of ancestors produced a large "don't know" or "no answer" group. About 20 per cent of the whites did not reply to the question.

Differences in attitude among the ethnic groups were more pronounced among Catholics than Protestants in both the Roper and the I.N.R.A. studies. In the Roper survey, Irish Catholics were 18 per cent more favorable to the Senator than unfavorable, while "old American" Catholics were 11 per cent more negative than positive. Among Protestants on the other hand, those of German origin were the most pro-McCarthy (2 per cent), while those of British ancestry were most opposed (−8 per cent).

Results from both surveys show that Irish and Italian Catholics were among the most pro-McCarthy groups. The Roper data indicate that Germans, both Catholic and Protestant, were disproportionately in favor of McCarthy, but the I.N.R.A. materials do not confirm this finding. The explanation for this seeming inconsistency may lie in the differing formulation of the questions on ethnicity. It may be that McCarthy appealed successfully to the "Roper" Germans whose family had emigrated to the United States within the past three generations, and consequently retained emotional ties to Germany that made them receptive to McCarthy's isolationist appeal. "I.N.R.A." Germans are more likely to have been old-stock Americans and, like other "old American" groups, predisposed to disapprove of the Wisconsin Senator.

In summary, it appears that the findings concerning ethnic and religious factors agree with the hypotheses suggested in the original essays—that is, McCarthy was generally opposed by descendants of old American Protestant families, and he drew disproportionately from Catholics of recent immigrant background. The two minority groups whose circumstances have led them to identify with liberal Democratic groups and leaders, the Jews and the Negroes, were among those most strongly opposed to McCarthy.

# Michael Paul Rogin: McCarthyism Not a Mass Movement

*In 1967 Michael Paul Rogin published an important book entitled* The Intellectuals and McCarthy. *Rogin used quantitative techniques to attack those pluralists (or New Conservatives) who contended that McCarthy's support in the Midwest was centered in regions formerly loyal to "agrarian radicalism." In the three Midwestern states that he examined, he found the electoral basis of early twentieth-century agrarian radicalism unrelated to midcentury McCarthyism. In Wisconsin, in fact, the heirs of rural progressives tended to vote for liberal Democrats, not conservative Republicans. Although Rogin conceded that McCarthy did have a lower-class following in the nation as a whole, he ascribed this support to uninformed anticommunism rather than to irrational status resentments.*

*The real blame for McCarthy, according to Rogin, belongs not to the lower classes, for McCarthyism was never really a mass movement. The fault lies instead with a portion of that very elite so admired by the pluralists—with the conservative Republican leadership, especially in the Midwest, which exploited McCarthyism for its own ends and supported McCarthy because he expressed its resentments. Rogin's book, therefore, had two purposes: to argue, as did Polsby, that McCarthyism was a movement within the traditional framework of American politics; and to refute the conservative views popularized by post-McCarthy pluralists.*[7]

From 1950 through 1954, Joseph McCarthy disrupted the normal routine of American politics. But McCarthyism can best be understood as a product of that normal routine. McCarthy capitalized on popular concern over foreign policy, communism, and the Korean War, but the animus of McCarthyism had little to do with any less political or more developed *popular* anxieties. Instead it reflected the

[7] Michael Paul Rogin, *The Intellectuals and McCarthy* (Cambridge, Mass., 1967), pp. 216–17, 241–44, 247–51. Editor's title. Reprinted by permission of The M.I.T. Press, Cambridge, Massachusetts. Footnotes have been omitted for reasons of space.

specific traumas of conservative Republican activists—internal Communist subversion, the New Deal, centralized government, left-wing intellectuals, and the corrupting influences of a cosmopolitan society. The resentments of these Republicans and the Senator's own talents were the driving forces behind the McCarthy movement.

Equally important, McCarthy gained the protection of politicians and other authorities uninvolved in or opposed to the politics motivating his ardent supporters. Leaders of the GOP saw in McCarthy a way back to national power after twenty years in the political wilderness. Aside from desiring political power, moderate Republicans feared that an attack on McCarthy would split their party. Eisenhower sought for long months to compromise with the Senator, as one would with any other politician. Senators, jealous of their prerogative, were loath to interfere with a fellow senator. Newspapers, looking for good copy, publicized McCarthy's activities. When the political institutions that had fostered McCarthy turned against him, and when, with the end of the Korean War his political issue became less salient, McCarthy was reduced to insignificance.

Politics alone does not explain McCarthyism; but the relevant sociopsychology is that which underpins normal American politics, not that of radicals and outsiders. Psychological insights are not relevant alone to the peculiar politics of the American Right. Equally important, the ease with which McCarthy harnessed himself to the everyday workings of mainstream politics illuminates the weaknesses of America's respectable politicians.

Attention to sociology and psychology must be concentrated within the political stratum, not among the populace as a whole. It is tempting to explain the hysteria with which McCarthy infected the country by the hysterical preoccupations of masses of people. But the masses did not levy an attack on their political leaders; the attack was made by a section of the political elite against another and was nurtured by the very elites under attack. The populace contributed to McCarthy's power primarily because it was worried about communism, Korea, and the cold war. . . .

The data, in sum, do not suggest intense, active, mass involvement in a McCarthyite movement. Efforts to relate status frustrations and psychological malformations to McCarthyism have not proved very successful. Party and political issue cleavages structured McCarthy's support far more than pluralist hypotheses predicted. But the ignorant, the deprived, and the lower classes did support McCarthy disproportionately. Were they expressing their animus against respectable groups and institutions?

To answer this question, we must ask two others: Why did Mc-

Carthyism attract a large popular following of this character, and what impact did support for the Senator have on political behavior?

Most people supported McCarthy because he was identified in the public mind with the fight against communism. In June 1952, a national sample was asked whether, taking all things into consideration, they thought committees of Congress investigating communism, like Senator McCarthy's, were doing more good than harm. In a period when less than 20 per cent of the population had a favorable personal opinion of the Senator, 60 per cent were for the committees and only 19 per cent against them. The more McCarthy's name was identified with anticommunism, the more support he got from the population. Perhaps because they themselves feared the Communist menace, the pluralists underplayed the anti-Communist component of McCarthy's appeal.

In the Stouffer study, respondents were asked to name someone whose opinions about how to handle communism they especially trusted. Most votes went to J. Edgar Hoover and Eisenhower—27 per cent and 24 per cent respectively. McCarthy was third with 8 per cent. Respondents were then asked whether they trusted this person because they knew his opinions pretty well or because of the kind of person he was. The results were

|  | *Opinions* | *Person* |
|---|---|---|
| Hoover | 33% | 55% |
| Eisenhower | 19 | 65 |
| McCarthy | 58 | 31 |

McCarthy's appeal was the functionally specific appeal of a single-issue promoter, not the diffuse appeal which mobilizes the "mass man." McCarthy's stress on communism may have suggested "the weakness of a single issue" for building a right-wing mass movement, but by the same token it explained the strength of McCarthyism.

Popular concern over communism could have symbolized a basic uneasiness about the health of American institutions. So it did for McCarthy and his most vociferous supporters, who saw a government overrun with dupes and traitors. For them, the Communist issue was the issue of Communists in government; internal subversion was the danger. For the American people, however, communism was essentially a foreign policy issue. In the 1952 election, less than 3 per cent expressed concern over Communists in government—fewer than referred to the Point Four program. Foreign policy, on the other hand, was an extremely salient issue, and those concerned over foreign policy were more likely to vote Republican. The external Communist threat and the fear of war benefited the GOP at the polls in the 1950's: the internal Communist danger, salient to committed Republicans alone, did not. Moreover, mass concern about foreign policy did not appear over the loss of China, which the right-wing invested with such peculiar moral significance. It was only when American soldiers went to Korea that foreign policy became salient at the mass level. And the desire there—as expressed in the election of Eisenhower—was for peace not for war.

Why then, if McCarthy's appeal had specifically to do with foreign policy and the Korean War, did he receive greater support among the poorer and less-educated groups? Had the working class been actively concerned about McCarthy, we might expect this support to overcome the relative lack of political knowledge among those of low socioeconomic status. But asked to name the man who had done the best job of fighting communism, the less-educated and poorer strata volunteered McCarthy's name no more than did the better-educated and rich. Highly conscionable McCarthy sentiments were as prevalent among the upper as the lower classes. (Those of higher socioeconomic status, with more political information and sophistication, were more likely to name McCarthy as someone who had done a particularly bad job.) Disproportionate working-class support for McCarthy thus only manifested itself when his name was actually mentioned in the polls; it was not powerful enough to emerge when workers had to volunteer his name on their own.

The evidence does not suggest that the Communist issue preoccupied the lower classes, or that they were using that issue to vent general grievances about their position in society. More likely, they simply had less information about McCarthy's methods, a less sophisticated understanding of their nature and less concern in the abstract about possible victims of the Senator's techniques. Therefore, when the pollsters specifically mentioned McCarthy's name, it tapped among the middle-class revulsion over McCarthy's crudities and opposition to his infringements of individual rights. Among the working class, it tapped an anticommunism relatively less restrained by these concerns. . . .

What are we to conclude, then, about McCarthy's "mass" appeal? McCarthy's popular following apparently came from two distinct sources. There was first the traditional right wing of the midwestern Republican Party. Here was a group to whom McCarthy was a hero. He seemed to embody all their hopes and frustrations. These were the militants in the McCarthy movement. They worked hardest for him and were preoccupied with his general targets. To them, communism was not the whole story; their enemies were also the symbols of welfare capitalism and cosmopolitanism. These militants were mobilized by McCarthy's "mass" appeal. Yet this appeal had its greatest impact upon activists and elites, not upon the rank-and-file voters. And while McCarthy mobilized the Republican right wing, he did not change its traditional alliances. This was not a "new" American Right, but rather an old one with new enthusiasm and new power.

McCarthy's second source of popular support [was] those citizens mobilized because of communism and the Korean war. Concern over these issues throughout the society increased Republican strength although this increase in popular support accrued not so much to McCarthy as to Eisenhower. McCarthy's strength here was not so much due to "mass," "populist," or "status" concerns as it was to the issues of communism, Korea, and the cold war. At the electoral level there was little evidence that those allegedly more vulnerable to "mass" appeals were mobilized by McCarthy to change their traditional voting patterns.

McCarthy had real support at the grass roots, but his was hardly a "movement in which popular passions wreaked their aggression against the structure of the polity." In a period in which the populace gave overwhelming support to Eisenhower, it can hardly be accused of failing to show deference to responsible political leadership. In so arguing, I by no means wish to minimize the danger of McCarthyism. But the pluralists, writing in a context of fear of the masses, have misunderstood both the source and the nature of that danger. They see a rebellious populace threatening the fabric of society. In fact, McCarthy did immense damage to the lives and careers of countless individuals. He exercised an inordinate influence over policy making. But popular enthusiasm for his assault on political institutions simply cannot explain the power he wielded. In so far as McCarthy challenged political decisions, political individuals, and the political fabric, he was sustained not by a revolt of the masses so much as by the actions and inactions of various elites.

### THE ELITES

Conservative Republican activists provided McCarthy with the core of his enthusiastic support. In addition, groups ranging from Catholic Democratic workers to conservative southern senators contributed to McCarthy's power—the workers by verbal approval in the polls, the senators by their actions and silences in Washington. Having examined the contribution of the masses to McCarthyism, we turn now to the elites.

The pluralists argue that McCarthy was not simply attacking Communists, but also had as his targets the eastern, educated, financial, political, and intellectual elite. There is merit in this view, nevertheless, McCarthy enjoyed the support of some wealthy and influential political elites, and even some of those he attacked played a role in augmenting his power. The existence of a powerful Republican right wing, the new appeal of the issues of communism and foreign policy, and McCarthy's own tactical brilliance raised McCarthyism to a place of national prominence. But there was more to McCarthy's success than this. The response of a variety of political elites—by no means simply allies of the Wisconsin senator—enabled him to harness himself to the everyday workings of American politics. Those already part of this machinery often did not approve of McCarthy. Some, like moderate Republicans in their battle with the Democrats, congressmen in their battle with the executive, newspapers in their search for news, thought they could use him. Others, like southern Democrats, saw no need to treat McCarthy differently than they treated other senators. Still others, moderate Republicans in their desire for party unity, liberal Democrats in their desire for reelection, were afraid of him. Political and psychological reasons made a variety of political elites anxious to avoid a confrontation with McCarthy. Until it became clear to them that McCarthyism was more than politics as usual, they failed effectively to challenge it.

We have already pointed to the importance of the political structure in influencing McCarthy's mass support. Regardless of attitudes toward civil liberties and even toward McCarthy in the abstract, traditional political allegiances kept the workers in the Democratic Party in the 1950's and business and professional men in the GOP. McCarthy's "mass" appeal did not register directly in politics because many who supported him cared more about the Democratic Party, the New Deal, their trade unions, or their wives and families than they cared about McCarthy. They therefore did not break their traditional political habits.

Just as the political structure limited the sustenance McCarthy could derive from the grass roots, so it influenced the behavior of political elites. We look now at conservative Republicans and GOP moderates, at the Senate and the southern Democrats, at the press and at the liberals.

Most of those who mobilized behind McCarthy at the national level were conservative politicians and publicists, businessmen and retired military leaders discontented with the New Deal, with bureaucracy, and with military policy. Of nineteen businessmen in the leadership of the Ten Million Americans mobilizing for McCarthy, only one had inherited wealth. These men had been part of the Republican right wing before McCarthy; they were joined by an occasional ex-agrarian radical like Burton Wheeler. Numbers of former Marxist intellectuals such as Louis Budenz, James Burnham, and John Chamberlain became McCarthy publicists, but they lacked political influence or popular support. The political conservatism of the elite supporters of McCarthy ran the gamut of domestic and international policy.

We have already discussed the historical reasons for McCarthy's conservative support. The evolution of politics in the Middle West and the nation had had two political consequences for conservatives. They were in heretofore unprecedented positions of political power at the state level and political weakness at the national level. Their desperation is suggested by Taft's famous advice to McCarthy, "If one case doesn't work, then bring up another." This political elite sustained McCarthy. It helped dramatize his issues and fight his fights. Conservative Republican activists provided money and enthusiasm for the Senator's cause. In Wisconsin, for example, McCarthy did not mobilize the mass of voters. But he did mobilize the local elites of the Republican Party. The near-hysterical enthusiasm with which they identified with the Senator gave the movement its emotional intensity. The regular Wisconsin Republican organization—in an action almost unprecedented in American politics—put up a candidate to oppose Wisconsin's other incumbent Republican senator because he had not voted against McCarthy's censure.

How to explain the mentality of these McCarthy supporters? Lipset, analyzing American politics as a conflict between values of achievement and egalitarian populism, argues that political excesses such as McCarthyism derive from America's egalitarian strain. Thus it is argued that Britain was spared a McCarthyite episode because the populace had deference for its established leaders. But a more important difference between Britain and the United States on this score is the character of conservative politics of the two countries. The British example suggests by comparison what American conservatives were willing to do. Certainly these conservatives were unrestrained by aristocratic traditions, but to ascribe this to populist values rather than to the capitalist-achievement ethic is perverse. In a Protestant, competitive society, an individual can blame only himself for failure, and the fear of failure appears at all levels of the social structure. The attendant insecurities and frustrations will often produce conspiracy theories, scapegoat hunting, and terrible resentments. McCarthy was supported by the activists of a party that emphasizes free enterprise, achievement, and individual responsibility. The politics of these people seems more sensibly explained by their preoccupations with achievement and failure than by their populistic concerns.

# Bibliographical Note

Students interested in the background of McCarthyism will find it useful to consult works about American communism. On the 1930s, Louis Coser and Irving Howe's *The American Communist Party* (New York, 1957) contains useful chapters. An influential but much exaggerated account of Stalinist influence in the depression on American intellectuals is Eugene Lyons' *The Red Decade* (New York, 1941). To correct Lyons' caricature, Frank A. Warren wrote *The Liberals and Communism* (Bloomington, Indiana, 1966), in which he examines three "left-wing" liberal magazines and finds a complex response in the 1930s to communism. See also parts II and III of Daniel Aaron, *Writers on the Left* (New York, 1961), and Ralph L. Roy, *Communism and the Churches* (New York, 1960). The subject of Communist espionage is surveyed in James Burnham, *The Web of Subversion* (New York, 1954), which is perhaps too uncritical of the testimony of former Communists and overestimates the harmful effects of espionage. Similar to Burnham's account are the relevant chapters in Nathaniel Weyl, *The Battle Against Disloyalty* (New York, 1951). See also David Y. Dallin, *Soviet Espionage* (New Haven, 1955). The story of the Canadian spy ring is told authoritatively in "Royal Commission to investigate disclosures of secret and confidential information to unauthorized persons" (Ottawa, June, 1946). Whittaker Chambers in *Witness* (New York, 1955) and Elizabeth Bentley in *Out of Bondage* (New York, 1951) relate their experiences as Communist underground agents.

On the postwar reverses of American communism, see David Shannon's helpful book, *The Decline of American Communism* (New York, 1959). For an account of how the CIO expelled the Communists, see Max M. Kampelman, *The Communist Party vs. the C.I.O* (New York, 1957). In Bert Andrews, *Washington Witch Hunt* (New York, 1948), the State Department is criticized for its early handling of security cases. Truman's loyalty program is carefully analyzed in Eleanor Bontecon, *The Federal Loyalty and Security Program* (Ithaca, 1953). The civil libertarian critique of the program appears in Alan Barth, *The Loyalty of Free Men* (New York, 1951), and Francis Biddle, *Fear of Freedom* (New York, 1951). Carey McWilliams' *Witch Hunt: The Revival of Heresy* (Boston, 1950) contains valuable material on the national obsession with loyalty in the years prior to McCarthy's advent. On Henry Wallace and the Progressive party, see Curtis D. MacDougall, *Gideon's Army* (New York, 1965). Useful material on New York's American Labor Party, which came under Communist domination in the mid-1940s and then declined, can be found in David J. Saposs, *Communism in American Politics* (Washington, 1960). The best book on the Hiss case is Alistair Cooke, *A Generation on Trial* (New York, 1950). See also accounts by the two principals: Chambers, *Witness,* and Alger Hiss, *In the Court of Public Opinion*

(New York, 1957). For a Red hunt before McCarthy, see Robert Carr's scholarly *The House Committee on Un-American Affairs, 1945-1950* (Ithaca, 1952) and Walter Goodman's entertaining *The Committee* (New York, 1968).

No scholarly biography of Senator McCarthy has yet appeared, and large gaps in our knowledge about him persist. The first book-length study of McCarthy was Jack Anderson and Ronald W. May, *McCarthy: The Man, the Senator, and the "Ism"* (London, 1953), a hostile, sometimes unfair, but still valuable source. The most famous biography is Richard Rovere, *Senator Joe McCarthy* (New York, 1959). A graceful bit of character assassination, this book rests on the assumption that nothing McCarthy ever did was right. For still another critical portrait, see the chapter on McCarthy in Reinhard H. Luthin's *American Demagogues* (Boston, 1954). In April, 1954, *The Progressive* (vol. 18) devoted an entire issue to the subject of McCarthy's career, which it found thoroughly condemnable. Another unfriendly but informative study is James Rorty and Moshe Decter, *McCarthy and the Communists* (Boston, 1954), which concludes that McCarthy actually helped the Communists. Michael Straight, *Trial by Television* (Boston, 1954), is a liberal's account of the Army-McCarthy hearings. McCarthy answered his critics in *McCarthyism: The Fight for America* (New York, 1952). In addition he published one other book, *America's Retreat from Victory* (New York, 1952), which is a reprint of his 1951 Senate speech attacking General Marshall. The best defense of McCarthy is William F. Buckley and L. Brent Bozell, *McCarthy and His Enemies* (Chicago, 1954). Mainly an analysis of McCarthy's charges against the State Department, this book conceded that McCarthy exaggerated his charges but contended that they had some substance. The periodical *Continuum* devoted most of its Autumn, 1968 (vol. 6), issue to McCarthy, with rather disappointing results.

Several men who at one time or another met up with McCarthy wrote about their experience. In *Ordeal by Slander* (Boston, 1950), Owen Lattimore answered the charges that McCarthy made against him at the Tydings hearings. Prompted by McCarthy's accusation that he was a conscious agent of the Communist conspiracy, James A. Wechsler wrote *Age of Suspicion* (New York, 1953), which told of his experience in the 1930s in the Young Communist League and his later appearance as a hostile witness before McCarthy's committee. A more cooperative witness, who later recanted his testimony and went to prison for perjury, was Harvey Matusow, who discusses McCarthy in *False Witness* (New York, 1955). Charles E. Potter, a conservative Republican and a member of McCarthy's committee, recalled the Army-McCarthy hearings and his private disgust for McCarthy in *Days of Shame* (New York, 1965). Dwight Eisenhower devoted part of one chapter in *Mandate for Change* (Garden City, 1963) to his unhappy experience with McCarthy. Sherman Adams' *First Hand Report* (New York, 1961) presented the same view from the White House. McCarthy was remembered fondly by Roy Cohn in *McCarthy* (New York, 1968).

Earl Latham, *The Communist Controversy in Washington* (Cambridge, Mass., 1966), attempted an overview of the problem that unfortunately is interpretatively weak. For a summary of a few early views of McCarthyism, see Dennis Wrong, "Theories of McCarthyism—A Survey," *Dissent*, 1 (Autumn, 1954), 385–92. Nathan Glazer, "The Method of Senator McCarthy," *Commentary*, 15 (March, 1953), 244–56, argued that the bulk of McCarthy's support came from ethnic isolationists. Leo B. Huberman and Paul M. Sweezy, "The Roots and Prospects of McCarthyism," *Monthly Review*, 5 (January, 1954), 417–34, offered a Marxist interpretation. Herbert Aptheker, a Marxist historian, devoted a chapter in his book *History and Reality* (New York, 1955) to McCarthyism and found that "it is the creation of giant monopolists just as Hitlerism was the creation of Germany's giant monopolists." John Steinke and James Weinstein, "McCarthy and the Liberals," *Studies on the Left*, 2 (1962), 43–50, located the origins of McCarthyism in the Cold War, "of which the liberals were the chief architects." To illustrate their thesis, the authors showed that the liberals Red-baited McCarthy himself by unfairly ascribing his 1946 primary victory to Communist support.

The classic inquiry into McCarthyism is Daniel Bell, ed., *The New American Right* (New York, 1955), later reissued as *The Radical Right* (Garden City, New York, 1963), which set forth the status anxiety hypothesis. Peter Viereck's *Unadjusted Man* (Boston, 1956) and Edward A. Shils' *The Torment of Secrecy* (New York, 1956) are good examples of the pluralist point of view. For a typical indictment of "mass democracy," see Will Herberg, "Government by Rabble-Rousing," *New Leader*, 73 (January 18, 1954), 13–16. C. Vann Woodward, "The Populist Heritage and the Intellectual," *American Scholar*, 29 (Winter, 1959–60), 55–72, found that the attempt by some pluralists to link Populism with McCarthyism was not always fair to the former movement. David A. Shannon, "Was McCarthy a Political Heir of LaFollette," *Wisconsin Magazine of History*, 45 (Autumn, 1961), 3–9, denied any important connection between McCarthy and LaFollette progressivism. Martin Trow, "Small Businessmen, Political Tolerance, and Support for McCarthy," *American Journal of Sociology*, 64 (November, 1958), 270–81, rejected the pluralist analysis and argued, on the basis of his study of Bennington, Vermont, that small businessmen, hostile to mature industrial society, were the strongest source of McCarthy's support. Nelson W. Polsby, "Toward an Explanation of McCarthyism," *Political Studies*, 8 (October, 1960), 250–71, offered a political interpretation. The most thorough rebuttal of the pluralists is Michael P. Rogin, *The Intellectuals and McCarthy* (Cambridge, Mass., 1967), which finds pluralist theory inadequate and their analysis of McCarthyism statistically untenable.

# Index

## A

Acheson, Dean, 8, 23, 25, 46, 49, 56, 59, 66, 113, 126, 145
Adams, John G., 83
*Amerasia*, 4
American Communist Party, 5
American Heritage Protective Association, 142
American League Against War and Fascism, 2
American League for Peace and Democracy, 53
Americans for Democratic Action (ADA), 3, 62
*Ancien Régime and the Revolution* (Toqueville), 146
Anderson, Jack, 10
Anderson, Sherwood, 1
Appropriations, Committee on, 69
Army Industrial College, 138
Army vs. McCarthy hearings, 82–104
Arundel, Russell M., 14

## B

Baldwin, Hanson, 57, 120
Baldwin, Raymond, 14
Banking and Currency, Committee on, 14
Barmine, Alexander, 76, 77
Barth, Alan, 5
Baruch, Bernard, 137
Bell, Daniel, 131
Bentley, Elizabeth, 6
Benton, William, 44, 114, 115
Berle, Adolph, 25, 43
Bohlen, Charles (Chip), 65, 67
*Boston Post*, 141, 143
Bozell, L. Brent, 20, 27, 37
Bradley, A. C., 109
Bricker, John, 108
Bridges, Styles, 8
Brownell, Herbert, 78, 138

Buckley, William F., 20, 27, 37
Budenz, Louis, 37, 172
Burke, Edmund, 132
Burnham, James, 172
Byrnes, James F., 19

## C

Caldwell, Erskine, 1
Calhoun, John C., 132
Capehart, Homer, 9
Carr, Frank, 95, 112
Central Intelligence Agency (CIA), 65, 79
Chamberlain, John, 172
Chambers, Whittaker, 2, 6, 25
Chiang Kai-shek, 1, 8, 23, 46, 49, 57
*Chicago Tribune*, 147
Childs, Marquis, 120
Churchill, Winston, 55
Clucas, Lowell, 77
Cocutz, John, 74–75
Coe, Frank, 64
Cohn, Roy M., 82, 90–93, 107
Coleman, Tom, 139
*Commentary*, 133
*Commonweal*, 122
*Communist Party vs. the C.I.O.* (Kampleman), 2
*Compass*, 47
Conant, James B., 69
Congress of Industrial Organizations (CIO), 2, 3
*Congressional Record*, 53, 97, 104
Connors, W. Bradley, 73, 76
Coplon, Judith, 7, 9
Coughlin, Father, 164
Cullen, Hugh Roy, 140, 142
Curran, Joseph, 3
Currie, Laughlin, 6

## D

*Daily Worker*, 30, 37, 45, 77, 78, 99
Daughters of the American Revolution, 151

178

Roosevelt, Franklin D., 2, 25, 56, 57, 136, 138, 160
Rosenberg, Ethel, 9
Rosenberg, Julius, 9
Rovere, Richard, 55, 113
Royall, Kenneth C., 133, 134
Rules and Administration, Committee on, 82, 104

**S**

St. Clair, Jim, 94
*Saturday Evening Post*, 141, 143
Service, John S., 23
Schenck case, 5
Schine, G. David, 82, 90
Schuh, Matt, 136
Schlesinger, Arthur, Jr., 62
*Senator Joe McCarthy* (Rovere), 55
Shapley, Harlow, 24
Smith Act (1940), 5
Sparkman, John, 65
Station, Admiral, 63
Stettinius, Edward, 25, 68
Stevens, Robert, 83, 107
Stevenson, Adlai E., 61, 107
Symington, Stuart, 110, 111

**T**

Taft, Robert A., 8, 13, 15, 46, 65, 73, 155, 173
Taft-Hartley Act, 15
*Time*, 112, 115, 129
Tobey, Charles, 14
Tocqueville, Alexis de, 132, 146
Truman, Harry S., 4, 5, 8, 9, 13, 24, 25, 33, 37, 46, 48, 49, 50, 58, 59, 78, 79, 136, 160
Tydings, Millard, 37, 44, 101

**U**

*Unadjusted Man, The* (Viereck), 144
Un-American Activities, House Committee on (HUAC), 25, 43, 53, 54, 95
Unions, Communist, 3
United Auto Workers, 2, 3
United Electrical Workers, 2, 3

United Mine Workers, 13
United Nations, 23, 29
United Nations Economic and Social Council (UNESCO), 24
United Nations Relief and Rehabilitation Agency (UNRRA), 25
United States Seventh Fleet, 48–49

**V**

Vincent, John Carter, 77
Voice of America, 31, 65, 73–76

**W**

Wadleigh, Julian H., 24
Wallace, Henry A., 3
War Industries Board, 138
War Production Board, 2
Ware group, 2
*Washington Post*, 45
Watkins, Arthur, 96, 144
Watkins Committee, 97, 145
Weizsäcker, Ernst von, 133
Welch, Joseph, 90–96, 129
Welker, Herman, 107
Werner, Edgar V., 11
Wheeler, Burton K., 172
Wheeler-Bennett, 121
Wheeling, W. Va., Speech, 19, 116
*Wheeling, W. Va., Intelligencer*, 19
Wherry, Kenneth S., 39
White, Harry Dexter, 6, 78, 81
Wiley, Alexander, 12
Wilson, Edmund, 1
Wilson, Richard, 138
*Wisconsin C.I.O. News*, 13
Woltman, Frederick, 117, 124
Wyatt, Wilson, 62

**Y**

Yalta, 25, 57, 68, 69
*Yates v. United States*, 6
Young Communist League, 62

**Z**

Zwicker, Ralph, 83–88, 97, 98